Patent Failure

Patent Failure

How Judges, Bureaucrats, and Lawyers
Put Innovators at Risk

James Bessen and Michael J. Meurer

Princeton University Press
Princeton and Oxford

Library of Congress Cataloging-in-Publication Data

Bessen, James, 1958–

Patent failure : how judges, bureaucrats, and lawyers put innovators at risk /

James Bessen and Michael J. Meurer.

p. cm.

Includes bibliographical references and index.

ISBN 978-0-691-13491-8 (hardcover : acid-free paper)

1. Patent laws and legislation—United States.   I. Meurer, Michael James.   II. Title.

KF3114.B47 2008

346.7304'86—dc22   2007048854

British Library Cataloging-in-Publication Data is available

This book has been composed in Adobe Garamond

Printed on acid-free paper. ∞

press.princeton.edu

Printed in the United States of America

1   3   5   7   9   10   8   6   4   2

To Irwin (with his 12 patents), Thelma, and Joyce

To Miyuki, Quinn, and Zach

Contents

Preface

This book is the product of its authors' unusual combination of skills, knowledge, and experience. We each have decades of different sorts of involvement with innovation: economics research, legal scholarship in patent law, and the practical business of being an innovator and entrepreneur in the software industry. This breadth of experience and knowledge has been essential to the primary intended contribution of this book: to bring a wide variety of evidence to bear on the questions of how well the patent system performs economically, what contributes and detracts from this performance, and how policy can improve it.

We were motivated to write this book by what we saw as the growing need to base patent policy on empirical evidence, to get beyond what law professor Jamie Boyle calls "faith-based policy." Over the last decade, a chorus of innovators has grown increasingly louder in its complaints about the patent system. This is especially true in some new-technology areas such as software. We suspect that the patent system is approaching an historic crossroads and we will soon see fundamental policy changes.

Yet as Congress began holding hearings on patent law in 2005, we heard mostly rhetoric and anecdote, despite a large body of empirical research that has been performed by legal scholars and economists. Although economists and law professors have brought some excellent empirical research to bear on specific policy questions such as patent-continuations practice or postgrant review of patents, general evaluation of the patent system and policy priorities do not seem to be based on any detailed empirical analysis.

Sometimes economists quote Machlup (1958) to suggest the futility of attempting to draw broad conclusions about the performance of the patent system: "If we did not have a patent system, it would be irresponsible . . . to recommend instituting one. But since we have had a patent system for a long time, it would be irresponsible, on the basis of our present knowledge, to recommend abolishing it." Yet in the half-century since Machlup wrote these words, empirical research has advanced dramatically. Researchers now have large, computerized databases of information on patents, patent prosecution, patent litigation, research and development (R&D), corporate financial variables, and so forth. They also have sophisticated econometric tools and models that they have used to analyze these data and measure key aspects of patent performance. One would hope that something a bit more definitive than Machlup's conclusion could be drawn from this extensive body of research.

This is what we attempt to do by synthesizing a wide variety of evidence from diverse sources. We draw on economics research that uses large databases of patents. We also draw on more detailed analyses of court cases and outcomes more familiar to legal scholars. Moreover, the significance of our contribution lies not just in that we use a wide range of empirical evidence, but that we measure that evidence against yardsticks that are grounded in the practical realities of the way the law and innovation operate. Empirical economics research on patents has faced two sorts of difficulties in evaluating performance of the patent system. First, it has proven difficult to isolate all of the components of "net social welfare," the gold standard of economics-policy evaluation. We do not attempt to measure net social welfare, but instead measure more limited aspects of patent performance that are nevertheless still quite informative regarding policy. Second, economic theory tends to use highly stylized concepts such as patent "strength," "breadth," and even "quality." These concepts have proven difficult to measure because, unfortunately, they do not unambiguously correspond to the actual practical realities faced by innovators. Instead, the measures we use touch on aspects of these characteristics (most notably, patent quality), but they result in estimates of economic costs and benefits that are directly relevant to decisions that business managers make about innovation.

Because this work is a synthesis, we owe a great debt to researchers who have come before us and especially to those who introduced us, inspired us, and taught us essential aspects of this subject. In this regard we acknowledge the great contributions of Eric Maskin and Eric von Hippel.

Our work would have been impossible without the development of large databases of patent and corporate information by Bronwyn Hall, Bob Hunt, and Manuel Trajtenberg. Many other researchers generously shared data, including Gwendolyn Ball, Jay Kesan, Megan MacGarvie, Kimberley Moore,

Lee Petherbridge, John Turner, Polk Wagner, and Rosemarie Ziedonis. Much of our data was extracted by research assistants and librarians, including Jay Cohen, Brian Costello, Annette Fratantaro, Deb Koker, Raquel Ortiz, Steve Rosenthal, and Dan Wolf.

Our work also would not have gotten far without our many discussions with friends and colleagues. Boston University School of Law is a wonderfully collegial place. So many faculty and students gave us things to think about. We especially thank Wendy Gordon and Maureen O'Rourke for their support. Many other people provided us with insights, questions, comments, criticism, and encouragement, including, Robert Barr, John Barton, Bob Bone, Jamie Boyle, Iain Cockburn, Wes Cohen, Dennis Crouch, Rochelle Dreyfuss, John Duffy, Beatrice Dumont, Rebecca Eisenberg, Lorna Flynn, Rich Gilbert, Andy Goldstein, Dennis Gorman, Dominique Guellec, Bronwyn Hall, Paul Heald, Rita Heimes, Bob Hunt, Brian Kahin, Karim Lakhani, Jenny Lanjouw, Mark Lemley, David Levine, Doug Lichtman, Bruce MacDougal, Megan MacGarvie, Eric Maskin, Peter Menell, Bill Meurer, Craig Nard, Robert Plotkin, Cecil Quillen, Arti Rai, Dan Ravicher, Jerry Reichman, Bill Ryckman, Pam Samuelson, Josh Sarnoff, Mark Schankerman, Solveig Singleton, Kathy Strandburg, Jay Thomas, John Turner, Eric von Hippel, Polk Wagner, and Rosemarie Ziedonis. We also thank conference and seminar participants at Benjamin Cardozo Law School; the Center for the Study of the Public Domain, Duke University; Emory University Law School; the "IP Scholars" conference, University of California, Berkeley; University of Michigan Law School; the "Designing Cyberinfrastructure for Collaboration and Innovation" conference, National Academy of Science; the NBER; the "Patents and Diversity in Innovation" conference, University of Michigan; the "Patent Law Conference," Santa Clara University; the "Software Patents: A Time for Change?" conference, Boston University; and the "Works-in-Progress" IP Colloquium, the University of Pittsburgh.

Finally, we thank Tim Sullivan of Princeton University Press and Krzysztof Bebenek for polishing the manuscript, and we gratefully acknowledge Joyce and Miyuki for putting up with us.

Patent Failure

1　The Argument in Brief

Zimbabwe, a country once considered the "breadbasket of Africa," now suffers widespread starvation. Much of this decline can be attributed to the tyrannical policies of President Robert Mugabe—in particular, his disregard for property. In 2000, Mugabe's followers seized land on over one thousand farms owned by white farmers. But when Zimbabwe's Supreme Court ordered the squatters evicted, Mugabe forced the chief justice to resign and physically threatened the remaining justices, who relented. Owners abandoned their property, severely disrupting agricultural production, and within a few years Zimbabwe was wracked by famine.[1]

Even with the rule of law, property systems can fail. A successful property system also requires supportive institutions, and the technical details of property law must make sense. Consider one particular country where many property owners had a hard time enforcing their rights and were often forced to resort to expensive litigation. In one notorious case, a property owner had to assert its rights against more than one hundred parties, an ordeal that involved forty-three separate lawsuits. With so many ostensible trespassers, one might assume the property owner's claim was weak, but as the courts found, this was not the case. Only one suit was dismissed on summary judgment, the owner's claims were largely upheld on appeal, and almost all the defendants settled.

This example does not come from a failed state or a "tinhorn dictatorship." The country in question is the United States; the property is U.S. Patent No. 4,528,643, granted in 1985; the owner who initiated the lawsuits was a company called E-Data; and the alleged violators included a roster of technology companies as well as thousands of small businesses and individuals operating e-commerce websites.[2] This failure of property rights cannot be attributed to a breakdown of the rule of law. Rather it was caused by the failure of patent-related institutions and patent law generally to get the details right. This widespread pattern of alleged violation and litigation would surely be unusual in real estate or personal property in the United States.

Such a rickety system of property rights seems unlikely to be an engine of growth. Burdensome means of enforcement lessen the value of property to its owners. Moreover, property disputes impose costs on other parties. Even though few are sympathetic to trespassers, squatters, and others who seek unjust enrichment, there is good reason to worry about costs imposed on innocent violators. In the case above, many of the defendants believed that they were not infringing upon the owner's rights, and they innocently made investments that turned out to be in violation. Those investments were exposed to unnecessary risk because of unclear property boundaries. A defective property system discourages trade and investment not just by property owners, but also by those who inadvertently face the threat of property related lawsuits.

This book considers patents as a form of property right. If patents work as property, they should reward innovators and encourage investment in innovation. Below, we explore how the laws and institutions of property, including patents, succeed and how they fail. The E-Data example suggests that even in an advanced society with well-developed legal institutions and strong respect for the law, property can fail. Yet this one example might not be entirely representative. We need to go further and ask whether patents work well as property overall.

This question is important because innovators have grown frustrated with the failings of the American patent system. Over the past several years, in newspaper articles and at hearings held by the Federal Trade Commission (FTC) and the National Academy of Sciences (NAS), industry executives have complained in growing numbers that the patent system is broken. In response, Congress has held its own hearings and debated reform. Critics argue that changes in patent law have created "a legal frenzy that's diverting scientists from doing science."[3] Some even believe that the patent system should be abolished.[4] Others say that the patent system can be fixed with some modest reforms.[5] Still others maintain that the patent system is not broken at all, and that current efforts to reform it are just an attempt to weaken the rights of small inventors.[6]

It is hard to tell who is right, however, because most evidence offered in support of these positions is anecdote, if not myth:

- Defenders of the current system tell stories about the role of patents in protecting small inventors from rapacious corporate giants. But most patents and most litigation do not come from independent inventors, so it is not clear how representative these stories are, or how important small inventors are overall.

- Critics of the system cite patents on a peanut-butter-and-jelly sandwich (U.S. Patent No. 6,004,596), a method of using a backyard swing (U.S. Patent No. 6,368,227), and a method of combing hair over a bald spot (U.S. Patent No. 4,022,227) as evidence of poor patent "quality." Standing alone, however, these patents are not evidence that anything is seriously wrong. Silly patents and patents on unworkable inventions, such as perpetual-motion machines, have been around for at least two hundred years.[7]

- Critics also raise the issue of lawsuits initiated by "patent trolls"— people who obtain broad patents not for purposes of innovation, but solely to ensnare real innovators who might inadvertently cross the boundaries of the trolls' patent. The label "troll" is potent rhetoric, but only a small percentage of patent litigation can be attributed to the most egregious trolls.

Stories about garage inventors are inspiring, while stories about frivolous patents and frivolous lawsuits are troubling, but better evidence is needed to guide patent reform. Without this evidence, it is hardly surprising that some reform proposals seem to be ad hoc.

This book moves beyond anecdote to provide the first comprehensive empirical evaluation of the patent system's performance. We measure patents against a simple, well-defined yardstick inspired by economic analysis of property rights. Our yardstick weighs the benefit of patents to an innovator against their cost, including the risk of inadvertent infringement. If the estimated costs of the patent system to an innovator exceed the estimated benefits, then patents fail as property.

Some readers might immediately find our objective to be somewhat oddly stated or, perhaps, overreaching. The key limiting qualifier here—the limitation that makes the empirical exercise feasible—is "as property." At the risk of getting a bit pedantic, this phrase requires more careful discussion.

Many readers might think the phrase is redundant in the present context. Some are likely to assume that patents *are* property. What, then, could it mean to ask if they work "as property"? For example, in a paper comparing different ways of providing incentives to innovate, theoretical economists Gallini and Scotchmer (2004) tell us that patents are "intellectual property," which they define as "an exclusive right to market an invention for a fixed time period." As such, it might seem sensible to call patents "property" because exclusion is a hallmark of property. Property rights in land give a farmer exclusive rights to grow crops and bring them to market. If patents provide exclusive rights to market inventions, how could they not work "as property"?

It is important, however, to distinguish idealized depictions of patents from the actual workings of the patent system. Patents do not actually provide an affirmative right to market an invention; they provide only a right to exclude *others* from doing so. This might seem an inconsequential difference, but it has practical significance: other patent holders can block even a patented invention from coming to market. The power to block innovation is especially troublesome when property boundaries are not well identified.

Some of the troubling issues raised by the E-Data patent are explained by this difference. E-Data's patent was for a kiosk that produced digital audio tapes and the like in retail stores, but they interpreted this patent to cover a very broad swath of e-commerce. On the other hand, IBM holds hundreds of patents related to e-commerce, but this did not prevent E-Data from threatening to block IBM from marketing its own innovative e-commerce products. To market its own patented technologies, IBM was forced to pay E-Data for a license. Similarly, Research in Motion (RIM) holds patents on its popular BlackBerry personal-communication device, but this did not prevent NTP, a patent licensing company, from famously suing RIM for patent infringement. To avoid being excluded from the market for its own patented invention, RIM paid NTP more than a half-billion dollars.

Gallini and Scotchmer present idealized notions of patents and property that might be useful for some theoretical inquiries.[8] Empirical investigation, however, requires us to be mindful of the ways in which real patents might fall short of such stylized concepts of property. If examples like E-Data and RIM are typical—and this is the kind of empirical question we explore in depth below—then patents will perform quite differently from the property ideal. Below, we estimate just how far actual patents fall short of that ideal. Patents work well as property for some kinds of technology and given the right institutional setting. Patents fail as property for other kinds of technology and given the wrong institutional setting.

Overall, the performance of the patent system has rapidly deteriorated in recent years. By the late 1990s, the costs that patents imposed on public firms outweighed the benefits. This provides clear empirical evidence that the patent system is broken. Both our empirical analysis and our comparative institutional analysis provide clues about the causes of this deterioration—and about what might be done to fix it.

Our focus is on the American patent system, and some of the problems we identify with the American patent system are unique. Nevertheless, there are two reasons that our analysis has relevance to innovation in other countries. First, many other patent systems are under some pressure to become more like the American patent system. For example, Japan and Europe have loosened restrictions against software patents. Second, patent rights and patent litigation are global matters. Important inventions are usually patented in all major markets. This means that patent holders can choose where to litigate. Increasingly, patent disputes are being litigated in the United States, usually resulting in worldwide settlement agreements. Indeed, European inventors file more lawsuits in the United States than they file in any European country other than Germany. This means that the United States patent system directly affects firms and innovators in Europe, Japan, and elsewhere.

PATENTS AS PROPERTY

We begin by comparing patents to tangible property. Lawyers and legal scholars—perhaps because they have endured at least a semester of training in property law and are therefore aware that things might not be so neat—tend to speak of patents not as a form of property, but as *analogous to* other forms of property. Some argue that the analogy might not be appropriate (Lemley 2005), others that the analogy is long-standing (Mosoff 2007), but most recognize that the law and institutions of property systems are complicated and patent law necessarily diverges from the law of tangible property.

We begin our inquiry in chapter 2 by looking at the appropriateness of this analogy, comparing the property-like features of patent law to features of the law of tangible property. We have already noted one important difference: patents do not provide an affirmative right to use an invention. More than one person can use an invention at a time and more than one inventor can claim rights over an invention. Many people can even invent the same technology independently at the same time. In contrast, tangible property is a "rival" good—that is, only one person can use it at a time. This means that the *right to exclude* others more or less conveys an affirmative *right to use* tangible property. As we shall see, this difference between inventions and tangible property is important.

In many other ways, however, patent law shares essential doctrinal features with the law of tangible property. Specifically, patents provide partial rights to exclude others from using an invention as well as rights to transfer ownership. Just as property rights provide incentives to invest in the acquisition, development, and maintenance of tangible property, patents potentially provide incentives to conceive a new technology ("invention"), develop it into a commercial product or process ("commercialization"), and put it to use ("innovation"). Such "innovation incentives" are central to the Constitutional mandate to "promote the progress of . . . the Useful

Arts," which the framers set out when empowering Congress to devise a patent system.

But property and patents only *potentially* provide these incentives. Our review finds well-known evidence that property systems sometimes fail to provide such incentives efficiently:

- Property rights can fail when their validity is uncertain. Such was the case when the transition from Mexican to American rule in California during the nineteenth century clouded the validity of land titles granted under Spanish and Mexican rule. This uncertainty led to squatting and a decline in agricultural productivity.

- Property rights can fail when rights are so highly fragmented that the costs of negotiating the rights needed to make an investment become prohibitive. Such was the case with Russian retail establishments in that country's transition to a private economy. Ownership rights to stores were granted to large numbers of parties, making it too difficult for any one group to obtain the required permissions to operate each store. The stores were often shuttered while street vendors conducted a busy trade nearby.

- Property can fail when boundary information is not publicly accessible. In many less-developed nations, cumbersome regulations discourage impoverished people from recording property boundaries. This limits their ability to trade that property or to use it as collateral for obtaining loans.

- Finally, property rights can fail when the boundaries of the rights are not clear and predictable. This problem sometimes arises with property extracted from nature, such as mineral rights. For example, mineral veins beneath the surface of the earth twist and intersect in unpredictable ways. Such a boundary-related failure in the copper mines of Butte, Montana, led to a violent struggle between rival claimants.

These failures emphasize the importance of implementation in property rights systems. The economic effectiveness of any property system depends not just on what it sets out to do, but also on the laws, regulations, institutions, and norms that implement the system. Consequently, the doctrinal similarity between patent law and the law of tangible property can obscure important differences in economic performance that arise because these doctrines are implemented differently. Patents might not work well as property if patent law is not implemented effectively; the messy details of how patents work matter.

The Notice Function: If You Can't Tell the Boundaries, It Ain't Property

We can identify one very important difference between the way property rights and patent rights are implemented. This difference concerns the "notice function" of property. An efficient property system notifies non-owners of property boundaries. For example, land rights have a well-developed and efficient system to notify third parties of boundaries. Because of this, only rarely does someone invest millions of dollars constructing a building that encroaches on someone else's land without permission. Far more typically, would-be investors "clear" the necessary rights before investing. They locate markers, check land deeds, conduct surveys, and so forth, in order to determine the adjacent boundaries. They then either negotiate rights to the needed land or design the building to avoid encroachment.

The notice function does not always work so well with patents. For example, the E-Data dispute arose because hundreds of parties, including some very large companies, ignored, did not see, or misunderstood the boundaries created by the patent in question. That patent, awarded to Charles Freeny Jr., was entitled a "System for Reproducing Information in Material Objects at a Point of Sale Location." Its unhelpful title obscures the fact that Freeny actually invented a kiosk for producing music tapes or other products in retail stores using digital information. But, as we have seen, the patent was asserted against thousands of companies doing e-commerce, a rather different technology.

Why did notice fail so completely in this case? For one thing, a prospective technology investor needs to check a very large number of patents. According to David M. Martin, CEO of a patent risk management firm, "if you're selling online, at the most recent count there are 4,319 patents you could be violating. If you also planned to advertise, receive payments for, or plan shipments of your goods, you would need to be concerned with approximately 11,000."[9]

But even if a website developer could check all these patents, it would be very difficult to know what their boundaries are. The boundaries of the E-Data patent depend on the meaning of abstract phrases such as "point of sale location," "information manufacturing machine," and "material object." Consider, for example, the meaning of "point of sale location." This is a bit of computer and retail-industry jargon first used when electronic terminals replaced cash registers. It refers to the location within a store where items are checked out and transactions take place. Did this term in the patent claim limit the patent to transactions in retail stores, or did it cover all e-commerce, including transactions that might take place in buyers' offices or even in their bedrooms? The district court limited the patent right to retail locations. In 2001, however, the Court of Appeals for the Federal Circuit, using legal rules that place little weight on actual industry usage or on dictionary definitions, concluded that the "point of sale location" included bedrooms, offices, and anywhere else with an Internet connection. Thus, sixteen years after the patent was granted, it was given boundaries that many people, including a district court judge, would find surprisingly broad. In the interim, the correct boundaries of this patent were essentially unknown. The patent offered poor notice.

Poor notice causes harm because it subjects technology investors to an unavoidable risk of disputes and litigation. The expected cost of inadvertent infringement imposes a *dis*incentive on technology investors. Potential innovators consider not only the reward that they might reap from owning patents, but also the risk of being sued for infringing upon the patents of others. Clearly, if the risk of inadvertent infringement is too great, the net incentives provided by the patent system will be negative, and patents will fail as a property system. This is similar to the failures that occurred with Mexican land grants in California, with Russian retail store ownership, and with the copper-mine war in Butte, Montana, noted above.

Establishing notice is often inherently easier for tangible property because, as opposed to patents, tangible property is a rival good. This means that active possession of tangible property is often sufficient to inform the world about what is owned and who owns it—consider, for example, the shirt on one's back. For nonrival inventions, such as RIM's technology, however, the fact that RIM independently developed and actively possesses the technology does not help clarify the relevant patent boundaries and ownership.

In addition, the implementation of patent notice suffers important deficiencies. In chapter 3 we explore several institutional differences between patents and the property system for land that might make the former particularly prone to notice problems. These institutional features affect patent notice and are thus central to our analysis:

1. *Fuzzy or unpredictable boundaries*: Surveying land is inexpensive, and the survey boundaries carry legal weight. While surveyors can plainly map the words in a deed to a physical boundary, it is much harder to map the words in a patent to technologies, as the E-Data patent dispute illustrates. Not only are the words that lawyers use sometimes vague, but the rules for interpreting the words are also sometimes unpredictable. Although innovators can obtain expensive legal opinions about the boundaries of patents, these opinions are unreliable. There is thus no reliable way of determining patent boundaries short of litigation.

2. *Public access to boundary information*: The documents used to determine boundaries for both land and patents are eventually available to the public. It is possible, however, for patent owners to hide the claim language that defines patent boundaries from public view for many years, a practice that is becoming increasingly frequent.

3. *Possession and the scope of rights*: Generally, tangible property rights are linked closely to possession, hence the well-known expression, "possession is nine points of the law." Patent law also requires possession of an invention, but often this requirement is not rigorously enforced. Courts sometimes grant patent owners rights to technology that is new, different, and distant from anything they actually made or possessed. Not surprisingly, this practice makes patent boundaries especially unclear in fast-paced fields such as biotechnology and computer software development. It certainly seems that E-Data was granted ownership of technology that was far removed from what Charles Freeny Jr. actually invented.

4. *The patent flood*: Clearance costs are affected by the number of prospective rights that must be checked for possible infringement.

Investments in land or structures rarely involve many parcels of land, and property law discourages fragmentation of land rights. In contrast, investments in new technology often need to be checked against many patents—even thousands, in the case of e-commerce. Although the patent system has features that discourage patent proliferation—notably the requirement that an invention not be obvious—empirical evidence suggests these are not working well.

These differences mean that patents might diverge significantly from an ideal property system that grants an inventor a well-defined, exclusive right to develop a technology and bring it to market. Because of such differences, patents might not work well as property. Whether or not they do is the empirical question at the heart of this book.

EMPIRICAL EVIDENCE: DO PATENTS WORK AS PROPERTY?

Do patents give inventors positive net incentives to invest in innovation? An answer requires careful attention to the details of the patent system and the markets for innovation. The empirical evidence must account for incentives from many sources, including exclusion of competitors, licensing, and sale of the patent. We must be careful to distinguish between patent based incentives and other incentives to invest in innovation. We must also account for disincentives that arise indirectly from the threat of litigation. We study how the pattern of incentives varies over time, and across industries, technologies, and types of inventor.

Our question is simpler and more basic than the questions economists often ask when evaluating policy. Economists like to ask whether policies increase "net social welfare," a generalized measure of the overall well-being of society. Short of that, economists like to ask whether innovation policies increase innovation or R&D spending. But these are even more difficult and complicated questions to investigate empirically. Many interrelated factors can influence R&D spending, innovation, and the resulting social welfare, so it is difficult to disentangle these to determine the independent influence of patents. Not surprisingly, economic studies that attempt to answer these more difficult questions typically have arrived at inconclusive results.

Our approach, instead, is to ask a more limited question. We can determine, with reasonable accuracy, whether or not patents provide net positive incentives for a given group of inventors. This does not tell us whether patent policy is optimal or not. To the extent that incentives are positive, we cannot tell whether they are too big or too small relative to the social optimum. There are many factors we cannot measure that go into a calculation of the optimal incentive. On the other hand, if patent incentives are negative, then they fail as property in a basic sense. In this case, patents do not do what they are supposed to do, and it is not likely that they will spur innovation and increase social welfare.[10] Even though society might receive benefits far beyond the innovator's profit, if patents discourage innovators on net, then patents will not help realize these benefits.

We begin our empirical analysis in chapter 4 by reviewing the literature. It has been almost fifty years since the empirical evidence on patents was last comprehensively reviewed. The reviewer, Fritz Machlup (1958), concluded that it was not possible to decide whether patents were good or bad policy instruments. In the interim, a wide variety of research has looked at the performance of patent systems.

We review this scholarship not to determine whether patents are good or bad policy instruments in general—the discussion above suggests that firm conclusions of this sort might be very difficult to reach. Rather, we simply ask whether a nation's patents seem to have a similar effect on its economic performance as do other property rights in that nation. If they do not, this suggests that the implementation differences between patents and other property rights might be significant. Even though economic performance is ultimately influenced by *global* property rights, the contrast between a nation's patents and its other property should reveal important differences or similarities.

Specifically, the research we review includes:

- *Historical research on the Industrial Revolution.* Although property rights and markets fostered economic growth and innovation throughout Europe and the United States, patents played a much more limited role. In Britain, few major inventors received much benefit from patents, although in the United States more did benefit. More generally, however, countries without patents were just as innovative during this period as those that had patents.

- *Statistical studies that compare the performance of countries over time.* These studies use indices of the strength of property rights or the strength of patent rights to explain each country's economic growth rate. Although general measures of property rights exhibit robust correlations with economic growth, measures of patent rights do not. Patents might still play an indirect role, however. Patent rights appear to be somewhat correlated with R&D spending, although this relationship exists only among more-developed countries, and it is not clear whether patents cause R&D or vice versa.

- *Studies of economic experiments.* These studies explore what happens when legal rights change. Some researchers have explored the role of property rights in the transition of former Soviet-bloc countries to market-based economies. Those countries that developed property institutions to support a robust market economy have experienced strong economic growth after an initial period of sharp decline. This success apparently depends, however, on the establishment of specific supportive institutions, including market-oriented legal systems, commercial banking, regulatory infrastructure, and labor-market regulation. Countries that introduced private property and markets without developing these institutions have experienced persistently declining per capita income. By contrast, economic experiments that extended or strengthened *patent* rights do not seem to show clear evidence of increased innovation, except, perhaps, to a limited degree among the wealthiest nations.

- *Miscellaneous research.* Case studies present a convincing argument that patents are critical for investment in R&D in the pharmaceutical industry. On the other hand, survey evidence suggests that in most other industries, patents do not pose much of a barrier to imitation, and firms rely mainly on other means, such as lead-time advantages and trade secrecy, to obtain returns on their R&D investments. Moreover, several studies suggest that a moderate degree of competition might actually spur innovation.

In summary, patents do not work "just like property." While they do play some role in promoting innovation and economic growth, that role is limited and highly contingent compared to the role property rights normally play in promoting economic growth. The laws and institutions that implement property rights might be harder to get right for patents than for tangible property rights.

Nevertheless, patents might still work effectively, even if they have a more limited impact on economic growth than property rights for other assets. To arrive at a more definitive evaluation, we need to perform a careful accounting of the incentives and disincentives for investing in innovation that patents provide. We do this by drawing on estimates found in the literature, and on some of our own estimates.

Figure 1.1, copied from chapter 6, conveys the basic calculations we make for United States public firms. Because chemical patents, especially on pharmaceuticals, are much more valuable and much less likely to be litigated, we display the chemical and pharmaceutical industries separately from other industries. The heavy, solid lines show the annual aggregate costs to these firms of defending against patent litigation. This estimate includes not only direct legal costs of litigation, but also business costs such as loss of market share or the costs of management distraction. The dashed lines represent an estimate of the incremental annual profit flow from all patents worldwide associated with inventions patented in the United States. We derive these estimates, based on a review of over twenty research papers, in chapters 5 and 6.[11]

The incremental profit flows represent the gross positive incentives provided to innovators by worldwide patents above and beyond the profits that could be earned without patents. Litigation costs represent an important disincentive to innovation. A firm looking to invest in innovation will consider the risk that the innovation will inadvertently expose it to a patent infringement lawsuit. Since infringement lawsuits are usually filed against firms exploiting new technologies, development of a new technology exposes the innovator to risk of inadvertent infringement if patent boundaries are hidden, unclear or unpredictable.[12] That risk weighs against the profits that can be made from innovation. Of course, firms are both patent holders and potential defendants, so a comparison of profit flows and litigation costs for a group of firms should reveal the sign of net incentives.[13]

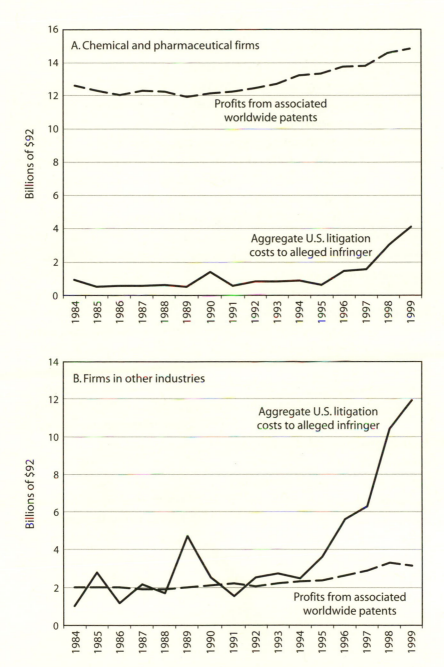

Figure 1.1. Aggregate Profits from Patents and Aggregate Litigation Costs for U.S. Public Firms. *Note*: This is a duplicate of figure 6.5, below.

The results in figure 1.1A show that chemical and pharmaceutical firms earn far more from their patents than they lose to litigation. But for other firms, figure 1.1B tells a simple but dramatic story: during the 1980s, these firms might have, at best, broken even from patents, but in the mid-1990s litigation costs exploded. By almost any interpretation, the United States patent system could not be providing overall positive incentives for these United States public firms by the end of the 1990s. The risk of patent litigation that firms faced in their capacity as technology adopters simply outstripped the profits that they made by virtue of owning patents. A firm looking to invest in an innovative technology during the late 1990s, taking this risk into account, would expect the net impact of patents to reduce the profits from innovation rather than to increase them. Moreover, preliminary data for more recent years suggest that this problem has gotten worse since 1999.

Note that patents *do* provide profits for their owners, so it makes sense for firms to get them. But taking the effect of *other* owners' patents into account, including the risk of litigation, the average public firm outside the chemical and pharmaceutical industries would be better off if patents did not exist.

Moreover, figure 1.1B understates the extent to which costs exceeded benefits for several reasons: disputes settled before a lawsuit was filed are not counted, nor are foreign disputes; this comparison ignores the costs of obtaining patents and clearance; and for a variety of reasons, the estimates of worldwide patent profits are biased upwards, while the estimates of litigation costs are biased downwards.

The patent system clearly provides large positive incentives for innovators in the chemical and pharmaceutical industries. Also, small firms generally receive benefits that exceed costs, but the net incentives for these patentees are not large. We will comment more on these exceptions below.

INTERPRETING THE RESULTS

To understand the meaning of the evidence in figure 1.1, we explore several related issues. First, what is driving this surge in the cost of litigation? In chapter 7 we look at a variety of alternative explanations. The increase in aggregate litigation cost is mainly driven by the increasing frequency of litigation, which has roughly tripled since the 1980s.[14] Yet when we look in detail at what determines the rate of litigation, we find that only a small part of this increase can be explained by measurable factors, such as how much the parties to a lawsuit spend on R&D or how many patents they have. This suggests that most of the increase arises from unmeasured factors that might include legal, institutional, and technological changes. We explore several possible factors, including deterioration of patent notice, industry-specific factors, greater rewards for litigation, a general increase in litigiousness, the rise of patent "trolls," and the declining quality of patent examination.

We can directly rule out several of these explanations. All industries appear to have experienced a rapid increase in patent litigation, although the increase seems somewhat more rapid in software-related industries. This means that industry-specific factors are unlikely to explain most of what is happening. Also, business-to-business litigation has not been increasing in general, so we cannot attribute the increase in patent litigation to an overall rise in litigiousness. In addition, we find no evidence to suggest that the rewards that patent holders gain from litigation increased in the 1990s, although they might have increased during the 1980s.[15]

We also considered the role of patent "trolls," which we define narrowly as individual inventors who do not commercialize or manufacture their inventions. One story claims that the increasing availability of patent litigators willing to work on contingency fees has spurred lawsuits by such trolls, who might otherwise be unable to afford litigation. The share of lawsuits initiated by public firms has not declined, however, nor has the share of lawsuits involving patents awarded to independent inventors increased. This suggests that the increase in litigation cannot be mainly attributed to patent "trolls," at least through 1999. Of course, if we use a broader definition of "troll" that includes all sorts of patentees who opportunistically take advantage of poor patent notice to assert patents against unsuspecting firms, then troll-like behavior might be a more important explanation. Indeed, if patent notice is poor, then all sorts of patent owners might quite reasonably assert patents more broadly than they deserve. But then it is more appropriate to attribute the surge in litigation to poor patent notice, not to trolls per se.

In fact, the distinctive pattern of litigation over time and across technologies does provide support for an explanation based on the deterioration of patent notice. Several changes to patent notice occurred during the mid-1990s, including the way that courts interpret patent claims, increased "hiding" of patent claims while applications are under review at the Patent Office, problematic legal decisions in software and biotechnology that extended the reach of patents to technologies far beyond what was actually invented, and the growing flood of patents that began during the mid-1980s and gathered strength during the 1990s. Many of these changes are the specific work of the Court of Appeals for the Federal Circuit, the specialized appeals court for patents that was established in 1982. In any case, these changes provide a natural explanation for the concurrent increase in litigation.

In addition, the pattern of litigation costs across technologies is consistent with differences in patent notice. Litigation costs are particularly low for patents on chemical compounds, including pharmaceuticals. At the same time, the value of these patents is much higher than the value of other patents—perhaps, in part, because litigation costs are low and enforcement is effective. Economists have long recognized that patents on chemicals work particularly well because these patents have very well-defined boundaries.[16] In contrast, economists recognize that complex technologies, such as electronics and computers, might have relatively poorly defined patent boundaries. Patents on complex technologies have higher litigation rates and lower values than chemical patents. By the late 1990s, these patents generated more litigation cost than profit.

Software patents, in particular, often have boundaries that are especially difficult to determine, for reasons we explore further in chapter 9. Software patents have even higher litigation rates and a high frequency of appeals over the meaning of patent claims. Not surprisingly, the costs of litigation for software patents far exceed the profits. The distinctive pattern of litigation rates across technologies thus supports the notion that patent notice might explain differences in patent value.

The deterioration of patent notice might also be roughly associated with a decline in patent quality, broadly conceived. Many critics equate low patent quality with frequent issuance of invalid patents. These critics contend that poor examination allows invalid patents to be issued for inventions that are obvious or lack novelty. Specifically, they assert that inadequate search of previous patents and publications causes examiners to overlook novelty and obviousness problems. Other critics attribute patent quality decline in part to the Federal Circuit's proclivity to weaken the legal test of obviousness. These two sources of patent quality decline contribute to the patent flood and make clearance difficult and costly, leading indirectly to litigation. Our broader conception of patent quality acknowledges problems with novelty and obviousness, but our evidence shows that quality problems are more fundamentally connected to problematic boundaries associated with patents that are vaguely worded, overly abstract, of uncertain scope, or that contain strategically hidden claims.

The narrow conception of patent quality decline does not explain the surge of patent litigation or the pattern of litigation across technologies. Perhaps there has been a recent surge of invalid patents granted, but no such surge appears in the data on litigation outcomes. Similarly, invalidation rates are not higher for technologies featuring higher litigation rates. This suggests that patent examination search quality is not primarily responsible for the increase in costly litigation by itself, although it might well be a contributing factor and it might also be a problem for other reasons.

This analysis leads us to the conclusion that during the late 1990s, the American patent system failed as a system of property rights for public firms. It did so because it failed to provide clear and efficient notice of the boundaries of the rights granted.

SMALL INVENTORS

But this evidence of failure applies only to one group of inventors— namely, those at public firms. Now this is a large and very important group of inventors, especially if we assume that the main purpose of patents is to provide incentives to invest in R&D—this group of firms is responsible for about 90 percent of R&D spending. Nevertheless, some important inventions are made by small inventors, including independent individuals and small nonpublic firms. Perhaps the patent system works sufficiently well for these small inventors to offset its other failures. Indeed, some people claim that almost all "breakthrough" inventions come from small inventors, and their interests should be paramount in debates about patent reform.

Chapter 8 explores several issues regarding small-inventor patents. There are good reasons to think that small inventors make important inventions. This is not true of all types of small inventors, of course; many small inventors patent games, simple machines, and other low-tech inventions. Nevertheless, many small inventors do make important high-tech inventions. But there is no evidence to suggest that *most* breakthrough inventions come from small inventors. What limited evidence exists—for example, the characteristics of inventors nominated to the National Inventors Hall of Fame— suggests that most recent major inventions originated in large organizations, although a significant minority of important inventions are developed by independent inventors or inventors working in small firms.

How does the patent system perform for small inventors? In our analysis of public firms, we find that small public firms enjoy positive incentives from patents—their litigation costs are lower than the profits they receive from patents, although their absolute level of profits from patents is not large. Other small inventors are also likely to enjoy a positive incentive, but we lack the data to estimate their litigation costs. Certainly, the many small inventors who do not commercialize any technology have little to fear as defendants in patent lawsuits. Even so, we find troubling evidence that patent notice adversely affects small inventors, too. Patent notice problems impair the market for technology and rob many small inventors of the larger reward they could get from licensing or selling their patents in a world with good patent notice.

The troubling evidence is this: all types of small inventors, including small firms, realize substantially less value from their patents than do large firms. This is true for the independent inventors who work in low-tech fields, as well as for small public firms in many high-tech industries. Indeed, relative to large firms, many small inventors, even small high-tech firms that go public, forgo patents entirely, relying instead on trade secrecy and other means of protecting their profits deriving from innovations. The patent system works for small inventors, but does so only weakly. Why? In part because small inventors do not have access to the resources needed to commercialize inventions. They cannot quickly ramp up manufacturing and marketing, they do not have established distribution channels, and they cannot easily finance acquisition of these assets.

Lack of such complementary assets would not be a problem if markets for technology worked better. Small inventors who lack resources should be able to sell or license their technology to large firms who have those resources. Indeed, technology markets are often the best means that small inventors can employ to capture value from their inventions. In a world with competitive and efficient technology markets, licensing royalties and sales contracts would deliver value to small inventors comparable to the value that large firms gain from their own patents. The fact that small inventors actually gain much less from their patents, however, indicates that these markets do not always work very well.

Better patent notice would improve technology markets in two ways. A direct improvement flows from clearer property rights. Unclear property rights increase bargaining costs and the probability of bargaining breakdown. Better patent notice makes technology markets more efficient, and hence more attractive to small inventors.

An indirect and possibly larger benefit flows from the impact of notice on buyers in technology markets. When potential buyers face substantial risk of patent litigation, they cannot profit as much from the technology they seek to exploit and are therefore unwilling to pay as much for the technology. Better notice would reduce the risk of inadvertent infringement and any ensuing litigation, increase the willingness of buyers to pay for technology, and increase the value of patents to small firms who sell in technology markets.

Small inventors and large firms alike suffer from poor patent notice.[17] The positive incentives that small inventors receive from patents give us no reason to be sanguine about the current state of the patent system.

The Particular Problem of Software Patents

As we noted above, the patent system performs particularly poorly for software patents. Software is a vital technology and, as we shall see, software patents contribute substantially to the overall failure of the patent system for public firms. We explore the reasons for this in chapter 9.

Software patents have been controversial in part because the software-publishing industry grew up largely without patents and most computer professionals oppose patenting software. But judicial decisions during the 1990s eliminated certain obstacles to software patents, and now close to 200,000 software patents have been granted.

Some argue that there is nothing different about patents on software, and if there are any problems, these will be resolved as the Patent Office adapts to this new technology. Some say that because the software-publishing industry remains innovative, patents cannot be hurting innovation. But evidence about the software-publishing industry is not definitive; the majority of software firms still do not obtain patents, and most software patents are awarded to firms in other industries, chiefly the manufacture of computers, semiconductors, and electronics.

Critically, software patents *do* seem to exhibit some marked differences from other patents when it comes to litigation costs. Software patents are more than twice as likely to be litigated as other patents; patents on methods of doing business, which are largely software patents, are nearly *seven* times more likely to be litigated. And, despite being a relatively new area for patenting, software patents accounted for 38 percent of the total cost of patent litigation to public firms during the late 1990s. This does not appear to be a temporary problem that is dissipating as the Patent Office adapts—the probability that a software patent will be litigated has been *increasing* substantially rather than decreasing.

Why are software patents more frequently litigated? In a word, abstraction. In chapter 9, we will elaborate upon what we mean by "abstraction" and how it affects patent notice, but for the present consider that software is an abstract technology, and this sometimes makes it more difficult, if not impossible, to relate the words that describe patent boundaries to actual technologies. In this context, it is helpful to recall the abstract concepts described in the claims of the E-Data patent—"point of sale location," "information manufacturing machine," "material object," and so on. These words reach far beyond the actual kiosk technology that Charles Freeny Jr. of E-Data invented, yet during the course of litigation it was not clear what, precisely, they covered. In other cases, the words in some broad software patents seem clear enough, but because the patents claim technology far beyond what was actually invented, judges will sometimes interpret the claims narrowly (for example, see the discussion of Wang's Patent No. 4,751,669 in chapter 9). But it is hard to predict which broad claims will be narrowed. This becomes another cause of boundary unpredictability that contributes to inadvertent infringement and, ultimately, to litigation.

Of course, software is not the only technology that can be described in abstract terms. Indeed, the problem of abstraction in patents has been recognized at least since the eighteenth century, when British law attempted to exclude patents on general "principles of manufacture" as opposed to specific inventions. In the United States, judges also developed doctrines to exclude patents with abstract claims during the nineteenth century.

Nevertheless, there are two major reasons why abstraction poses a particular problem for software. First, as we will discuss in chapter 9, the Court of Appeals for the Federal Circuit has tolerated more abstraction in software patents than seems warranted by these patent doctrines. Second, software is inherently more abstract than other technologies. Indeed, it is well known among computer scientists that software technologies (algorithms, system structures) can be represented in many different ways, and it might be difficult to know when alternative representations are equivalent. This means that the technology claimed in a patent can be difficult to distinguish from alternatives; it might be hard to know whether a given patent claims an invention that is different from previous inventions, or whether an allegedly infringing program is different from the claimed technology. If computer scientists cannot unambiguously make these distinctions, there is little hope that judges and juries can do better.

Although not all software patents suffer from abstract or overly broad claims, software technology is especially prone to these problems. Indeed, software patents are much more likely than other patents to have their claim construction reviewed on appeal—an implicit indication that parties to lawsuits have fundamental uncertainty over the boundaries of these patents. This uncertainty leads to more frequent litigation and substantially higher litigation costs.

Software patents are not just like other patents. The problems of software patents—problems arising partly from the nature of the technology and partly from the way the courts have treated this technology—are a substantial factor in the overall poor performance of the patent system. The problem of implementing patent law to deal with abstract patents appears to be particularly stubborn and is unlikely to go away unless it is addressed directly.

MAKING PATENTS WORK LIKE PROPERTY

What, then, will it take to fix the failure of patent notice and make the patent system an effective tool for encouraging innovation in all industries? At first glance, this might not seem too difficult a task, given that patents seem to have performed reasonably well as recently as the 1980s. Indeed, many people have been quite optimistic that the current round of draft legislation and recently renewed attention from the Supreme Court will soon lead to a rebirth of effective patent policy.

In chapter 10, however, we suggest that effective reform might well prove surprisingly difficult to achieve. Many reform advocates believe that the poor performance of the patent system flows from deterioration of patent "quality" (narrowly defined) that can be fixed by improving the patent examination process. We agree that invalid patents are a problem, and that patent examination can be improved; however, we see this as only *part* of the problem. We suspect that many people focus on patent quality because there has been so much publicity about bad patents on inventions that lack novelty or seem obvious, such as those mentioned previously involving the peanut butter and jelly sandwich or the backyard swing. Patents of doubtful validity create social costs, but our evidence suggests that concerns about validity are not the main drivers of the patent litigation "explosion."

Moreover, we think that attempts to improve patent quality, including review procedures involving third parties, will not be very effective unless there are broader improvements in patent notice. This is because patent examination *depends* on clear, predictable patent boundaries. For example, critics of the E-Data ruling contend that e-commerce had been discussed and practiced before Freeny's invention. Under patent law this "prior art" should have invalidated the E-Data patent. But if the patent examiner, like almost everyone else, interpreted the patent narrowly in 1983 as claiming only in-store kiosks and vending machines, not e-commerce, then that prior art would not have seemed relevant. Thus, patent quality depends on well-defined patent notice, which involves much more than simply improving the examiners' access to prior art.

Finally, improving patent notice will be challenging because it cannot be achieved merely by a few court decisions or statutory changes; rather, it requires changing institutions. As we discussed above, the institutions of the patent system fail to perform basic functions required for notice—functions other property systems perform smoothly. Indeed, the institutions of the patent system actually seem to have contributed to the deterioration of notice over the last two decades.

In particular, the structure of the courts—specifically, the designation of a single court for patent appeals—appears to have undermined notice in at least two ways. First, a specialized court is more likely than a typical appellate court to take actions to expand its influence. This seems to have been the case with the changes in the interpretation of patent claims. The Federal Circuit downgraded the role of the Patent Office and the district courts in claim interpretation while increasing its own. We will show that this shift has decreased the predictability of patent boundaries. The Federal Circuit has also increased its influence by expanding the range of patentable subject matter to include software, business methods, early-stage inventions, and more.[18] Increased patenting of these new technologies might have created problems because of a second institutional shortcoming: a single appellate court might not be well suited for developing new law. Because power is concentrated in the Federal Circuit, patent law misses the benefits of the intercircuit competition that exists in most other areas of federal law.

We thus think it likely that effective reform will require structural changes, including, possibly, multiple appellate courts, specialized district courts, and greater deference to fact-finders. What other changes might improve patent notice? In chapter 11 we consider many reforms, most of which have also been advanced by others who have preceded us. These include:

- *Make patent claims transparent.* We recommend changes in the way patent claims are defined, published, recorded in the application process, and used for subsequent determinations so that innovators have clear, accessible, and predictable information on patent boundaries. This includes strong limits on patent "continuations," a procedure used to keep patent claims hidden from the public for extended periods. We also consider a new role for the Patent Office where, for a fee, innovators can obtain opinion letters on whether their technology infringes a patent.

- *Make claims clear and unambiguous by enforcing strong limits against vague or overly abstract claims.* This includes a robust "indefiniteness" standard that invalidates patent claims that can be plausibly interpreted in multiple, fundamentally different ways. Also, we recommend reforms to limit overly abstract patents in software and other technologies. At the very least, patent law should prevent software patents from claiming technologies far beyond what was actually disclosed as the patented invention. If this proves inadequate, then we suggest subject-matter tests to limit the range of software inventions that can be patented, tests similar to those used during the 1970s and 1980s.

- *Make patent search feasible by reducing the flood of patents.* This includes a strong requirement that patents should not be granted on obvious inventions, coupled with substantially higher renewal fees. Ideally, patent renewal fees should be set by a quasi-independent agency and should be based on empirical economic research. These reforms will help stem the patent flood by screening out unwarranted patents and discouraging renewal of low-value patents. Reducing the number of such patents should help notice by reducing the cost of clearance search.

- Besides improving notice, we also favor reforms to mitigate the harm caused by poor notice. These include an exemption from penalties when the infringing technology was independently invented, as well as changes in patent remedies that might discourage opportunistic lawsuits.

In presenting these policy suggestions, we admit that we cannot know with any certainty what it will take to substantially improve patent notice.

These policy reforms move us in the direction of an effective patent system, but we cannot as yet tell whether they are sufficient to get us there.

Some have argued strongly that our policy prescriptions will not suffice. Economists Boldrin and Levine (2007) argue that the patent system does not work at all and should be abolished. We doubt that such an extreme move is warranted. Our evidence suggests that the patent system *does* provide positive innovation incentives for small inventors, and, on a larger scale, for chemical and pharmaceutical inventions. It seems likely that reform can improve notice and overall patent performance in some areas, especially since the patent system did provide positive innovation incentives as recently as the 1980s.[19]

On the other hand, we are troubled by the expansionist view of the courts that "everything under the sun made by man" should be patentable, including software, business methods, and even mental correlations. Tangible property systems are not so expansive. They restrict property to assets that can be clearly defined with unambiguous boundaries. A landowner receives no rights to untapped oil flowing beneath her land, or to migratory ducks that set down on it, or to the airplanes that fly over it. Similarly, we doubt that all types of inventive ideas can have clear boundaries, and our empirical evidence shows that many software and business-method patents fail to provide efficient notice. We are quite sure that the patent system needs to recognize the limits to its grasp, even if we are not sure of the best way to implement those limits.

Perhaps many of these reforms are not politically feasible today. Perhaps the political will to thoroughly fix patent notice does not yet exist. The patent bar has long dominated patent policymaking, and its interests—at least in the short run—do not always coincide with improved notice.

Yet there is some reason to think that this impasse is temporary and that some of the patent bar's opposition to improved notice will prove to be shortsighted. Our estimates suggest that the litigation burden imposed by patents is growing, and the performance of the patent system will continue to deteriorate. Moreover, the trends suggest that the deterioration might be particularly bad for software patents and other patents used in information technology (IT) industries—not only is the rate of litigation per software patent rising, but the share of software patents out of total patents continues to grow rapidly. It is no accident that computer, semiconductor, software, Internet, and finance companies have begun to lobby for patent reform.

If this prognosis is correct, then the political landscape will continue to change. In the end, the survival of the patent system will require major improvements in the notice function. Despite all the rhetoric calling for "protection of inventors' property," today's patents fail as property, and tomorrow's might yet do even worse. Too often, such rhetoric is used to justify policies that actually undermine the property nature of patents. We hope our message and our empirical evidence succeeds in distinguishing actual patent performance from rhetoric. But in the long run, the pressures of market competition will determine the fate of the patent system based on its performance. If patents fail to work as property, over time they will make the United States economically less competitive, and industry will demand change.

Note to the reader: We wrote this book for a non-specialist audience, however, in several chapters we added sidebars on some advanced topics that might interest economists or lawyers. The main text can be understood without reading these.

2 Why Property Rights Work, How Property Rights Fail

ARE PATENTS PROPERTY?

Most people understand patents to be a type of property. The notion that inventors should reap the benefit from their inventions has great intuitive appeal. There is a complementary sense of outrage when the interests of inventors are trampled, especially when the villains are big corporations. Many scholars share these sentiments.[1] Economists routinely treat patents as property rights. Even most lawyers who do not specialize in intellectual property readily accept the characterization of patents as property. It is curious, then, that scholars in intellectual property law are not completely comfortable applying the property label to patents.

Scholars critical of the recent expansion of intellectual property rights place part of the blame for the expansion on the rhetoric of property. They note that patents and copyrights have existed from the founding of the United States but the label "intellectual property" has become popular just in the last twenty years (Lemley 2005a).[2] The critics contend that invoking the "property" label has aided the expansion of patent rights because judges mimic real property rights too closely when crafting patent or copyright rights.[3]

Today there is a vigorous debate among intellectual property law scholars between those who generally approve of the *propertization* of intellectual property law, and those who do not. For example, Mark Lemley claims that "the economics of intellectual property law should focus on the economic characteristics of intellectual property rights, not on inapposite economic analysis borrowed from the very different case of land" (Lemley 2005a). In contrast, William Landes and Richard Posner claim that "there is a danger of losing sight of the continuity between rights in physical and intellectual property and thus the utility of using what economics has learned about the former to assist analysis of the latter" (Landes and Posner 2003).

Like Landes and Posner, we contend that the economics of property has valuable lessons for the economics of patents, but there is a danger of overstating the *continuity* between physical property rights and patents. We think much can be learned about the relatively poor performance of the patent system by understanding the sources of discontinuity between physical property and patents. We start by comparing the main features of property and patent law.

Use and Exclusion

The rights to use and exclude use by others are the hallmarks of tangible property under the law. An owner has the right to wear his shirt and live on his land. He also has the right to exclude others from use of his shirt and his land. Thus, property law gives an owner rights against strangers. In contrast, contract law creates rights only between parties who assent to be bound by the law. Patents are like property in that they create rights to exclude use by others, including strangers.

Patent law departs from tangible property law by granting only the negative right to exclude use by others and not the affirmative right to use an invention. This distinction matters when someone invents a patentable improvement or a new use of a currently patented invention. The second inventor can get a patent on her invention but the patent is subservient to the patent on the earlier invention. In other words, the second inventor cannot lawfully use her invention unless she gets permission from the owner of the patent on the first invention.[4]

Patents share another crucial feature with tangible property: liability does not depend on a defendant's knowledge or intent. A trespasser is still liable regardless of whether she was mistaken about a property line or took care to avoid trespass. Similarly, a technology-adopter is still liable for patent infringement regardless of whether she independently invented, or made a good-faith effort to avoid intruding on someone's patent rights.

Neither tangible nor patent property rights offer absolute rights of exclusion and under some circumstances these rights are curtailed.[5]

Division and Transfer

Property rights are the cornerstone of a market economy. Property law supports exchange by allowing property owners to divide and transfer their rights. Patent law follows tangible property law in this regard; in fact, patent law arguably goes further to promote exchange than tangible property law.

Owners of tangible property can sell, divide and sell a portion, or rent their property. Thus, Hertz Corporation owns a fleet of cars that it rents for a period of time and then sells. Similarly, patent owners can sell, divide and sell a portion, or rent their patent rights. In patent law jargon, a sale is called an "assignment," and a rental is called a "license."

The rental-to-licensing parallel is not exact because the inexhaustible quality of information means that a patent owner can license multiple users without degrading the use value of the information; this is not possible with rental cars. Sales and rental contracts might contain conditions that restrict permissible use of the tangible property. For example, a car rental agreement prohibits the renter from using the car recklessly, and typically sets payment terms that influence the distance driven and locations visited. Patent assignments and licenses might contain similar restrictions on permissible use of the patented invention. For example, a patent license might impose geographic, quantity, field-of-use, and even pricing restrictions on the licensee. Patent law is more generous to an owner than tangible property law in the sense that antitrust regulation of contract terms is relaxed in the context of patent licenses. Therefore, actions that a patent owner takes that might inhibit competition are more likely to survive antitrust scrutiny when they are linked to a contract involving a patented invention than to a contract involving unpatented tangible property.

Scope and Duration of Rights

Patents and tangible property display significant differences in terms of duration and scope. The property right in land is perpetual—personal property rights last as long as the property—but in the United States the patent right is generally limited to twenty years. The scope of tangible property is relatively easy to define in terms of physical attributes. For example, the scope of land rights is defined by a boundary traced on the earth. Defining the scope of patent rights is extremely difficult, because it is hard to draw a boundary around an idea. In chapter 3 we will explain the difficult and uncertain process used by courts to construe the claim language in a patent and determine the scope of a patent.

Acquisition and Ownership

The rules of acquisition and ownership for patents and tangible property exhibit some important differences, and the practical significance of acquisition rules is dramatically greater in patent law than it is for tangible property. Both tangible property and patents can be acquired through a properly conducted sale or assignment by a previous owner. Legal disputes usually focus on the integrity of the chain of title. Tangible property and patents can also be newly acquired from "the state of nature." Newly manufactured personal property is owned by its maker. Other new personal property that is captured, harvested, or extracted from the public domain usually belongs to the person who first took possession of the item.

The rules governing acquisition of patent rights are complex, but generally the first inventor is entitled to a patent, and subsequent inventors of the same invention receive no rights. Patent law contains a significant limitation on acquisition missing from the law of tangible property—not all inventions are patentable. A government agency, the Patent and Trademark Office (PTO) must examine patent applications and will grant a patent only if an invention is new, useful, non-obvious, and falls into one of the appropriate subject-matter categories. Furthermore, an inventor can

spoil his right to a patent by choosing to exploit his invention as a trade secret, in which case the next inventor might be able to patent the invention.

Remedies

The final major feature of property is the generous set of remedies available
to an owner whose property rights have been violated. Most notably, courts
are quite willing to award injunctive relief and disgorge the defendant's
profits arising from the violation.[6] In contrast, in contract law injunctions
are rare, and the usual damage measure awards the plaintiff his expected
payoff, and usually will not force disgorgement of the defendant's profit.
Patent law also favors injunctive relief, but is not so generous with damages,
and comes closer to the approach of contract law to damages.[7]

In summary, patents *do* appear to share many of the key features of tangible property. A patent owner can exclude others from using his invention.
Patent infringement claims are effective against strangers, even if they are
innocent—indeed, even if they have independently invented the patented
technology. Infringement lawsuits are backed by the threat of injunction.[8]
In addition, patent law has rules of acquisition, ownership, division, and
transfer that are patterned after the comparable rules from tangible property law.

There are some notable differences between patents and tangible property, which we have touched upon above. Patent law offers weaker rights
than property law along four dimensions. First, patents in the United
States are limited to twenty years. Second, there is no affirmative right to
use a patented invention. Third, patent law only extends to inventions
that are new, useful, non-obvious, and of the proper subject matter.
Fourth, patent damages do not include a defendant's profit.

Patent law offers stronger rights than property law along two dimensions. First, patent owners have more freedom in their design of contracts
because of a limited antitrust immunity. Second, patent law supports a variety of indirect forms of liability that allow the patent owner to bring suit
against parties above and below the direct infringer in the value chain.

Specifically, a patentee can sue an input supplier who contributes to inducing a customer to infringe a patent. Also, a patentee can sue anyone who buys or uses a patented product that was made by an infringing manufacturer. Indirect theories of liability are neither so well developed nor so important in tangible property law.

These doctrinal discrepancies are interesting, but, as we shall see, the truly significant differences between patents and tangible property are not linked to differences in doctrine, but rather to differences in *application*. The intangible nature of invention makes innocent infringement much more likely in the world of patents than in the world of tangible property. If two people grab the same black umbrella, they will immediately recognize the conflict and normally they will resolve it amicably. But two people can independently invent the same technology and not become aware of the conflict for a period of years. This problem is exacerbated because certain operational features of the patent system make patent rights much less clear than tangible property rights and certain critical institutions are dysfunctional or virtually non-existent. But this is getting ahead of our story . . . To understand the economic significance of these differences, we must first explore the ways that the main features of property can generate substantial economic benefits.

BENEFITS OF PROPERTY RIGHTS

Investment Incentives

Investment incentives are an easily recognized benefit provided by private property rights. Secure ownership of property assures an owner that he will appropriate a significant share of the return on his investment. For example, a farmer would be discouraged from cultivating crops on his land if his neighbors were free to harvest and consume his crops. If he can exclude others from the harvest, he can capture the market value of the crop, bolstering his investment incentive. Private property rights mean that the farmer's crop is secure from expropriation by other private parties and, under normal circumstances, secure from government expropriation, as well. It also means that the farmer gets the full value he can realize from consuming or selling his crop. Under other property regimes, such as feudalism and collective ownership, investment incentives are dampened because the farmer cannot be sure he will capture much of the return from his investment.

Several of the features of property law identified above contribute to securing these returns on investment. Obviously, the right to exclude others, backed by strong remedies like a quick and effective injunction, enhances the security of a property owner. Less obviously, clear boundaries for property rights minimize wasteful disputes and, to return to the example of the farmer, reduce any uncertainty concerning his claims to the crop. And the rules of acquisition ensure that the crop is owned by the farmer who planted it on his land. This sensible policy assigns the rights to the crop to the party best positioned to make socially desirable investment decisions.

Generally, efficient acquisition rules vest ownership in a party who has some degree of control over goods acquired from nature. Clear acquisition rules based on control and other indicators of possession mitigate harm caused by premature or redundant investment by parties who are competing to acquire property rights. Clear acquisition rules also limit disputes and opportunistic behavior that might arise from granting rights to parties who are not able to make the investments needed to develop property extracted from nature. The copper-mine war in Butte, Montana, mentioned in passing above and discussed later in this chapter, provides a dramatic illustration of the costs of inefficient acquisition rules.

Transfer to Higher-Value Users

The second benefit of private property is so intuitive and fundamental that it sometimes goes unnoticed by non-economists: private property rights promote exchange. Private property regimes allow owners to *alienate* or sell their property. The market economy facilitates efficient trade and reallocation of property from a seller with a lower value to a buyer with a higher value from use of the property.

Property law also encourages transactions, and complements contract law in less visible ways. Property rights can be divided and transfers can be made contingent. Lawyers think of property as a bundle of rights; they often unpack these rights and design complicated transfers involving a subset of the rights in the package. The use of property as collateral to secure a loan is an example with particular relevance to patents and innovation. Such complex transactions are much more difficult in regimes without private property.

In another vein, property rights encourage information-disclosure during contract negotiations. To see why, suppose Alan has gold nuggets in a stream on his land. Suppose it would be efficient for him to sell the land and let someone else extract the gold. Given insecure property rights, Alan would be reluctant to disclose his private information to Bonnie, a potential buyer. If the negotiations broke down, Bonnie might try to steal the nuggets or sell the information to a third party. Secure property rights make it profitable for Alan to disclose the information, and this disclosure promotes efficient transfer (Merges 2005).

Financial Markets

Economic historians and growth economists tend to define private property broadly enough to include partnerships and corporations. These organizational forms enable private shared ownership of firms. Economists suggest that partnership and corporation law play an important role in promoting financial markets and economic growth. (Rosenberg 2003) The availability of these organizational forms relaxes liquidity constraints and risk-bearing costs on new ventures and encourages entrepreneurship. Relatedly, mortgage and similar laws increase the liquidity of financial markets by drawing wealth from real property owners—wealth that remains locked up in less-developed economies. The rule of law plays a critical role in assuring passive investors that their ownership rights will be respected by those in control of a business.

Alternatives to Private Property

Private property is not absolutely necessary to achieve the social benefits described above. There are other ways that, say, a farmer can secure a full market return on his investment. He might use private protective measures like guards and fences to protect his crop. Perhaps social norms could also provide a secure environment for investment without property rights. For example, miners' protective leagues formed in western U.S. mining communities that lacked effective law enforcement in the early days of the gold and silver rushes. The protective leagues effectively used force and promoted social norms to protect the mineral rights of miners. In a contemporary example, Robert Ellickson (1991) studied Shasta County, California, during the 1970s and found that social norms largely displaced property law as the tool regulating stray livestock. When stray livestock caused property damage, the ranchers in the community relied on local norms to fix liability and enforce compliance. Ellickson found this homegrown regulatory regime systematically departed from the liability rules of California property law. Thus, the ranchers effectively opted out of property law for these disputes.[9]

Beyond investment incentives, formal property rights are not a necessary predicate to flourishing exchange. There is evidence of exchange between tribes of hunter gatherers going back thousands of years before agricultural civilization (Seabright 2004). Such exchange was likely facilitated by social norms of reciprocity and by private sanctions. Even today, criminals engage in many forms of commerce without the benefit of state-sanctioned property rights using private enforcement to secure transactions.

So the economic advantage of private property must be measured *relative* to these alternatives. An interesting question is whether an effectively implemented private property system significantly increases social benefits compared to a system that relies solely on the combination of private policing and social norms to protect property. There are two reasons to think the answer must be yes. First, public enforcement is often more efficient. There are fixed costs and economies of scale in setting up a police force. It is generally more efficient to provide a single police force for an entire county than for each property owner to set up his own force or purchase protection from private security forces.

Second, public enforcement can reinforce social norms. Well-implemented property rights are *self-policing*. Because the boundaries are clear, perceived as fair, and the remedies are swift and strong, tangible property rights are almost always respected without requiring expenditure on protective measures or enforcement. Only rarely do farmers call on law enforcement to stop neighbors from stealing their crop.

Property rights can be inexpensively enforced because they combine the threat of government force with social norms that support respect for property rights. On the other hand, social norms, enforced only with less effective private sanctions, can break down, leading to "tragedies of the commons." For example, norms limiting catches in certain New England fisheries broke down and a commonly managed resource was overfished to the point of near-extinction for several species (Woodard 2004). Despite the occasional instance where commons are effectively managed (Ostrom 1991), well-implemented property rights provide important incentives for investment in many cases.

WHY DOES PROPERTY SOMETIMES FAIL?

The economic benefits we have outlined above make property rights superior to a system relying solely on private enforcement and social norms. But clearly, the ability of any property system—either for inventions or for other sorts of property—to deliver these benefits depends on the details of the statutes, case law, regulations, and supporting social institutions. Each of the benefits depends on fast, efficient enforcement buttressed by social norms. If the property system fails to provide these things efficiently, then property can fail on its own terms.

This section considers some of the ways property systems have failed and some of the ways they are designed to avoid failure.

Uncertain Rights, Unreliable Enforcement

The transition from planned to market economies in Eastern Europe and the former Soviet republics created a set of natural experiments that economists have studied to gain a better understanding of the relationship between property law and the performance of market economies. Corruption and cronyism can make enforcement more costly or arbitrary and, at the same time, undermine social support for property rights. This, in turn, undermines the self-policing of property, requiring more costly overt enforcement. Johnson, McMillan, and Woodruff (2002) used surveys to obtain firm-level evidence of the role of property rights in spurring investment by small manufacturing companies in Poland, Russia, Slovakia, Romania, and

Ukraine. They find that firms with the "least secure property rights invest 40 percent less of their profits than those with the most secure property rights." Chapter 4 reviews other empirical evidence confirming the link between property rights and economic growth in formerly communist countries.

Economic historians reach similar conclusions in their studies of American economic history.[10] For example, the transition from Mexican to U.S. rule in California in the 1850s and 1860s disrupted property rights in agricultural land, and provided an important natural experiment for testing the investment incentives of secure property rights. Land rights were uncertain because the effectiveness and impartiality of the courts was unclear, and because the status of land titles previously granted by Spain and Mexico was clouded. Clay (2006) explains that the legal uncertainty was aggravated because of "widespread squatting on agricultural land held by the owners of Spanish and Mexican land grants." She gathered data on grain production in California farms and found insecure property rights adversely affected agricultural productivity. Also, the ambiguous status of property claims apparently undermined the social norms supporting those claims, leading to lawlessness and violence.

Severe uncertainty about ownership, the scope of rights, and the effectiveness of the courts causes significant deterioration in the performance of property. Mature property systems are resilient, however, and can perform quite well in the face of more moderate uncertainty. Landowners are generally free to use their land as they please, but there are restrictions on land use that adversely affects neighbors. The stringency of these restrictions under nuisance law is determined on a case-by-case basis. This creates some uncertainty about acceptable uses, but this sort of uncertainty does not seem to create much of an impediment to efficient investment and land use, because neighboring parties can find each other and usually negotiate a mutually beneficial agreement.

Informational Costs and Clearance Problems

A regime of private property imposes informational costs on putative property owners, the government, and third parties who wish to avoid infringing on the property rights of others. There are public and private costs of maintaining accurate information in registries. Property owners take steps to identify their property: surveying and fencing land, branding livestock, and fixing serial numbers on personal property, among others. Third parties bear the costs of identifying property rights and obtaining permission to use private property. Occasionally, ownership or use rights are disputed and parties litigate to clarify property rights.

De Soto (2000) argues that property rights often fail in developing economies because the administrative costs of recording a property transaction are ridiculously high. He notes, for example, that getting a title to a home in Peru takes 207 administrative steps. Red tape invites corruption and makes it harder to buy and sell property or to use it as collateral for a loan.

Effective property law takes steps to minimize these costs. It reduces the informational burden on the courts and litigating parties by favoring injunctive remedies. Damage remedies require expensive property valuations that can be avoided by reliance on injunctive relief (Smith 2004).[11] Property law mitigates informational costs to third parties by making property rights easily recognizable and facilitating the clearance of rights by third parties who would like to use another's property.

Recording statutes and standardization of the forms of property help diminish informational costs to third parties. Property law is more formal than contract law; it imposes restrictions on the forms of property and the ways that property rights can be created. In contrast, contract law allows contracting parties to craft most any sort of agreement that complies with other relevant laws. Arguably, these constraints reduce the burden on strangers to a property who must be able to recognize a property right and discern its boundaries.[12] They might also reduce the informational burden on those who wish to contract with a property owner (Hansmann and Kraakman 2002). Henry Smith argues that recording and standardization are complementary: standardization makes the search of the chain of title easier and more reliable (Smith 2003). He notes that land title specialists have emerged who efficiently inform third parties about the contours of potentially relevant property rights.

Fragmentation of property rights creates a different barrier to clearance that can arise even when property rights are relatively clear. In certain circumstances, socially valuable economic activity requires the use of the property of a large number of different owners. For example, when an aircraft travels any significant distance, it passes over many parcels of land. It would be difficult for the aircraft operator to get permission from every landowner in a flight path. Fortunately, the traditional rule which gives a landowner rights to all the space above his land was modified to allow aircraft to fly over land without permission from the landowners. Similarly, property rights are limited by the possibility that the state will use its power of eminent domain to create a corridor of land (a right-of-way) that can be used for transportation or a public utility.

Property law also takes certain steps to avoid a proliferation of property rights that are apt to generate high clearance costs. Generally, property law encourages people to divide, transfer, and recombine property interests to suit their preferences. Sometimes the process of division goes too far, and it becomes difficult to transfer and recombine property rights efficiently. Heller (1998) popularized the term "anti-commons" to describe high levels of fragmentation that frustrate both transfer and use of property. Use is discouraged when set up costs for uses are high compared to the value of the property; investment might be further discouraged if the fruits of investment spill over to the owners of neighboring fragments. Transfer is discouraged by transaction costs and hold-out problems.[13]

Heller illustrated the tragedy of the anti-commons by pointing to Moscow storefronts during the transition away from central planning. He noted that storefronts stood empty in the Moscow winter even though retail trade flourished in kiosks on the streets in front of those stores. He explained that store leases were too costly because the ownership of any one store was fragmented. A retailer needed to arrange a lease with too many distinct property owners. The resulting transaction costs made such leases uneconomical.[14] In other situations, fragmented rights might not completely deter investment, but instead simply provide disincentives. When rights are highly fragmented, people might invest without conducting thorough clearance of rights because that is simply too expensive. In this case their incentive to invest is reduced because of the risk of wasteful disputes.

Property law discourages harmful fragmentation through various rules. Heller (1999) discusses several of these rules, including primogeniture, limits on future interests, property taxes and registration requirements, and zoning and subdivision restrictions. When land was the main source of wealth, landowners devised complicated schemes for distributing their land to their heirs. Besides dividing the land geographically, they often divided ownership rights over time and included contingencies linked to births and deaths of potential heirs. Primogeniture was a feudal rule that restricted inheritances of land to the oldest son. The rule was intended to preserve the feudal order but it also had the effect of preserving large estates. The common law of both England and the United States abandoned primogeniture but developed other, more subtle doctrines to regulate temporal fragmentation and weaken the grip of the "dead hand of the past" on transactions by the living. Property taxes and registration fees obviously discourage fragmentation when the fixed minimum taxes or fees are large relative to the value of the property. The registration fees imposed under the federal mining law forced the abandonment of stale mining claims prevalent on federal lands. Finally, minimum lot size and setback requirements prevent the land in residential neighborhoods from fragmenting too much.

Newly Acquired Property Rights

Devising efficient property rights is particularly difficult in the context of newly acquired rights—a constant challenge for patent law. New property rights should be clearly defined to provide adequate notice to strangers who might be affected by the rights and who might want to contract for permission to use newly created property. Also, the law should strive to minimize social losses that might accrue as parties compete to acquire new property rights.

To a great extent, property law addresses the notice problem by relying on possession to govern allocation of new rights. The law often adopts nonlegal intuitions about physical control over an asset as the key sign of ownership. Simple possession rules make it easier for third parties to recognize the existence and scope of a property right. In the classic case, *Pierson v. Post*, a court was called on to award ownership of a fox to one of two hunters. Post was in hot pursuit of the fox with a pack of hounds. Pierson stepped in, killed, and took possession of the fox knowing Post was in hot pursuit. The court favored Pierson, perhaps because his possession of the fox left no doubt about when the property right was established and who the owner was. Critics of this outcome would have preferred an award to Post because it would have provided better incentives for parties to invest in hunting (and generally, the creation of a new property right). This interesting and difficult tradeoff will command much of our attention when we discuss the acquisition of patent rights in chapter 3.

We here pursue analogous problems that arise during the acquisition of new mineral rights. We will look back to mining and the mining law in America during the second half of the nineteenth century. We find that acquisition rules are difficult to calibrate; they sometimes cause social loss from excessive and duplicative mineral prospecting, and sometimes by chilling investment incentives.[15] Furthermore, vague rules of acquisition create notice problems and might result in disputes and litigation over neighboring mineral claims, which ultimately might lead to inefficient extraction of the minerals.[16]

We examine three different kinds of natural-resource extraction that yielded different kinds and frequencies of disputes because of differential information and enforcement costs. First, the California gold rush was dominated by placer claims, in which deposits were largely found on the surface in a fixed location (Libecap 1989; Lueck 1995). The mining camps set rules defining relatively small and clearly defined claims. Disputes were not too severe even though the mining camps were initially outside the reach of the law.

Second, a different set of rules emerged for oil and gas rights because these natural resources are migratory; that is, each well in a field draws from the same reserve that can flow from one location to another. Here it was impossible to enforce rights based on surface claims. Property rights granted to the underlying reserve based on surface claims could not be efficiently delineated and enforced. Instead, property rights were tailored to cover only the oil and gas drawn from the ground (so-called rules of capture) rather than the underlying reserve. This rule of capture creates a tragedy of the commons, and owners have an incentive to extract the mineral too rapidly, leading to losses from evaporation and fire and to inefficient extraction. To combat this problem, states developed regulations to limit the number of wells and to encourage "unitization" of the reserve where owners of surface claims shared jointly in the profits from the entire field.

Claims to veins of minerals create the third, hybrid case, where surface claims can not entirely avoid costly disputes and the tragedy of the commons might occur, even when miners hold fairly broad rights. A remarkable example is the so-called War of the Copper Kings in Butte, Montana (Glasscock 1935). The mountain standing outside of Butte was once known as the Richest Hill on Earth. It was mined for gold, silver, and, most notably, copper. The early miners at Butte exhausted the relatively small supplies of gold and silver in the 1860s and 1870s. At that point four large mining interests began to buy old claims in a search for copper ore. By the mid-1880s it was becoming clear that the mountain was laced with a rich tangle of copper veins that penetrated deep into the mountain. It was very difficult to trace the copper veins to the surface of the mountain. As a result, it did not become clear until about twenty years later who owned what copper.

Glasscock explains the source of uncertainty:

> The federal mining laws . . . protect[ed] the prospector who first located an outcropping mineral vein. Such surface indication of valuable ore was known as the apex of the vein. The owner was guaranteed the right to follow that vein downward, even when it led under the holdings of claims located behind it. That would have been fine if veins were always continuous from the surface down, but too frequently they are not. They are broken or faulted, cut off here and elsewhere by worthless rock. If a vein leading down from the surface is lost near the vertical side wall of a claim, and a similar vein of identical ore is found below it or to one side in the adjoining claim, who is to decide whether the second discovery is a geological continuation of the first? Who but the courts, basing decision on the expert testimony of geologists and engineers?

The interlaced veins meant that different mining companies often dug tunnels beneath or beside the tunnels of their rivals. Occasionally, miners would break through into a neighboring tunnel. Sales (1964) reports that gun fights and chemical warfare occurred in the mines. Sales and Glasscock both suggest malicious blasting by one mining company injured miners in other mines. Glasscock reports that one company would develop its claims so that the water in its mines would drain into rivals' mines. And both writers relate that the mining companies would use inefficient extraction methods in their race to mine a contested vein before their rival was able to. Legal control over these socially harmful tactics was difficult to achieve because ownership was unclear and litigation was protracted and costly.[17]

These varied natural-resource examples show that the effectiveness of property rights is sensitive to the details of implementation. The benefits of private property derive from the promise of efficient, non-arbitrary enforcement. The details of the rules of acquisition and the determinants of the scope of the rights affect this efficiency. Poorly designed rules of acquisition, ownership, and scope can cause property to fail. In chapter 3 we look at how the rules determining patent scope and acquisition fare.

These failures are failures of property rights on their own terms—that is, property rights failing to deliver on their promise of efficient enforcement to make investment and trade secure. In chapter 4, we examine empirical evidence on the performance of the patent system. We show that patents do not fare well as property, and we identify some likely reasons for the failure. The analysis in this chapter provides us with the appropriate yardstick with which to measure the performance of patents. If patents work efficiently as a form of property, they will provide net incentives to invest and trade. But if the patent system is not well implemented, then excessive disputes will arise, imposing large costs relative to the benefits. We can evaluate the performance of the patent system as a property system by estimating these private benefits and costs.

3 If You Can't Tell the Boundaries, Then It Ain't Property

Introduction

A successful property system establishes clear, easily determined rights. Clarity promotes efficiency because "strangers" to a property can avoid trespass and other violations of property rights, and, when desirable, negotiate permission to use the property. The concepts in the last sentence are critical to understanding the performance of the patent system. As we shall see, increasingly, patents fail to provide *clear notice* of the scope of patent rights. Thus, innovators find it increasingly difficult to determine whether a technology will infringe upon anyone's patents, giving rise to inadvertent infringement. Similarly, they find it increasingly costly to find and negotiate the necessary patent licenses in advance of their technology development and adoption decisions. Thus, clearance procedures that work well for tangible property are undercut by a profusion of fuzzy patent rights.

An ideal patent system features rights that are defined as clearly as the fence around a piece of land. Realistically, no patent system could achieve such precision, but our current system appears to be critically deficient in this regard. The comparison to tangible property is informative. In the last chapter, we suggested that patent law shares many doctrinal features with the law of tangible property, but that the *application* of these doctrines might be substantially different.

This chapter compares in detail the law and institutions that promote patent notice with the corresponding law and institutions that provide notice for tangible property. The patent system fares badly in this comparison; certain institutions that contribute to clear notice are pitifully underdeveloped. It is hardly surprising, then, that patents, unlike tangible property, have a significant problem with inadvertent infringement. Moreover, we find some evidence that notice problems have been getting worse.

BAD FENCES MAKE BAD PATENTS

Two Kinds of Inadvertent Infringement

We begin by looking in detail at inadvertent infringement, notice, and clearance. Inadvertent patent infringement often arises either when a firm independently invents a technology that was previously patented, or when a firm attempts to design non-infringing technology that competes with a patented technology. Disputes arise in some cases because alleged infringers are not aware of the earlier invention and the purported patent rights. Other disputes arise because the set of potentially relevant patents is large, the scope of the claims is vague, and many of the claims might be invalid. Under these conditions, designing around patents is difficult and clearing the rights can be prohibitively expensive.

The recently decided case involving the BlackBerry personal digital assistant illustrates the first type of inadvertent infringement. RIM, maker of the BlackBerry, was ensnared in a long-running patent infringement lawsuit with a company called NTP.[1] NTP co-founder Thomas Campana Jr. tried and failed to commercialize wireless e-mail but he did acquire several patents relating to the technology. Mike Lazaridis, the founder of RIM, independently invented similar technology, which he patented, and turned into the BlackBerry without getting permission to use Campana's patents. After five years of litigation, and facing the threat of injunction, RIM settled with NTP and agreed to pay $612.5 million.

The momentous dispute between Kodak and Polaroid nicely illustrates the second type of inadvertent infringement.[2] Kodak was the dominant firm in American photography from the earliest days of the industry. Newcomer Polaroid introduced instant photography in the late 1940s—with help from Kodak—and for several years they had no significant competition in the U.S. market. Kodak explored instant photography and even produced an instant film technology that was used on the Lunar Orbiter in 1966, but they delayed entry into the consumer market until 1976. One factor that slowed Kodak's entry was the great care they took to invent around Polaroid's patents. Kodak started research in 1969 on an instant photography product that would compete with Polaroid's in the consumer market. From the beginning they consulted with patent lawyers to make sure they steered clear of Polaroid patents. Kodak believed its technology was very different from Polaroid's. Kodak's former senior vice president and general counsel Cecil Quillen Jr. stated: "The Kodak chemistry worked exactly backward from the Polaroid chemistry." Nevertheless, Kodak eventually lost the patent suit that Polaroid filed one week after Kodak entered the market. They paid Polaroid about $900 million and subsequently exited the instant photography market.

Patent Clearance

Of course, RIM and Kodak could have avoided these problems if they had licensed the patented technology up front (assuming, that is, that the other parties had been willing to license)—they could have cleared the rights in advance. This sort of thing happens routinely with tangible property and even with other intellectual property, such as copyrights.

The world of movie production and copyright clearance provides a glimpse of what the patent system should aspire to achieve in terms of notice and clearance. Movies often incorporate a variety of pre-existing copyrighted works. They contain pre-existing sound recordings, new versions of old songs, special effects video, art work displayed in sets, and dialogue based on screenplays, and sometimes plots based on plays, novels, even other movies. A movie producer must be careful to obtain copyright permission from the owners of the copyrights on these other works. If a producer fails to clear the rights, even to a work that plays quite a minor role in the movie, the owner of the infringed copyright can stop all performance of the movie.

Experienced Hollywood movie producers manage copyright clearance without much trouble. The transactions to acquire the necessary rights are relatively standardized.[3] The producer usually gets a license to use pre-existing art, music, video, and text. Copyrights to copyrighted work created during the production of the movie are usually assigned to the movie producer through contracts signed by the many collaborators who contribute to the movie.

Motion picture producers and technology developers share comparably complex intellectual property environments. But technology developers have far more difficulty negotiating clearance contracts and steering clear of problematic patents. The BlackBerry and instant photography sagas are two of many examples of sensational failures of patent notice and clearance. Below we try to understand why these failures occurred.

Why didn't RIM clear patent rights in advance of the BlackBerry introduction the way movie producers clear copyrights in advance of movie distribution? One reason is that Lazaridis did not build on Campana's technology the way a movie screenplay builds, for instance, on the plot of a novel. Campana and Lazaridis independently invented various aspects of the technology, likely without knowing their future rival existed.[4] RIM first learned about NTP and Campana's patents in early 2000 when NTP sent letters to several companies, including RIM, warning them about NTP's wireless e-mail patents. This was ten years after RIM started developing wireless technology, four years after RIM introduced its prototype of the BlackBerry, and two years after RIM signed contracts with Canadian and American telecommunications companies to supply wireless e-mail service.

But surely, a sophisticated business like RIM was aware that independent invention is not a defense allowed in a patent infringement lawsuit. In fact, an innovator can even get a patent on his technology (as Lazaridis did), and still be liable for infringement of someone else's patent. Why didn't RIM search for patents that they might infringe upon? After finding such patents, they could have negotiated a license or redesigned their technology to avoid infringement. We do not know why RIM did not find and deal with Campana's patents at an earlier date, but we can make an educated guess. If RIM had searched, they would have found many patents granted to many inventors with uncertain scope and validity that might apply to various aspects of the BlackBerry.[5] Further, RIM would still have to worry about unpublished applications that might mature into patents covering their technology. We suspect that often, it is simply bad business to search for patents and negotiate licenses in advance of technology adoption. The costs of sorting through a large number of uncertain property rights is larger than the expected cost incurred when any one patent is asserted against the innovator. We cannot be sure, but we would not be surprised if RIM's failure to do a patent search was, at the time, the best business decision available to the company.

Kodak chose the opposite path, but fared no better. They retained a leading patent expert named Francis T. Carr to advise them on how to avoid patent infringement. Carr conducted an exhaustive review of potentially relevant patents and Kodak carefully developed technology they thought was outside the domain of Polaroid's patents.[6] Nevertheless, Polaroid asserted that Kodak had "willfully" (knowingly) infringed upon its patents, but the trial judge refused to award enhanced damages for willfulness and concluded: "The uncontroverted facts demonstrate that Kodak consulted Mr. Carr early and often as it developed its instant integral photography system."[7]

Kodak's patent review was thoroughly integrated with its R&D on consumer instant photography. The review started seven years before a commercial product was introduced. Carr studied more than 250 patents, many owned by Polaroid and many owned by others. He "rendered 67 written and countless oral opinions on both the film and camera patents." In the lawsuit, Polaroid focused on thirty-four claims contained in ten of their patents. Three of the patents were invalidated. Kodak was held liable for infringing upon twenty claims in the remaining seven patents.

Carr had advised Kodak that the claims in those seven patents were either invalid or not infringed upon. "Over the course of three years Mr. Carr reviewed more than 50 potential imaging chemistries for Kodak. Eventually, after working closely with Mr. Carr and performing tests he requested to make certain he understood how the chemistry worked,"

Kodak chose an imaging technology that was later ruled to be infringing. Kodak also incorporated design changes to mechanical features of its camera that Carr thought would keep them clear of Polaroid's patents. The trial judge concluded that Carr "discussed the Kodak technology with Kodak engineers, and gave his considered advice. . . . That advice simply turned out to be wrong."

These two examples show that the patent notice function breaks down for two sorts of reasons. First, a technology investor might not be able to unambiguously determine the scope and validity of a set of patents, as in the Kodak example. Second, even if scope and validity could be determined with reasonable accuracy, it might be too costly to do so. Below we look at the law and institutions that give rise to both of these situations.

Land versus Technology

The RIM and Kodak cases illustrate how patent notice and patent clearance failure cause expensive patent disputes. Regrettably, such problems are widespread. One good way to recognize the size of the problem is by comparing property rights in land to patents.

Real property law gives landowners a clear view of property boundaries. Before building a costly structure near the perimeter of one's land, a sensible landowner will consult a lawyer and conduct a survey of the land. Land records, a survey, and a title search give a potential builder clear notice of where her property ends and her neighbor's begins. We rarely hear about lawsuits caused because someone inadvertently built a structure on, or made some other investment within the boundaries of, another's property.[8]

A prospective land-buyer will take the same steps before buying land. Normally, any clouds on the title to the land will be cleared before the sale is completed. The process of examining property rights to land is routinely provided by a robust market that combines title examination with title insurance. In contrast, patent search and clearance is hardly routine. The process is costly and inconclusive. Typically, the risk of infringement that remains after a competent patent review is so unpredictable that it is virtually uninsurable.[9] Similarly, uncertainty about scope and validity undermine the market for patent enforcement insurance.

Overall, the legal infrastructure supporting patent law performs poorly compared to the infrastructure supporting real property law. A few numerical comparisons lay bare the stark contrast. Title insurance on a $150,000 mortgage runs about $450 in Iowa, a state with a relatively efficient system.[10] The revenue from these policies is more than adequate for the insurers to cover their costs of searching and examining the title, defending against future lawsuits, and paying losses that result from lawsuits. Impressively, search and examination is so effective that insurers nationwide pay only about 5 percent of premium dollars on claims.[11]

Now imagine that an innovative firm purchases insurance against patent lawsuits that might arise after it adopts a new technology. What would it cost an insurance company to search and examine patent databases, pay to defend patent lawsuits, and pay for damages (and perhaps even the costs from an injunction)? We do not have an estimate of the search and examination costs, but unlike title insurance, the lion's share of the cost would probably arise from lawsuits. We estimate in chapter 6 that the expected cost of defending patent lawsuits is now at least 13 percent of the cost of R&D investment. This ratio is a lower bound on the cost of our hypothetical infringement insurance. The cost of search and examination plus the expected cost of defending title lawsuits is much less. Dividing $450 by $150,000 gives a ratio of 0.3 percent, which is less than one-fortieth of the ratio for patents.

A similar comparison between patents and copyrights would probably be equally discouraging, but we are not aware of any data on either copyright infringement insurance or copyright litigation costs. Two pieces of information suggest that copyright does far better than patent in providing notice and facilitating clearance. First, copyright clearance is relatively standardized in the motion picture, music, and publishing industries. Second, copyright infringement insurance is available to protect against risks created by errors or omissions in the clearance process.[12]

The software industry is especially interesting because patent and copyright lawsuits are both possible. The IT Compliance Institute notes that sound IT policy can avoid most copyright infringement and trade-secret misappropriation, but patent infringement is virtually impossible to avoid; insurance against copyright infringement is affordable, but patent infringement insurance is prohibitively expensive for most companies.[13]

Differences in Law and Institutions

The costs of insurance and clearance are much lower for tangible property than for patents. Why? There are sharp differences between patents and tangible property regarding the law and institutions that promote clear notice. Consider the following contrasts between patents and land, repeated from chapter 1:

- *Fuzzy and unpredictable boundaries.* Land can be inexpensively surveyed and the survey boundaries carry legal weight. In contrast, innovators must cope with expensive and unreliable legal opinions about the boundaries of patents that get no deference from the courts. Surveyors can plainly map the words in a deed to a physical boundary; it is much harder to map the words in a patent to technologies. Not only are the words that lawyers use sometimes vague, but the rules for interpreting the words are also sometimes unpredictable. There is no reliable way of determining patent boundaries short of litigation.

- *Public access to boundary information.* The documents used to determine boundaries for both land and patents are publicly available. It is possible, however, for patent owners to hide the claim language that defines patent boundaries from public view for many years—this is being done with increasing frequency.

- *Possession and the scope of rights.* Generally, tangible property rights are linked closely to possession. Patent law also requires possession of an invention, but often this requirement is not rigorously enforced. Consequently, courts sometimes grant patent owners rights over technology that is new, different, and distant from anything they actually made or possessed. Not surprisingly, this practice makes patent boundaries especially unclear in fast-paced technologies such as biotechnology and computer software.

- *The patent flood.* Clearance costs are affected by the number of prospective rights that must be checked for possible infringement. Investments related to a new land use rarely implicate very many parcels of land. Also, as we noted in chapter 2, property systems include features that discourage fragmentation of land rights. Investments related to new technology frequently need to be checked against large numbers of patents. Although the patent system has features that discourage patent proliferation (notably the non-obviousness requirement), empirical evidence suggests these are not working well.

The combination of these four factors explains the poor performance of the notice function in the patent system, and the associated high rate of inadvertent infringement. We explore these factors in more detail over the remainder of this chapter.

Fuzzy and Unpredictable Boundaries

Institutional Failure: Why the Notice Function Works for Property but Not for Patents

Property law provides good notice to potential purchasers about the property rights relevant to a contemplated new land use. Patent law often fails to provide good notice to innovators about the patent rights relevant to adoption of a new technology. Property law has stable doctrine and flourishing institutions designed to transmit clear notice. Patent law lacks both.

Suppose a real estate investor wants to acquire a certain parcel of land and build a mall. Her lawyers should be able to tell her that she will need to acquire rights to parcels A and B, but not nearby parcels C and D. They should also be able to tell her whether there are any mortgages, easements, future interests, or other interests in the relevant property. To a great extent, public documents give notice of these interests and provide evidence of their validity or invalidity.

The work of real estate lawyers is complemented by the work of title agents and surveyors. Both are licensed professionals who contribute in important ways to the success of property law in providing clear notice. Surveyors work from the plot description found in the deed or in a registered survey and, using well-recognized and standardized methods, plot out the boundary lines. In most states, surveyors' boundaries are legally recognized. A typical survey for a residential property costs several hundred dollars. Title agents search deeds and other public information to help lawyers judge the validity of property titles. A title search for a residential property with title insurance also typically costs several hundred dollars.

The patent system also has licensed patent agents and patent lawyers. They can also render a judgment on whether a proposed investment (technology) infringes on valid patents owned by others. They judge both the boundaries and the validity of these patents. They also work by reading legal documents—issued patents—and applying them to the matter at hand. Two crucial differences between the systems are worth noting here. First, a legal "opinion letter" on a technology typically costs about a hundred times more ($20,000 to $100,000). Second, this finding carries little legal weight.[14]

Indeed, no one except appeals court judges seems to be able to provide a definitive answer on potential infringement; predictably, even their opinions are often in conflict (Wagner and Petherbridge 2004). It is true that patent examiners determine the boundaries of each patent—this is necessary for them to determine whether the patent meets the criteria of patentability, that is, whether the patent is truly novel. But patent examiners do not record their interpretation of the boundaries of the patent and, even though courts presume that their decisions about patent validity are correct, courts pay little heed to the boundaries that patent examiners use to make these determinations.

District courts hold hearings to interpret the boundaries of patents in lawsuits. In some cases they call on expert witnesses to provide understanding of the technology and industry usage of technical terms. But these determinations get no deference at the appellate level, either. In fact, the Federal Circuit reverses the district court judge's construction of 34.5 percent of the claim terms appealed and this percentage increased during the 1990s.[15]

These difficulties arise, of course, because it is much more complicated to map the boundaries of a technology from a verbal description than it is to map a plot of land using a standardized surveyor's description. This problem arises partly from the nature of the subject matter and partly from the difference in techniques used to do the mapping. We look at the law of patent claim interpretation in the next section.

But the hard fact is, innovators cannot quickly and easily obtain a reliable judgment on whether prospective technology infringes on others' patents. Perhaps in an earlier time, when technology was simpler, this was not such a serious problem because the ambiguity of patent claims was not so great. But as we discuss below, there are reasons to think that this ambiguity has been increasing substantially in recent years. In addition, changes made during the 1990s in the legal methods used to determine the boundaries of patents appear to have made the uncertainty even greater.

A Nose of Wax?

Patent documents are typically long and obscure. The most obscure and most important part of each patent is the set of claims found at the end of the document. Patent claims create property rights. Each claim is a single sentence—an odd sort of sentence, to be sure, which might run on for several paragraphs. Collectively, the claims determine the scope of the owner's right to exclude—they are the fences that mark the inventor's property. Giles Rich, the most famous patent judge of modern times, observed: "[T]he main purpose of [patent] examination . . . is to try to make sure that what each claim defines is patentable. To coin a phrase, *the name of the game is the claim.*"[16]

The game is stacked in favor of inventors and against examiners and the public. Examiners get an average of eighteen hours to read and understand the application and make sure that each claim is valid.[17] Patent law imposes many validity requirements. Time pressure means that inventors will often be able to push through questionable claims. Critics of the patent system quite properly complain that the Patent Office frequently approves of claims that are obvious or lack novelty.

We want to highlight a different problem that has not attracted much comment—the issuance of vague claims. In order to be valid, the claims must meet the requirement found in paragraph 2, section 112 of the patent statute, United States Code Title 35: "pointing out and distinctly claiming the subject matter which the applicant regards as his invention." The Supreme Court long ago recognized that "[t]he claim is a statutory requirement, prescribed for the very purpose of making the patentee define precisely what his invention is; and it is unjust to the public, as well as an evasion of the law, to construe it in a manner different from the plain import of its terms."[18]

Nevertheless, patent applicants sometimes game the system by drafting ambiguous patent claims that can be read narrowly during examination, such that they avoid a novelty rejection, and broadly during litigation, which supports a finding of infringement. The E-Data patent discussed in chapter 1 is such an example. Limited resources mean that the Patent Office does a poor job of monitoring the clarity of patent claims, and thus notice suffers.

The Federal Circuit, the appeals court that sets most patent law standards, has not promulgated rules to restrict vague claim language effectively. In fact, the court itself is reluctant to invalidate an indefinite claim. Allison and Lemley (1998) find that only 5.8 percent of invalidations are based on claim indefiniteness. The Federal Circuit explained:

> We engage in claim construction every day, and cases frequently present close questions of claim construction on which expert witnesses, trial courts, and even the judges of this court may disagree. Under a broad concept of indefiniteness, all but the clearest claim construction issues could be regarded as giving rise to invalidating indefiniteness in the claims at issue. But we have not adopted that approach to the law of indefiniteness. We have not insisted that claims be plain on their face in order to avoid condemnation for indefiniteness; rather, what we have asked is that the claims be amenable to construction, however difficult that task may be. If a claim is insolubly ambiguous, and no narrowing construction can properly be adopted, we have held the claim [to be] indefinite. If the meaning of the claim is discernible, even though the task may be formidable and the conclusion may be one over which reasonable persons will disagree, we have held the claim sufficiently clear to avoid invalidity on indefiniteness grounds. (*Exxon Research and Engineering Co. v. U.S.*, 265 F.3d 1371, 1375 [2001])

The Federal Circuit's approach appears to be inconsistent with the statute and contrary to the policy concern expressed by the Supreme

Court. The Court recognized the social value of a rigorous indefiniteness doctrine in a 1942 case, Justice Robert H. Jackson stated: "A zone of uncertainty which enterprise and experimentation may enter only at the risk of infringement [that is, litigation] would discourage invention only a little less than unequivocal foreclosure of the field. Moreover, the claims must be reasonably clear-cut to enable courts to determine whether novelty and invention are genuine."[19] As the Federal Circuit admitted, tolerating vague language at the Patent Office yields difficult questions of claim interpretation. The Supreme Court anticipated contemporary claim construction problems when it warned: "Some persons seem to suppose that a claim in a patent is like a *nose of wax* which may be turned and twisted in any direction, by merely referring to the specification, so as to make it include something more than, or something different from, what its words express."[20]

Some ambiguity would not be too harmful if the public could rely on a predictable method of claim interpretation. Unfortunately, the Federal Circuit has not formulated such a method. Recall that district court judges do a poor job of predicting Federal Circuit claim interpretation. Certainly, it follows that lawyers will have difficulty counseling potential infringers how an ambiguous claim term will be interpreted. The discussion in Sidebar 3.1 illustrates the difficulty of this interpretative task.

The Federal Circuit is keenly aware of the notice problems created by uncertain claim construction. The law governing claim construction has long been in flux as courts have searched for satisfactory methods. A significant development occurred twelve years ago in the case *Markman v. Westview Instruments*.[21] The case and its progeny made claim construction a question of law subject to *de novo* review in the Federal Circuit. Essentially, this means that the judges in the Federal Circuit have the power to choose the meaning of patent claims anew, ignoring lower-court decisions. Alternative approaches would have distributed power among fact-finders, trial court judges, and appellate judges.

Consolidating power in the appellate court offers the benefit of the experience of the Federal Circuit judges, but reliance on their experience reviewing patent cases has not paid off. The goal of predictable claim interpretation has been thwarted by three problems. First, members of the Federal Circuit have been feuding over appropriate methods of claim

Sidebar 3.1. Claim Construction

Good patent policy analysis is not possible unless one has a basic understanding of patent claims, how they are interpreted, and how they create property rights. So, in this section, we present the highlights from a patent lawsuit involving a claim relating to a simple invention. Even though the invention is simple, you will soon see that understanding and applying the claims can be quite difficult even for experienced patent judges.

U.S. Patent No. 4,018,260 relates to a home improvement invention, specifically a set of border pieces used to attach a fabric wall covering to a wall. Drawings from the patent are displayed on the left-hand side of figure 3.1. The patent suggests the advantage of the invention is that it makes it easier for an inexperienced person to hang wall covering. The relevant portion of the disputed claim 1 reads as follows:

1. An assembly of border pieces for creating a framework attachable to a wall or other flat surface for mounting a fabric sheet which is cut to dimensions at least sufficient to cover the surface, said assembly comprising
(a) linear border pieces and
(b) *right angle corner border pieces* which are arranged in end-to-end relation to define a framework that follows the perimeter of the area to be covered . . .

The patentee, Unique Concepts, sued Kevin Brown for patent infringement. The defendant made and sold a set of border pieces for hanging wall covering. The outcome of the case turned on the interpretation of claim 1, and in particular of the italicized language: "right angle corner border pieces," labeled 15 in the figure.[44] The claim also describes linear border pieces (labeled 14) and distinguishes them from the right angle corner border pieces. Brown's set of border pieces contained trapezoidal pieces with a forty-five degree cut (labeled 4 on the right-hand side of figure 3.1). Two trapezoidal pieces could be connected to serve the same function as the right angle corner border

(Continued)

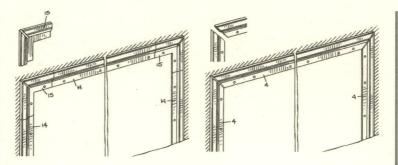

Figure 3.1. U.S. Patent No. 4,018,260
(left) The Patented Frame from Unique Concepts
(right) The Alleged Infringer's Frame

pieces. Brown did not use corner pieces as in the patent. Thus, the court needed to decide whether the scope of claim 1 was broad enough to include the defendant's product.

The majority of judges ruled there was no infringement, but Judge Giles S. Rich dissented and offered an alternative claim construction that was broad enough to support a finding of infringement. In effect, Judge Rich argued that the term "right angle corner border pieces" is not restricted to preformed corner pieces and thus includes the alleged infringer's configuration. The disagreement concerned not only the language in the claims themselves, but also what the patentee's original language claimed, how this was changed in response to Patent Office objections, and how the invention was described elsewhere in the patent.

This dispute reveals the troubling indeterminacy of claim construction. We suspect the uncertainty about claim boundaries is even greater for patents featuring more complex technologies, abstract claim terms, and early-stage technologies.

construction.[22] One camp takes a very formal approach to interpretation, and the other is more willing to rely on contextual clues to aid interpretation. Second, the appellate court is too distant from the expert testimony and other facts that should be used in sensible claim construction. Judge Haldane R. Mayer of the Federal Circuit laments: "Because claim construction is treated as a matter of law chimerically devoid of underlying factual determinations, there are no 'facts' on the record to prevent parties from presenting claim construction one way in the trial court and in an entirely different way in this court."[23] Third, in its formalist vein, the Federal Circuit has been skeptical about the use of "extrinsic evidence" in claim construction. Extrinsic evidence comes from outside the patent document and proceedings in the Patent Office. It includes expert testimony, journal articles, dictionaries, and other outside evidence that might reveal industry usage. Much of this extrinsic evidence is available to parties interested in mapping out the scope of a patent before they get near a courtroom. Potentially, greater use of extrinsic evidence would strengthen the notice function, but, importantly, it would also reduce the power of the Federal Circuit.[24]

Fuzzy boundaries are still possible even when claims are relatively precise and their literal scope is clear. *Warner-Jenkinson Co. v. Hilton Davis Chemical Co.* illustrates this point. The case featured yet another instance of inadvertent infringement; the parties independently invented an improved process for purifying dye. Hilton Davis claimed a version of the process operating at a pH ranging from 6.0 to 9.0. Warner-Jenkinson's technology operated at a pH of 5.0, outside the range of the relevant claim. Nevertheless, a jury found Warner-Jenkinson infringed under the doctrine of equivalents.[25] This doctrine expands the scope of a claim beyond the scope identified through claim construction.[26] The original goal of the doctrine was to protect inventors against the risk that a pirate would spot a poorly drafted claim, introduce a slight variation in a patented technology that was outside of the claim, and escape literal infringement. Such evasion could occur if the patent owner did not foresee the manner of imitation chosen by the pirate, and therefore drafted its claim too narrowly. Today the doctrine applies without regard to the motives or methods of the alleged infringer—in particular, it applies to independent inventors and those who make a good-faith effort to invent around a patent, as well as to pirates.

The doctrine of equivalents corrodes the notice function of patents and increases the risk of inadvertent infringement. Warner-Jenkinson might have thought a pH of 5.0 was outside the fence erected around processes with pHs ranging from 6.0 to 9.0, but they were wrong. The Supreme Court admitted: "[t]here can be no denying that the doctrine of equivalents . . . conflicts with the definitional and public notice functions of the statutory claiming requirement."[27] Nevertheless, they confirmed the availability of the doctrine against inadvertent infringers.

PUBLIC AVAILABILITY OF BOUNDARY INFORMATION

Determination of boundaries depends on publicly available information. Land deeds are available in county registries. Most patent documents are also publicly available, but inventors can delay release of important boundary information. Many inventors act strategically to hide their claims from potential infringers. Inventors are allowed to draw out the patent application process for years if that serves their interest—and not infrequently it does. They often monitor the technology choices of other firms and write their patent claims to cover the technology of potential licensees. The targeted firms might get locked into a technology choice and find themselves in unfavorable bargaining positions with the patent owner.[28]

In a notorious recent example, the firm Rambus participated in a semiconductor standard-setting organization while the same firm was secretly pursuing a patent on the same technology. By participating in the standard-setting process, Rambus learned information that it used to write claims that covered the standard. This strategy worked because the company added the claims to a patent that was pending when the standard-setting process began. Thus, the "invention" was completed before the standard was set, but the claims were written *after* the standard was set. Rambus dodged private suits alleging fraud and antitrust violation and was successful in enforcing its patent.[29]

It appears that hidden claims are becoming much more prevalent. One practice used to keep claims hidden is to file "continuing" applications. Under United States Patent Office rules (most other nations lack comparable procedures), once an original application is filed, one or more continuing applications based on the same invention, but with different claims, can be filed. This gives the patent applicant additional opportunities to change the claims over time, possibly catching unsuspecting innovators by surprise. The number of continuing applications, shown

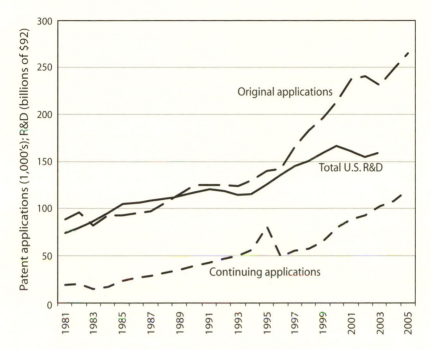

Figure 3.2. The Growth in Original and Continuing Patent Applications
Sources: Quillen and Webster (2006); NSF

as the heavy dashed line in figure 3.2, has increased seven-fold since 1984, to about 120,000 per year (Quillen and Webster 2006). Continuing applications now constitute about one-third of all patent applications.

The patent system was reformed about ten years ago to reduce some of the problems created by hidden claims. The term of the patent was changed from seventeen years from issue to twenty years from application date, and patents are published after eighteen months, unless the applicant refrains from patenting outside the United States. These reforms probably had a significant positive effect, but hidden claims are still a problem. Applicants can change claim language in patents without updating the published applications. The final claim language is published only after the patent is issued, and the gap between application date and issuance is growing.[30] Moreover, publication does little to prevent patent applicants from introducing unanticipated new claims via continuing applications.

Possession and the Scope of Rights

In general, in order to own, one must possess. Although possession is not sufficient to guarantee ownership, the law by and large assigns initial property rights only to the extent that one possesses—exerts some control over—a property. A possession requirement means that the owner of a property is actually in a position to make the socially desirable investments or transactions that are the key economic benefits of property.

Simple possession rules also make it easier for third parties to recognize the existence and scope of a property right. If farmer Jones owns and possesses a shirt, a tractor, a house, and a farm, then neighbor Smith should know that he must ask permission before using that property. Furthermore, Smith probably will not have any trouble figuring out that Jones is the owner.

The scope of most tangible property is easily described. Fences, surveys, and land records provide clear notice of the scope of rights to land. The physical structure of goods, machines, buildings, and the like defines those kinds of property—and gives clear notice of the scope of rights. Rental, securitization, liens, and other legal devices might complicate the allocation of rights to use tangible property, but they are *not* relevant to what we here mean by "scope." Clear scope is present when a stranger recognizes when she is about to use someone's property and puts her on notice to seek whatever permissions are necessary. Everyone recognizes that an unattended boat tied to a dock is someone's property, and that it should not be used without permission.

In some cases, when tangible property is taken from nature, the scope of the property rights is not so clear. In these cases, simple physical characteristics are not so useful for establishing legal boundaries because the relevant characteristics change over time or are not fully known initially (that is, they are revealed over time). The mining disputes discussed in the previous chapter make this point. Another example comes from water law. In certain jurisdictions, the right to use water from a stream running through a property depends on the consumption of others elsewhere on the streamcourse. Hence, a newcomer will need to investigate her neighbors' water use to determine whether and to what extent property rights already exist for the stream flow.

In the case of migratory wild animals, property law follows the "rule of capture": you can own what you capture, but not the stock from which it came. Thus, when someone shoots a wild duck, she does not gain rights to the flock. It is easy to see how the rule of capture promotes clear notice. Suppose the first hunter to shoot a duck in a flock actually gained ownership over the flock. It would be virtually impossible for hunters in the next county to recognize the flock was owned. Furthermore, the counterfactual property rule would invite endless disputes about who was the true owner of the flock, and which ducks belong to which flock.[31]

Similarly, the possession rule in patent law is designed to mitigate notice problems. Paragraph 1, Section 112 of the patent statute, United States Code Title 35, requires that the patent describe how to make and use the invention in sufficient detail so that others can do so. This "enablement" requirement makes the patentee demonstrate the practical knowledge needed to usefully own the claimed invention.[32]

This possession requirement allows courts to invalidate patent claims that are "too broad" insofar as the inventor did not really possess all the claimed technology. A famous example concerns patents on the light bulb. Thomas Edison was not the first inventor of the incandescent light bulb. He had many competitors, and his light bulb built on many earlier contributions.[33] William Sawyer and Albon Man together obtained a light bulb patent before Edison achieved his famous invention and they sued Edison. Their patent claimed a light bulb with a "conductor of carbon, made of fibrous or textile material." Edison made a light bulb with a bamboo filament that fell within the language of the broad Sawyer and Man claim. The court ruled in favor of Edison because Sawyer and Man had actually only made a light bulb using carbonized paper as a filament. They did not make light bulbs with other filaments drawn from the wide range of fibrous and textile carbon-based filaments—in fact, most of those filaments would not work. Edison labored mightily to find a bamboo filament, which worked very well—he tried over six thousand different substances before settling on bamboo. But the Sawyer and Man patent did not describe this important detail. They possessed the specific invention of a light bulb using carbonized paper, but they did not possess the claimed knowledge to make and use all "fibrous or textile" forms of carbon, including the bamboo later discovered by Edison. Therefore, the court invalidated Sawyer and Man's claim because it claimed more than they actually possessed—they claimed technology that had not yet been invented.[34]

Ideally, enablement restricts patent scope so that inventors' property rights do not stray far from the invention they actually possess. In the past, inventors had to demonstrate a working prototype or scale model of the invention in order to demonstrate possession. Inventors no longer need to provide a working prototype in order to obtain a patent; the general possession requirement, however, remains central to patent law.

Thus, we are troubled by the many recent examples of patent claims that have been read broadly to cover infringing technologies that are distant from the invention actually possessed by the patent owner. Many of these infringers have arrived at significant inventions independent of any information contained in the patent at issue. Consider, for example, the following two cases.

In a biotechnology case, Amgen obtained broad coverage from its patent claim on the protein erythropoietin (EPO), a naturally occurring hormone that promotes the production of red blood cells.[35] EPO had been previously isolated and purified but attempts to obtain therapeutically useful quantities of the hormone from urine or blood had failed. Instead, Amgen isolated the human DNA that coded for EPO and inserted it into Chinese hamster ovary cells. These genetically engineered cells produced human EPO that could be efficiently isolated and purified. As a result, Amgen launched the blockbuster drug Procrit™ and they obtained a patent that claimed all "non-naturally occurring" EPO.

Later, an innovative biotech company, Transkaryotic Therapies, Inc. (TKT), developed an entirely different method of producing EPO. TKT did not insert human DNA in a foreign host cell, but instead figured out a way to trick human cells into directly producing large amounts of EPO. Amgen successfully sued TKT (and its co-defendant Hoechst) for infringement.

Amgen faced two main obstacles en route to an infringement judgment. First, the claim to all "non-naturally occurring" EPO had to be read broadly enough to cover the EPO made in human cells using TKT's technique. Second, this broad claim had to meet the enablement requirement—that is, Amgen had to show it possessed the relevant technology. Amgen overcame these obstacles even though they clearly were unable to replicate TKT's technique. All that these two technologies had in common was that they shared the objective of producing large quantities of EPO outside of the human body.

A second case concerns the patent granted over relatively abstract ideas to E-Data, discussed in the chapter 1. Freeny actually invented a kiosk for generating audio tapes and the like at retail stores. Nevertheless, because his patent claims were highly abstract, they were interpreted to apply to a broad swath of e-commerce, even though nothing in his patent described general-purpose transactions over the Internet.

Arguably, the E-Data and Amgen patents suffer from the same defect as the patent of Sawyer and Man: they do not demonstrate possession of the broad range of technologies that they claim. There are two clear problems with this policy. First, it makes patent boundaries incredibly fluid over time. Third parties cannot rely on the plain meaning of a term at the time of patent application: *claim terms are allowed to change meaning over time as technology advances*. Second, it penalizes real innovators who operate in the shadow of early, broad claims. Both of these factors tend to generate costly disputes.

Many of the troubling cases in which patent claims are untethered from actual inventions arise in biotechnology. This is no accident. Several factors have contributed to a "flood" of biotech patents on very early-stage technologies: the Patent Office has granted thousands of patents on gene fragments, the Bayh-Dole Act (1980) has encouraged patenting by academic researchers even though most of these inventions are inchoate (Thursby and Thursby 2003), and the Federal Circuit has changed patentability standards to permit patents on technologies that are still a great distance from practical application.[36] Inevitably, a large number of patents on early-stage technologies leads to attempts by patentees to assert these patents over later-developed technologies.

Patenting of early-stage technology is not the only situation where patents are asserted against later-developed technologies. For a variety of reasons, which we explore separately in chapter 9, abstract patent claims are particularly endemic to computer-related patents. Of particular importance, the law has changed to permit the patenting of abstract software ideas, and the number of software patents granted has increased dramatically. The growth in the number of these patents also contributes to the frequency with which patents are asserted over fundamentally more advanced, later-developed technologies.

The increase in patents on early-stage technologies and the increase of patents with abstract claims has lead with increasing frequency to lawsuits against later-developed technologies. This in turn has made clear possession rules more important than ever. But judges have not consistently limited ownership to the technologies actually possessed, perhaps because some jurists have felt an impulse to reward "pioneer" inventors. But the court has not been uniform about this, and some judges have developed controversial new rules to limit the reach of patents over later-developed technologies. Feldman (2005) documents the state of tumult this issue has engendered in patent law with respect to biotech patents.[37] Unfortunately, we suspect that the net effect of the expansive reading of patent rights taken together with recent corrective measures has been to increase uncertainty and costly disputes.

The Patent Flood

A large number of property rights held by many different owners can make the clearance of rights for new investment costly. If clearance costs grow too large, then complete clearance becomes infeasible, and firms will only do a cursory clearance or, perhaps, none at all.

In the previous chapter we discussed how property law uses various rules to limit fragmentation of rights, including primogeniture, limits on future interests, property taxes and registration requirements, and zoning and subdivision restrictions. Patent law also has rules that limit the proliferation of rights. First, an inventor must demonstrate an invention has sufficient practical utility in order to receive a patent. Also, patents are not granted for inventions that are obvious improvements on previous technology. These patentability requirements work to weed out the potential clutter of patents on inchoate or minor inventions. In addition, patent renewal fees work to sift out less valuable patents.

The evidence suggests, however, that over the last two decades the number of patent rights has proliferated dramatically. The number of patent applications more than tripled between 1980 and 2004, from 104,329 to 356,943. That would be great news if it represented dramatic growth in American innovation, but the story is not so simple. The growth was *not* caused mainly by a surge in R&D spending. Instead, the number of original patent applications has outstripped the growth of United States R&D spending (see figure 3.2), especially since the mid-1990s.

Empirical research by Hall (2005) found that patent application growth data displays "a very significant structural break between 1983 and 1984," which she attributes to the pro-patent policies of the Federal Circuit. Indeed, Henry and Turner (2006) identified a pro-patentee structural shift in court rulings that occurred at about this time. Furthermore, Hall (2005) found that growth comes from U.S. firms in the "electric machinery, electronics, instruments, computers, and communication equipment" industries. Much of this growth took place during the 1990s and might be associated with subject matter expansion for software-related inventions (Bessen and Hunt 2007).

The growth in patent applications and grants has been accompanied by comparable growth in the number of claims per patent. Even though each patent is supposed to protect only one invention, patents can have multiple claims—indeed, many patents have dozens of claims. Inventors write claims to protect different aspects of an invention, for example, by claiming a product and also processes for making and using the product. Furthermore, they write claims of varied coverage to hedge against the risk that certain claims will be invalidated or read narrowly. Allison and Lemley (2002) compared patents from the mid-1970s to patents from the mid-1990s and found that the mean number of claims had grown from 9.94 to 14.87, a nearly 50 percent increase.

The growth in the number of patents and the number of claims do not necessarily imply a comparable increase in search costs associated with clearance. If, for example, patents could be neatly divided into technology classes so that only a small class needs to be searched, then search costs might remain reasonable despite the huge increase in numbers. But evidence from litigation suggests that this is not so. Bessen and Meurer (2005) found that about a quarter of all lawsuits between public firms involved firms that patented in very different technology classes *and* which were in unrelated industries. Indeed, it is not hard to find examples where firms are sued over patents covering distant technologies. For example, Amazon.com has been sued by a firm with a patent covering cable TV movie selection and another firm with a patent on a bank ATM interface.[38] This implies that a complete clearance procedure requires careful examination of very large numbers of patents, indeed. As noted in chapter 1, David Martin of M-Cam estimates that a typical web shop might need to check over 11,000 patents. Clearly, costs of clearance can be substantial.[39]

Moreover, the law actually imposes penalties that discourage thorough clearance. Knowledge gained through a patent search increases the risk of a finding of willfulness in a patent lawsuit. Firms are discouraged from reading patents because of fear of the financial penalties that might follow a finding of willfulness. The disincentive is greatest when a firm believes there are a large number of weak patents in the technological vicinity of its innovation. If the firm is unlikely to license the patents, then reading them simply increases the risk of a finding of willfulness. On the other hand, when a firm believes there are a small number of strong patents nearby, it would read and license them or be careful to invent around them.[40]

The cost of clearance ratchets up even more when patents have fuzzy boundaries and when many patents are likely to be found to be invalid. With these uncertainties, a technology investor will have to examine many patents of vague scope and dubious validity. Note that even though the Federal Circuit has strengthened patent rights by making changes to the law that reduced the probability of invalidity, the share of district court decisions that invalidated a patent is still 27 percent.[41] This introduces an element of risk into clearance decisions and it disrupts attempts to invent around patents. As noted earlier, Kodak relied on expert opinion that several Polaroid patents were invalid. If they thought those patents were likely to be valid, they would have chosen another product design, or perhaps stayed out of the market altogether.

There is abundant evidence that many technology firms follow the same path as RIM and invest little in patent search and clearance. A recent survey of the members of the Intellectual Property Owners organization found that 65 percent of respondents disagreed with the statement, "We always do a patent search before initiating any R&D or product development effort" (Cockburn and Henderson 2003).

Finally, in addition to the costs of searching and identifying rights to clear, a technology investor might also face substantial costs in transacting for those rights.[42] Semiconductor manufacturing is one industry where this problem is felt acutely.

> Semiconductor manufacturing is . . . notoriously complex, integrating an array of process and product technologies that cover aspects of the circuitry design, materials used to achieve a certain outcome, and methods used in the wafer fabrication process. As several industry representatives pointed out, a given semiconductor product (say, a new memory or logic device) will often embody hundreds if not thousands of 'potentially patentable' technologies that could be owned by suppliers, manufacturers in other industries, rivals, design firms, or independent inventors. (Hall and Ziedonis 2001)

Ziedonis (2004) found that fragmentation is such a serious impediment to licensing that it all but drives patenting behavior by certain firms in the semiconductor industry.[43]

In this chapter we have uncovered four aspects of the notice problem. To begin, inventors can hide patent claims, and thus boundary information, from the public. Next, even when the relevant public has access to the patent claims, they are frequently very difficult to interpret. Even assuming the claims are available and clear, there is a danger that the meaning of claim language will change (and become broader) over time. Finally, even when claims are available, clear, and fixed over time, the cost of searching for relevant patents can be quite high. High search costs arise directly because of the high number of patents that potentially apply to certain technologies, and indirectly because of the high rate of invalidity and the willfulness doctrine both discourage innovators from initiating a patent search. In combination, these four problems can reinforce each other—for example, a large number of fuzzy or unpredictable patents make clearance procedures especially fruitless.

The law and institutions that support notice in the patent system fall far short of similar institutions supporting notice for tangible property rights. It is hardly surprising that land title insurance is cheap and readily available while patent infringement insurance is limited, expensive, and not widely offered. Nor is it surprising that inadvertent infringement is a serious problem for patents but not for tangible property. In the next chapter we begin our examination of empirical evidence on the performance of patents as a property system in order to shed further light on the economic significance of patent notice problems.

4 Survey of Empirical Research: Do Patents Perform Like Property?

INTRODUCTION

Perhaps one of the clearest lessons of the Cold War was that private-property and market economies can be powerful engines of economic growth and innovation. While centralized economies have mustered impressive economic efforts, especially during times of war, they have generally failed to provide a high and rapidly growing standard of living. Moreover, what they have achieved has sometimes come at a horrible human cost.

The experience of the Cold War seems to lend force to arguments that intellectual property, too, promotes economic growth and innovation. Indeed, it is now often argued that the institutions responsible for the success of Western economies are "the rule of law and private property rights, including intellectual property."[1] Similarly the Intellectual Property Owners Association suggests that property-based incentives explain U.S. technological leadership: "The possibility of patent rights gives incentives to inventors and their employers to create new technology and to invest in commercializing technology. Policy makers have generally agreed that the American tradition of strong patent laws has contributed to making this country the world's technological leader, a position it has held for more than a century."[2] This is a seductive argument. There is solid empirical evidence that secure property rights are conducive to economic growth. So it might seem to follow that "strong" patent laws should also promote innovation and economic growth. But what is the actual empirical evidence that patents and other forms of intellectual property are responsible for the technological leadership of the United States in particular and the West generally?

Casual observation suggests that the United States and other Western nations share both technologically advanced economies and well-developed patent systems. But this is a correlation, not evidence of causation. That is, well-developed patent systems might cause economic growth in these nations. Or it might be, instead, that successful technology companies or other groups, such as the patent bar, have lobbied for patent protection. In this latter case, economic success promotes the expansion of the patent system, not the other way around. Indeed, the patent systems in advanced nations today consist of highly sophisticated institutions supported by substantial funding. These institutions were not simply legislated, but rather developed, along with a wide variety of other legal and social institutions. Their evolution required both extensive experience and a large allocation of resources and they would seem as out of place in nineteenth-century America as they would in many of today's less-developed nations. Thus the correlation between the sophistication of a nation's technology and the sophistication of its patent system does not provide evidence of a causal link in and of itself; a more advanced analysis is required.

It might well be true, as the Intellectual Property Owners maintain, that most policymakers see a link between "strong" patent laws and U.S. technology leadership.[3] But as James Boyle acerbically notes, policymakers have too often ignored empirical evidence, basing policy, instead, on "faith-based" reasoning about property rights with regard to such matters as software patents, broadcast rights, copyright term, and database rights.[4]

The problem with this sort of reasoning is that it is based on analogy: because property rights promote economic growth, then patents, which are like property, are assumed to promote economic growth and technological advancement, as well. Patents are called "intellectual property," but, as the previous chapters discussed, there are important differences between patents and traditional forms of property. Indeed, the term "intellectual property" only gained wide usage during the last two decades, and only recently has the term mostly shed the quotation marks (though not, alas, in a discussion, as here, of terminology) that explicitly remind us of the analogy being made.[5] Although patents share important features with tangible and financial property, the differences between them can critically affect the link between patents, innovation, and economic growth.

On the other hand, not all policymakers ignore the evidence. At least one group of policymakers at the World Intellectual Property Organization has looked at the evidence and concluded, "Current data regarding the importance of IP [intellectual property] in economic development is still limited, however. Visible and demonstrable evidence of economic payoff attributable to IP protection is currently not sufficiently developed."[6] But if intellectual property acts just like tangible property, shouldn't the evidence of economic payoff be just as clear and obvious?

This chapter surveys previous empirical research on the economics of patents, comparing this research to similar research on property rights. Our objective in this chapter is not to obtain a conclusive finding on whether patents are good policy instruments or not. Nor do we attempt to evaluate how well patents work as property; that we discuss in chapters 5 and 6. Instead, here we simply aim to compare the evidence of economic payoff from general property rights to the evidence of the economic payoff from patents. If the analogy to property is close, then we should see similar evidence of economic payoff.

We reject the conclusion that the evidence is "not sufficiently developed" or that the evidence is inconclusive, at least regarding this limited inquiry. Instead, there is a substantial and well-developed literature and we find clear and consistent evidence of private economic benefit from patents. The evidence, however, also suggests that these benefits are limited in important ways and often depend on other factors and other institutions, and that patents might also impose significant social costs. The evidence for economic payoff is far more tenuous for patents than it is for other property rights.

In short, patents are *not* just like property; the benefits of the patent system are much more qualified. Moreover, the empirical economic evidence strongly rejects simplistic arguments that *because* patents are property, they universally spur innovation and economic growth. Instead, the effectiveness of patents as a form of property depends on the details of the laws, institutions, technologies, and industries involved.

THE EVIDENCE ON PROPERTY RIGHTS AND PATENTS: A COMPARISON

In what ways might we expect patent rights to perform similarly to rights in tangible property? As discussed in chapter 2, property rights provide incentives to invest, to trade, and to finance. There are other arguments made in favor of property rights, for example, some people argue that property is a moral right. But our concern here is with economic performance, and these incentives are the essential economic benefits of property.

Similar economic benefits are ascribed to patents; indeed, the main economic arguments in favor of patents stress such benefits.[7] Patents provide incentives to invest in R&D and other innovative efforts, as well as in the commercialization and further development of an invention; further, they encourage investment in companies that hold them. In addition, patents provide security in the licensing and sale of technology. These incentives are widely held to promote innovation and economic growth.

In this chapter we look for evidence that patents and property rights provide private incentives to invest and trade, promote investment (specifically, in the case of patents, in R&D), and spur economic growth. We look at four sorts of evidence pertinent to the links between property, patents, and innovation and economic growth: that from economic history, especially the Industrial Revolution; cross-country econometric studies; and "natural economic experiments," observing the impact of discrete changes in patent law. Finally, we look at a variety of evidence about whether imitation and competition really do threaten innovation.

The evidence we look at concerns individual nations or industries within nations. Considering the global nature of modern economies, this might strike some readers as suspect—investors and innovators within a nation are influenced by more than that nation's property rights. Innovators and investors in England are influenced by property rights and patents in Spain, to the extent that England trades with Spain. Stronger rights in Spain might provide a bigger, more secure market for British goods. But that fact does not undermine the validity of our investigation; British property rights matter for British investors and British patent rights matter for British inventors. Since we are comparing, say, British property rights to British patent rights, we can evaluate the relative effects of these on British economic growth, notwithstanding the fact that Spanish rights might also influence the British.

Historical Evidence

Economic historian and Nobel-laureate Douglass C. North (1981) has argued persuasively that the British Industrial Revolution was facilitated by secure property rights. Many European nations were hobbled with feudal customary rights that were often disputed, undocumented, and hard to establish. In contrast, by the time of the Industrial Revolution, Mokyr (1999) writes, Britain's government was "one of, by, and for private property."[8] Britain had well-defined private property rights, less arbitrary courts and police, and institutions that limited confiscatory taxation (North and Weingast 1989). This reduced transaction costs and encouraged the growth of markets, allowing for greater specialization, economies of scale, and more secure returns on investment. These benefits are seen as important preconditions for the innovations and, ultimately, the economic growth that arose from the Industrial Revolution.

North includes patents among Britain's advantageous property rights during the Industrial Revolution. Britain's patent law dates from 1624, while most other European countries did not have patent laws until the end of the eighteenth century. But more than a few economic historians are skeptical about the significance of patents for the British Industrial Revolution, as Mokyr (1999) notes.[9]

One reason for Mokyr's skepticism is that relatively few inventors of key technologies prior to the mid-nineteenth century seemed to benefit from patents. James Hargreaves and Samuel Crompton, inventors of cotton spinning machines, did not obtain patents (Crompton was later compensated by Parliament). Crompton did not obtain a patent because Richard Arkwright held a broad patent on spinning technology. Arkwright had patents, but his key patent was challenged and invalidated; he nevertheless made a fortune. Edmund Cartwright, inventor of the power loom (an automatic loom), and Richard Roberts, inventor of a successful automatic spinning machine, both obtained patents on these inventions, but were unable to earn profits from them, despite the eventual wide adoption of their machines. John Kay, inventor of an improved weaving shuttle, and the Fourdrinier brothers, inventors of a paper-making machine, were both nearly ruined by the costs of patent litigation.

James Watt is a happy and prominent exception: Watt obtained a patent on his improved steam engine design and, thanks in part to Parliament's extension of their patent term, the firm of Boulton and Watt made a substantial return on the investment needed to commercialize the invention. But we should not overestimate the significance of Watt's example. His reputation appears to have outpaced the merit of his inventions (MacLeod 1998), which made only a limited contribution to economic growth (von Tunzelmann 1978).[10] Most of the impact of the steam engine on economic growth appears to have come much later, after many additional improvements had been made in steam engine efficiency (Crafts 2004). This is significant because Nuvolari (2004) shows that most of this later increase in efficiency can be attributed to "collective invention," where engineers actively shared inventions rather than patented them.

Economic historians have suggested several reasons why patents might not have played a role more similar to that of other property rights in Britain. A major problem was that patent litigation was costly and risky.[11] Courts were not always sympathetic to patent holders, patent law was complex, and patents could be invalidated (Mokyr 1999). One early problem— one that has recurred through patent history, as we shall see—was legal uncertainty about whether patents could be issued for abstract principles of manufacturing or only for specific applications of manufacturing processes (Dutton 1984). Litigation might have been more common than necessary because Britain had a registration system instead of patent examination. British patents were not examined for novelty or inventiveness prior to the twentieth century. One study found that 42 percent of patents were either partly or wholly anticipated by earlier patents and many inventions were patented multiple times (MacLeod et al. 2003). Also, prior to 1883, the British patent system was very costly, both in fees and in the indirect costs resulting from bureaucratic red tape.

Dutton (1984) is perhaps the economic historian with the most optimistic interpretation of the British experience. He cites evidence that hundreds of inventors did patent, many obtained multiple patents, and that there was even some trade in patents. This suggests that some inventors obtained *some* benefit from patents. But, as we elaborate in the following chapters, this does not mean that they received a *net* benefit from patents—the costs of litigation and disputes can easily offset the gains. Dutton and others recognize that these latter costs were substantial. He floats the idea that despite these major problems, patents might have encouraged innovation because perhaps inventors accepted the "socially wholesome illusion" that the patent system was more perfect than it really was. But MacLeod et al. (2003) found that about nine out of ten patents arose in industries that saw little innovation, and that patenting was at best loosely related to technological innovation. And although there were some inventors who obtained ten or more patents, and although there was some trade in patents, the numbers were small, especially in comparison to those in the United States, and this even though the United States lagged in economic development during this period.[12] Moser (2006), using information on inventions exhibited at the 1851 Crystal Palace World's Fair, found that only 11 percent of British inventions were patented. So it seems particularly hard to argue that British patents played a very *significant* role during the Industrial Revolution, even if some inventors had irrational expectations of the patent system.

Indeed, the experience in the United States was quite different from that in Britain.[13] The United States initiated patent examination in 1836 and its patent fees were quite low. When examination standards were relaxed during the 1850s, patent applications soared (Post 1976), leading to what Khan (2005) has called "The Democratization of Invention." Individual mechanics and farmers could and did obtain patents in large numbers and an active market for patents developed that lasted until the end of the century. And although there were some well-known cases where patents were "invented around," such as Eli Whitney's cotton gin and Francis Cabot Lowell's power loom (which he himself copied from British models), many of the famous inventors in the United States did make profits from patented inventions (Khan and Sokoloff 1993).

So patents might have played a more positive role in the economic growth of the United States, although research has not yet established the extent of this contribution. On the other hand, the ready availability of patents also had a possible deterrent effect on economic growth insofar as small groups or individual firms were able to accumulate patent "thickets," or to set up patent pools, which might have substantially extended their market power and posed entry barriers or disincentives to other innovators. The first patent pool was formed for sewing machines in 1856 after extensive litigation. Also in the 1850s, the Draper Company perfected the technique of amassing a large number of patents to extend their monopoly, first with patents on loom temples, then with spinning spindles in the 1870s, and later with the Northrup automatic loom in the 1890s (Mass 1989). They controlled over 400 patents on spindles and over 2,000 patents on the automatic loom. This arsenal and their aggressive litigation posture allowed them to monopolize key textile equipment for many decades.

Despite its faults, the United States patent system possibly had a much more positive effect on innovation and economic growth than the British system. But the differences only underline the contingent nature of the benefits of a patent system. They depend very much on the details of the system and the nature of the institutions that support it.

There were also important differences across industries and technologies. This is evident in Moser's (2002) quantitative research on the effect of patents on innovation in different countries during the nineteenth century. Moser looked at differences in innovation across countries during the mid-nineteenth century. She measured national innovation by looking at the inventions displayed by different nations at the World's Fair of 1851 and that of 1876; she looked specifically at the number of inventions that were rated as important by panels of experts at the Fairs. She found that nations with patent systems were no more innovative than nations without patent systems. Similarly, nations with longer patent terms were no more innovative than nations with shorter patent terms. Patents did seem to make a difference in national patterns of specialization, however. In countries without patents, innovation was centered in industries that appeared to have strong trade-secrecy protection; in countries with patents, this was not the case.

So, in contrast to general property rights, patents had a much more uneven and limited effect on economic development during the nineteenth century. The role of patents seems to have varied depending upon the specific features of patent institutions, as well as upon the technologies and industries involved.

Cross-Country Studies

In recent years, economists have developed a large literature comparing the economic performance of different countries as a means of identifying factors that influence economic growth. These studies have used panels of data that typically consist of dozens of countries observed over several decades. They conducted multiple regression analyses to control for a wide variety of factors that are thought to influence growth. Property rights institutions have featured prominently in this literature. The multiple regression approach allows one to assess the extent to which property rights affect economic growth independently of other factors. A few studies have also used measures of a country's patent rights and intellectual property rights, but the results for these measures have been quite different from the results for more general measures of property rights.

Early studies used measures of political instability and measures of civil rights as proxies for the quality of property rights institutions. Keefer and Knack (1995, 1997) developed indices that capture contract enforceability, risk of government expropriation, rule of law, constraints on the executive branch of government, and bureaucratic quality. They incorporated these in a regression of each country's per capita economic growth rate, including additional controls for education, labor-force growth, and other factors. Across a variety of specifications, they found that the quality of property rights institutions is strongly and positively correlated with a nation's economic growth rate.

Keefer and Knack did not control for "reverse causality"—that is, for the possibility that economic growth might have caused improvements in property rights institutions instead of the other way around. As above, this might be the case if, say, wealthier nations tended to allocate more resources to improving property institutions because wealthier nations have more property potentially at risk from bad institutions. Hall and Jones (1999) built a similar model that does control for reverse causality.[14] Again, the property variables show a strong relationship with economic growth.

Sidebar 4.1. Multiple Regression Analysis

Multiple regression analysis is a statistical technique used when researchers want to analyze a phenomenon that might be associated with
multiple independent factors. Such a setting poses some tricky issues.
Consider, for example, a researcher estimating the gas mileage of different
models of cars. The researcher wants to estimate the relationship between
the vehicle model (an "independent variable") and the gas mileage (the
"dependent variable"). If the researcher has data on the actual mileage
and gas consumption for a sample of vehicles, the researcher could simply
calculate the mean gas mileage for each model.

This might be misleading, however. Suppose, for example, that pickup
trucks are driven mainly on highways in rural areas. Since highway driving is generally associated with higher gas mileage, the pickup trucks in
the sample might get better mileage than, say, compact cars driven in the
city, even though pickup trucks would get lower mileage than compacts if
they were driven under the same conditions. Since the researcher wants to
estimate the effect of vehicle model independently of how the car is
driven, simple estimates of mean mileage per model are misleading. This
is known as "omitted variable bias." If the variable representing highway/
city driving is omitted, the resulting estimate is biased.

Multiple regression analysis allows the researcher to "control" for the
effect of highway driving by including this variable as an independent
variable in addition to the vehicle model. More generally, when the dependent variable is associated with multiple factors, researchers attempt
to add control variables for all factors that might plausibly be associated
with the dependent variable. Then the estimates obtained for the effect
of the variable of interest—in this case, the vehicle model—should not
suffer from omitted variable bias.

Several studies have also included measures of patents or intellectual
property rights, but the results are quite different. Gould and Gruben
(1996) used a measure of a country's strength of patent protection in a regression similar to that of Keefer and Knack. In their base model the
patent index has a positive coefficient, but it is not statistically significant
(that is, given the statistical precision of their estimate, they cannot reject

the hypothesis that the true value of the coefficient is zero). They tried a wide variety of other specifications and interactions and in a few cases they obtained coefficients that are statistically significant, but most results are only weakly significant. Moreover, this study has some important limitations that make any results difficult to interpret. In particular, these regressions do not include measures of other property rights—one might expect patent rights to be correlated with other property rights, which, as above, are known to have a positive effect on economic growth—nor do they control for reverse causality.

Park and Ginarte (1997) conducted a more elaborate study that included measures of general property rights, specifically an index of "market freedom." They also used a more sophisticated measure of a country's patent rights,[15] as well as a more sophisticated estimation technique. In their base regression, they found that the market freedom variable has a positive and statistically significant effect on economic growth but the intellectual property rights index has a negative coefficient that is not statistically different from zero. Although intellectual property rights do not appear to have a direct positive effect on economic growth, the authors did, however, find some limited evidence that intellectual property rights are correlated with a country's R&D spending (see also Kanwar and Evenson [2003]). It might be the case that intellectual property rights encourage R&D spending but that this effect is too small to show up as a major direct influence on economic growth. But even this result is limited for two reasons. First, Ginarte and Park found that it only holds among the wealthier countries in their sample.[16] Second, they did not control for reverse causality—that is, firms that spend a lot on R&D might, after they become established, lobby for stronger patent laws.

In a separate paper Ginarte and Park (1997) looked at the factors that determine a country's intellectual property rights (the same index). They found, in fact, that lagged R&D (R&D from five years earlier) is positively correlated with subsequent intellectual property rights strength. This suggests that there is, indeed, a significant reverse causality.

In summary, the qualitative difference between regression results for general property rights and those for intellectual property rights is striking. General property rights have a strong and direct influence on economic growth that is robust to a wide variety of specifications and to controls for reverse causality. In contrast, intellectual property rights appear to have at best only a weak and indirect relationship to economic growth; this relationship appears to apply only to certain groups of countries or certain specifications, and the direction of causality is unclear.

Intellectual property rights are *not* just like other property rights, and simple casual observations about the correlation between United States or Western technology and patent systems can be misleading. On the other hand, this does not mean that patents have no measurable effects, but rather that it appears that their effects might be more tentative, being contingent upon the details of the patent system or the particular technology, industry, or state of economic development.

Natural Economic Experiments

One way that researchers have sought to untangle the direction of causality is to look at "natural economic experiments": they compare economic activity before and after a discrete change in the law. Even though economic policy might have changed in response to "endogenous" factors, such as successful firms lobbying for stronger property rights, when the change occurs as a sharp break, the effect of that change should be observable immediately after it goes into effect. There are studies of natural economic experiments both for changes in property rights, generally, and for patent rights, specifically.

Perhaps the biggest economic experiment in recent years is the transition of Eastern European economies from centralized planning to market-based economies that began with the collapse of the Soviet system in the late 1980s. Svejnar (2002) studied the economic performance of the countries making this transition twelve years hence. Per capita GNP growth had fallen steadily in Soviet Bloc countries for decades to a level of 0.8 percent growth per annum during the 1980s.

Economists had high expectations that moving to a market system would generate a rapid increase in economic growth. This did not happen. Per capita GNP fell rapidly in all the countries, but some eventually recovered and entered a period of positive, and in some cases rapid, economic growth. The outcome apparently depended on the particular set of reforms each country put into place. Svejnar distinguished two levels of reforms. Almost all of the countries initiated "Type I" reforms involving macroeconomic stabilization policies, removal of price controls and subsidies, and dismantling of the institutions of the communist system. Some countries—notably Poland, Hungary, Slovakia, and Slovenia—also pursued "Type II" reforms that permitted the development of government policies and institutions to support a robust market economy. These included privatization of large enterprises and establishment of effective market-oriented legal systems, commercial banking, regulatory infrastructure, and labor market regulation. These latter reforms were critical in providing a reliable tax base for government agencies and for limiting corruption and rent-seeking behavior. And they appear to have made the crucial difference in economic performance—the countries that initiated Type II reforms now have strong economic growth in contrast to those countries that put into place more limited institutional changes.

This analysis suggests that when it comes to the economic effects of property, the devil is in the details. It is not enough to eliminate centralized control and to provide legal rights to property. Effective economic performance depends on well-developed public and private institutions to support the property system and these are often more difficult to develop.

The evidence from changes in patent law further suggests that the devil might be even more deeply hidden in the details of patent institutions. Sakakibara and Branstetter (2001) examined the effect of a 1988 law that increased patent scope in Japan. They found no evidence of an increase in either R&D spending or innovative output that could be plausibly attributed to the patent reform. Bessen and Hunt (2004) looked at the effect of changes in the United States treatment of inventions that involve software. They found that the number of software patents grew dramatically. Firms in the software industry acquired relatively few patents, however; instead, most were obtained by firms in electronics and computer industries known for stockpiling large arsenals of patents to use as bargaining chips. Moreover, the firms that acquired relatively more software patents tended to actually *reduce* their level of R&D spending relative to sales.

Several studies have looked at the effect of extending patent protection to pharmaceutical products and processes. Many countries historically have limited patent coverage of pharmaceuticals, but they extended coverage in recent decades under pressure from trade negotiators. Scherer and Weisburst (1995; see also Challu [1995]) studied the effect of a program to strengthen drug patents introduced in Italy in 1978. They found no evidence that drug R&D accelerated within the well-established Italian drug manufacturing industry after the law change.[17] Lanjouw and Cockburn (2001) studied the effect of the TRIPS treaty (1995), which required about forty less-developed signatory countries to implement pharmaceutical patent protection by 2005. Among other things, they looked at the R&D allocated to products specifically directed to markets in less-developed countries. They found some increase in spending during the mid- and late 1980s, perhaps in anticipation of the changes. These trends, however, actually appear to have leveled off or reversed during the 1990s, when the TRIPS changes went into effect.

All of these studies are subject to the caveat that other, simultaneous changes might have possibly caused a reduction in innovation or in R&D, potentially confounding the results. The similarity of results across these various studies suggests that confounding factors are not responsible for most of what has been observed. One study used the power of numbers to limit the explanatory role of possible confounding effects. Lerner (2000, 2002) examined 177 changes in patent law that "strengthened" patents in a panel of sixty countries over 150 years. In such a large sample the role of confounding factors should be limited—positive confounding events will tend to be offset by other, negative confounding events in estimates of the average response. In his accounting of events that strengthened patents, Lerner included changes in substantive law that improved the scope or extent of patent rights and he also included reductions in patent fees.[18] Although the latter does not strictly imply an increase in patent rights, inventors have been found to increase their rates of patenting in response to cheaper patents (MacLeod et al. 2003). Lerner was not able to directly measure the effect of these changes on innovation. Instead, he measured their effect on patenting within the country making the change and also the effect on patenting by domestic inventors at Great Britain's Patent Office. He found that, overall, foreign inventors increased their patenting in countries that strengthened their patent laws (figure 4.1). *Domestic* inventors, however, actually patented *at a lower rate* after the change, both within their home country and at the British Patent Office. Exploring alternative specifications, Lerner found that this decline applied more to

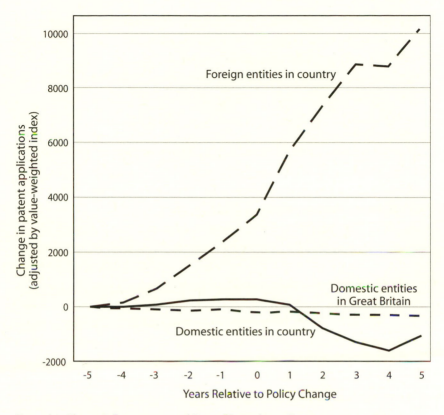

Figure 4.1. Change in Patenting around Patent "Strengthening"
Source: Lerner (2002)

poor nations and nations with initially lower levels of patent protection. Nevertheless, the overall results seem consistent with the studies of changes in pharmaceutical patent coverage: it might benefit foreign inventors who trade in patented goods, but it is not clear from these studies that stronger patent laws improve domestic innovation.

Qian (2006) conducted a detailed cross-country study of changes in pharmaceutical patent coverage from 1978 to 2002, controlling for general property rights and other variables that might affect pharmaceutical innovation. As did Lerner, she found that, in general, changes strengthening patent coverage for pharmaceuticals do not increase domestic innovation. She also found some evidence of a positive effect on innovation among more-developed countries with greater educational attainment and more market freedom. Even this effect is limited, however: at high levels of patent "strength," additional strengthening measures actually decrease innovation.

Empirical Evidence on Free-Riding

Before we attempt to draw overall conclusions from our review of the literature, it is helpful to ask whether patents do, in fact, play the role prescribed for them in economic theory. The standard argument is that without patents, inventions will be quickly copied by imitators. Competition from these "free-riders" will drive down prices, making it impossible for the inventor to earn sufficient profits to recoup his investment in developing the invention. Without the promise of secure profits, inventors will not invest in the first place, or so the argument goes.[19] This is a plausible and oft-told tale, but what is the actual evidence to support it? Do patents prevent the market entry of free-riders who would otherwise destroy or reduce incentives to innovate? Empirical research suggests that the answer is "sometimes" and "to some extent." This might help explain the nature of the findings described above.

The canonical example of the free-riding problem is traditional drug development (biotechnology is different in some important respects). DiMasi, Hansen, and Grabowski (2003) estimate that the average out-of-pocket cost for a drug company to develop a new drug, including the costs of research projects that were initiated and then abandoned, is $402 million (valued in year 2000 dollars and undiscounted). About 70 percent of this cost is incurred during the clinical trials necessary to obtain government approval. Generic drug manufacturers are not required to repeat these same clinical trials, so their R&D costs are far less than those of the original manufacturer. This means that when patents expire, generic manufacturers can enter the market and compete at lower prices. Grabowski and Vernon (2000) find that prices drop to 37 percent of their original level two years after the entry of generic manufacturers. The higher prices that pharmaceutical firms charge while they are still "on-patent" allow them to earn above-normal profits, or "rents," that more than recoup their development investments (Dimasi, Hansen, and Grabowski 2003).

But the pharmaceutical industry might be atypical. Certainly, few other industries have such a high regulatory burden on initial innovation. Typically, imitators do not operate at such a large cost advantage relative to initial innovators. Mansfield, Schwartz, and Wagner (1981), using survey data, found that imitation cost and time are about two-thirds of the original development cost and time on average. This is still an advantage for imitators, but not a terribly large one; imitators, too, have significant entry costs.

Further, the very nature of pharmaceutical patents—patents on small, well-defined molecules—might enhance the effectiveness of patenting in this industry. These patents have clear boundaries that, as we develop below, promote efficient enforcement of the patent rights. Survey respondents told Mansfield, Schwartz, and Wagner that patents increased imitation costs only 7 percent for electronics and machinery inventions at the median; the figure was 30 percent for pharmaceutical inventions.

More generally, imitation costs are high apart from issues related to patents because firms have means other than patents for protecting their innovations. Innovators might earn above-normal profits because they have lead-time advantages, or because they descend a learning curve first. They might earn additional profits from complementary products and services, or rely on trade secrecy. Surveys find that in most industries (pharmaceuticals are the exception here), R&D managers report that these other means of appropriation are more effective than patents in obtaining returns on their R&D investments (Cohen, Nelson, and Walsh 2000; Levin et al. 1987). For this reason, it is not surprising that survey research has also found that most inventions are *not* patented (Arundel and Kabla 1998; Cohen, Nelson, and Walsh 2000). On average, large European firms applied for patents on only 36 percent of product innovations and 25 percent of process innovations. Again, pharmaceutical firms are outliers—they applied for patents on 79 percent of pharmaceutical products.

Also, it is not clear that the entry of imitators is necessarily detrimental to innovation as in the canonical reward theory model. If firms can obtain some rents even when competing against a limited number of other firms, then competition might actually increase innovation. As long as there is not too much competition, entrants might spur incumbents to not rest on their laurels (Aghion et al. 2005) and entrants might bring diverse knowledge that increases the odds of future innovation success

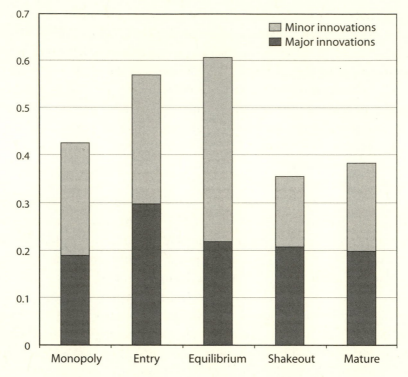

Figure 4.2. Rates of Innovation over Technology Life-Cycle
Source: Gort and Klepper (1982)

(Bessen and Maskin 2007). Aghion et al. found that innovation is greatest when firms earn moderate rents; too much or too little competition reduces innovation rates. Gort and Klepper (1982) studied the industry life-cycles of a number of major new technologies. Most of these industries follow a pattern: beginning with only one or a few firms in the market, there is a phase of rapid entry of new firms. This is followed by a leveling-off and a shakeout, reducing the number of firms and leading to a mature phase featuring a small number of dominant firms. They found that innovation rates, for both major and minor innovations, are greatest during the second and third phases when there is considerable market entry (figure 4.2). Less innovation occurs when firms face less threat of competition. On the other hand, *patenting* rates are greatest during the shakeout phase (figure 4.3). This suggests that much innovation is not dependent on patenting.

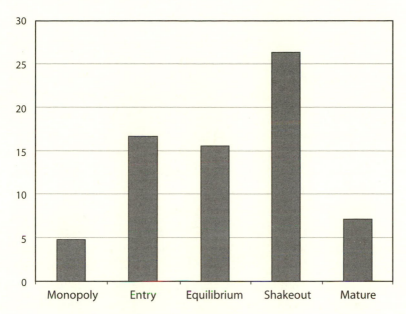

Figure 4.3. Patenting Rates over Technology Life-Cycle
Source: Gort and Klepper (1982)

This evidence does not mean that patents have no value. Rather, the effectiveness of patents varies by industry and technology and for many industries and technologies their effectiveness *is* limited. This assessment is supported by estimates of the private value of patents. We find in the next chapter that the private value of United States patents is about 3 percent of the value of R&D spending; the private value of worldwide patents held by United States firms is about 9–18 percent of R&D. This is consistent with the survey results above—in most industries, most of the value of R&D is appropriated by other means than patents. Nevertheless, patents have substantial value and might play a critical role in protecting some innovations.

THE BOTTOM LINE: IMPLEMENTATION MATTERS

The empirical evidence we have surveyed does not portray patents as positively and unambiguously as some patent advocates might prefer. The performance record of the patent system is clearly spotty and weak. Some suggest that the deficiency might be in the data or in the methods used to analyze it. It might be, as WIPO suggests, that the evidence is just "not sufficiently developed."

We argue, to the contrary, that the evidence is indeed conclusive, at least regarding the specific focus of our inquiry: patents *do not* deliver the same kind of economic payoff as do property rights. We make two points. First, the economic effect of patents is distinctly different from the effect of general property rights on economic growth. Second, the evidence of this difference is consistent across a large number of studies using a variety of methodologies.

The historical evidence, the cross-country evidence, and the evidence from economic experiments all point to a marked difference between the economic importance of general property rights and the economic importance of patents or intellectual property rights more generally. With the cross-country studies in particular, the quality of general property rights institutions has a substantial direct effect on economic growth. Using the *same* methodology and in the *same* studies, intellectual property rights have at best only a weak and indirect effect on economic growth.

The research also suggests a reason why patents differ from general property rights in motivating economic growth overall: the positive effects of patents appear to be highly contingent. Differences in technology and industry seem to have mattered considerably for twentieth-century R&D managers, as also for the innovative performance of nineteenth-century World's Fair exhibitors. Some results from the cross-country studies suggest that less-developed countries have a harder time realizing benefits from patents and that countries that participate actively in international trade might benefit more.

Some of these differences arise because of differences in the relative costs and effectiveness of alternatives to patents. Patents might contribute more to economic growth in the pharmaceutical industry than they contribute in electronics industries because the latter can more effectively earn returns on innovation through lead-time advantage, sales of complementary products and services, and so forth. Other differences might arise because of subtle differences in patent institutions. Patents might work better in the pharmaceutical industry because patents on chemical entities have much sharper boundaries than patents on software. Patents might have worked better in the United States of the nineteenth century because patent institutions performed better than their British counterparts.

Of course, the economic effectiveness of all forms of property depends on details of the supporting institutions—this is evident from the disparate growth-paths of Soviet Bloc economies. But the economic effectiveness of patents might be much more sensitive to the details of the relevant institutions than are general property rights. Perhaps this is because patent law might be much more specialized, complex, and sophisticated than, say, real property law, and thus effective institutions might be more difficult to develop and maintain.

In any case, the empirical economic evidence strongly rejects simplistic arguments that patents universally spur innovation and economic growth. "Property" is not a ritual incantation that blesses the anointed with the fruits of innovation; legislation of "stronger" patent rights does not automatically mean greater innovation. Instead, the effectiveness of patents as a form of property depends critically on the institutions that implement patent law. And there appear to be important differences in the effectiveness of the implementation across different technologies and industries.

On the other hand, we can also reject the view that patents uniformly stifle innovation. In the pharmaceutical industry and in the nineteenth-century United States, we see definite evidence that patents do and did sometimes provide positive private incentives for innovation.

Of course, we have asked and answered an intentionally narrow question here. We have not asked whether the patent system is the *best* way to encourage innovation. Nor have we even asked whether the total net effect of the patent system is positive. Some argue, for instance, that mechanisms such as rewards or purchase contracts would be more socially efficient ways of encouraging pharmaceutical research. Others, such as Boldrin and Levine (2005), argue that even though patents provide some individuals with rewards, they are not necessary to encourage innovation and that they are socially wasteful because they make subsequent innovations more difficult. These are interesting and important questions, but we doubt that they can be answered very well at this time based strictly on the empirical evidence. That is, the evidence *is* inconclusive with regard to these questions.

Our approach in the following chapters is to focus on the narrower questions of whether and where today patents do function effectively as a property system, what factors affect this performance, and what institutional changes might improve the effectiveness of the patent system. We limit our inquiry to the extent that we seek to obtain definitive answers. We do, however, think that the effectiveness of patents as a property system is central in any case to some of the other considerations noted above. If the patent system can be made more effective, then this necessarily affects any comparison to alternative policies. It also affects any assessment regarding the balance between private incentives for initial innovation and those for follow-on innovations. If patents can be made to work like property, then this constitutes a powerful argument in favor of the patent system.

5 What Are U.S. Patents Worth to Their Owners?

Introduction

A common argument one hears, especially from patent lawyers, is that they know that the patent system works because they regularly see people who benefit from it. For example, Dennis Crouch, a patent attorney and law professor, made this argument in his popular *Patently-O* weblog. Responding to a *Wall Street Journal* editorial calling for an overhaul of the patent system, he wrote,

> I had two companies approach me this week about patent work. They are both small businesses who want to go global. They believe that they have great innovations, but the only way that they will have [to] get a fair shake in the world of investors and business development is if they begin the process of securing their IP rights.
>
> As you may know, I am upbeat about our patent system. Despite the bad press, there are genuine success stories that continue to drive the uniquely American innovative spirit. Let's bring about legislative and PTO reforms to fix the problems—and I believe that there are problems—but the system is far from broken. A complete overhaul makes interesting press, but it is not the right solution.[1]

Now, we do not wish to pick on our colleague Dennis—we like his weblog after all—but we do think his logic in the quotation above is misleading as a policy argument. Even accepting that his anecdotes are representative, we do not believe that an accurate conclusion about the overall effectiveness of the patent system can be drawn from any number of such "success stories."

No doubt Dennis, like most patent attorneys, delivers real value to his clients. Indeed, in this chapter we show strong quantitative evidence that patents *do* deliver significant value to their owners. These estimates of value are not as large as some advocates might like. Patent values vary considerably across different technologies and types of owners, and they have not been increasing in recent years, as some have suggested. Nevertheless, this evidence does support our colleague's contention that there are indeed many genuine success stories.

But the difficulty with his argument is that the patent system also imposes costs on these same clients as well as on others. As we discussed in chapters 2 and 3, a badly functioning property system imposes costs that arise from unanticipated disputes, including litigation costs. Innovators can benefit from patents and at the same time be burdened with dispute costs that exceed the value of those benefits. Their own patents might produce "success stories," so that it is worthwhile for them to get patents, yet, at the same time, other people's patents might generate disputes that are so costly, innovators might be better off without patents altogether. Some disputes arise from the innovator's own patents; these tend to reduce the ex ante value of those patents. Other disputes arise because an innovator might inadvertently infringe upon someone else's patents; these disputes can arise even if the innovator has no patents of her own. An empirical assessment of the patent system needs to estimate both the benefits and the costs from both types of disputes and then compare them. Undoubtedly, some innovators will receive net benefits and some will not, but any judgment about the rigor of patent reform should, ideally, be based on a careful assessment of the overall net benefits.

We begin that assessment in this chapter, estimating the positive incentives that innovators receive from the patent system. Then, in the next chapter, we estimate patent dispute costs. As discussed in chapter 1, our approach is not to estimate the entirety of social benefits and costs of the patent system, but rather just the more limited effect of the patent system on innovators' incentives to invest in the development and commercialization of new technology. At the end of the next chapter, we estimate the net private incentive, positive or negative. We obtain this estimate by subtracting dispute costs from the economic rewards of owning or licensing a patent.

Of course, in any inquiry of this sort, there must remain some uncertainty and ambiguity in the estimates. When facing a range of estimates, our approach is to make upper-bound estimates (that is, estimates that are at or near the top of the range) on the benefits and lower-bound estimates (that is, estimates near the bottom of the range) on the costs. When making assumptions we try to be neutral or to make choices that overstate net patent benefits to innovators. We hope our conservative methodology gives readers confidence that our negative assessment of the current state of the U.S. patent system is appropriate.

What Kind of "Value" Do We Want to Measure?

Property works by providing incentives to owners to invest and trade. The value of these incentives, in the case of patents, is the "reward" that patents provide. The private value of patents is a measure of the size of this reward. We can thus measure the positive incentives that patents provide to their owners by estimating the value of patents to their owners.

Since the word "value" can refer to several different concepts in regard to patents, it is helpful to make a few distinctions. First, we do not distinguish whether or not the value is derived by directly excluding others from the market or by licensing or selling the patent; ultimately, in both cases, the value derives from the ability to exclude.[2] If a firm can exclude rivals from selling a patented product or from using a patented process, then that firm can, in many cases, earn greater profits than it would otherwise. The firm can charge a higher price for a product with limited competition, or the firm can earn greater margins if it has at its disposal a more cost-effective process than is available to its rivals. These extra profits are called "rents." The firm does not need to be a complete monopolist in order to earn rents. But the firm does need to be able to exert some market power—to exclude rivals at least partially—in order to receive direct value from a patent.

But even where a firm does not market a patented product itself and even when it does not use a patented process, it can still extract value from a patent by licensing or selling it. Even in this case, the value of the patent depends on the ability of the licensee or purchaser to extract rents—this is what makes them willing to pay a royalty or purchase price.

Second, the value of a patent is measured relative to the alternative means an innovator has for profiting from her invention. As discussed in the previous chapter, innovators can earn rents without patents via lead-time advantage, profits on complementary goods and services, secrecy, among other means. In general, patents are *not* the only way that innovators can "get a fair shake in the world of investors and business development," in Crouch's formulation. Firms do not patent a majority of their inventions and about 15 percent of all R&D is performed by firms that obtain no patents at all. So the private value of a patent is the value of the *incremental* rents above and beyond the rents earned by other means. As we shall see, a very substantial part of firm rents from innovation are obtained by other means. It follows from such observations as the above that the value of the patent per se is not the same as the value of the technology to which it is attached. The private value of the technology is the value of the rents obtained by all means, so this is generally larger than the value of the relevant patent, often much larger. Additionally, we are only concerned here with the private value of the patent, not the social value of the technology. These two can differ significantly. For instance, there are likely many instances in which patent owners capture only a fraction of the value an invention gives to society; this happens because patent owners capture only part of the value their inventions deliver to consumers, and because useful information about the invention "spills over" to other innovators, who use the information without infringing the patent. On the other hand, if a patent on an obvious invention allows a firm to steal business from a rival, then the private value of the patent could actually exceed the social value of the patent.

Such discrepancies between private value and social value are important, but they are not, however, the focus of our investigation. Our limited aim is to estimate the net incentives that patents provide to innovators. If the net private incentives are not positive, then patents are not likely to do a good job of generating net social value either, regardless of whether social value is greater or smaller than private value.

ESTIMATES OF VALUE

How can we estimate the value of a patent? One obvious approach is to ask patent owners. Researchers have surveyed patent owners and asked at what price they would be willing to sell their patents (Gambardella, Giuri, and Luzzi 2006; Gambardella, Harhoff, and Verspagen 2006; Harhoff, Scherer, and Vopel 2003). These studies contain helpful information on the distribution of patent values but they actually measure the value of the patent *plus* the underlying value of the technology.[3] For this and several other reasons, the available survey data are not suitable for our purposes.[4]

Fortunately, economists have devised at least two clever methods to infer patent value from observed behavior—the behavior of patent owners, in one case, and the behavior of investors, in the other case. Basing the estimates on observed behavior has several advantages. First, such estimates may be superior to survey-based estimates if economic actors behave differently than they say they do. Second, the estimates apply quite generally regardless of the actors' motivations. For example, if patent owners value the status of having a patent certificate to hang on the wall, then this value is reflected in their behavior and captured in our estimates. Finally, these methods evaluate patent value independently of the value of the underlying technology.

We estimate the value of recent United States patents to their owners using each method and find that the estimates correspond reasonably well. We also check these estimates by computing the rents implied by these estimates of patent value and comparing these rents to the actual profits of patent owners for several important examples. These, too, correspond well.

Estimates of United States Patent Value Based on Renewal Behavior

The first method, devised by Pakes and Schankerman (1984), uses data on patent renewal behavior. Most patent systems require that patent owners pay maintenance fees during the term of a patent in order to keep the patent in force. In Europe, those fees are typically annual. In the United States, beginning in 1980, patent owners had to pay fees after 3.5, 7.5, and 11.5 years in order to keep patents in force beyond 4, 8, and 12 years, respectively.

The idea behind this method is very simple. If we observe a patent owner who, say, declines to pay a fee of $1,000, then we can infer that the patent is worth less than $1,000. With many such observations over a large number of patents, we can estimate the distribution of patent values, including average values.

Here are some representative data for all the United States patents granted in 1991:

	4th Year	8th Year	12th Year	17th Year (Full term)
Percent expired in year	20%	21%	17%	42%
Average fee due in 1992 $U.S.	$814	$1,562	$2,327	—

Nearly 60 percent of these patents are not renewed to term even though the renewal fees are not large. This suggests that the majority of patents are not worth more than a few thousand dollars.

How, then, can we derive an average patent value from such data? Although the basic idea is quite simple, sound econometric practice must address two major complications. First, the value of a patent changes over time. Technologies become obsolete. Rivals can figure out ways to "invent around" a patent. Several researchers have studied the pattern of change and found that an assumption of constant depreciation is reasonably accurate.[5] Most of the studies that use renewal data make this assumption, but those studies that consider more general patterns of depreciation nevertheless obtain similar estimates of patent value.[6]

Second, from one patent to another, values can vary considerably. The distribution of patent values is quite "skewed"; that is, most patents have little value, but a small number are very valuable. Researchers have studied the distribution pattern of a variety of measures of patent and invention value, including survey estimates, case studies of inventions and start-up companies, and university licensing royalties. These values tend to adhere to the "80-20" rule: 80 percent of the total value is contributed by 20 percent of the inventions.

A sample distribution is shown in figure 5.1. This distribution comes from a survey of German inventors who reported the values of their

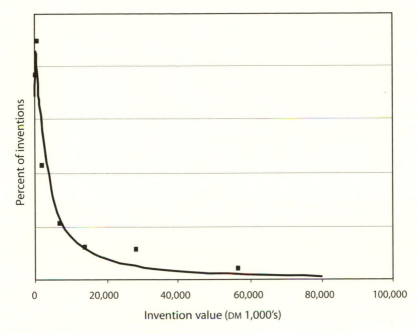

Figure 5.1. Percentage of Inventions of a Given Value
Source: Harhoff, Scherer, and Vopel (2003)

inventions. The figure shows the relative percentage of inventions at each given value in thousands of deutsche marks. As can be seen, this distribution has a long "tail," representing the small number of inventions with very large values; a much larger percentage of inventions have low values. This is important because it means that no single number can represent the value of patents for all the possible inquiries we might want to make about patent value. Instead, we estimate the distribution and estimate mean and median averages. The details of this estimation procedure are described in the sidebar 5.1, "Estimating Renewal Values," (pp. 115–17).

Table 5.1 shows estimates of mean and median patent values for the United States and European countries from a variety of different studies using this and some closely related methods. The mean value of a United States patent across all groups of United States patent holders (United States patents are more valuable to foreigners) at the time of the patent

Table 5.1.
Estimates of Patent Value

Study	Patent Issue Year	Patent Country	Group	Patent value ($U.S. 1992) Median	Mean
U.S. Studies					
Barney (2002)	1986	U.S.	all	5,849	61,896
Bessen (2006)	1991	U.S.	all U.S. patentees	7,175	78,168
	1985–91	U.S.	U.S. public firms, manufacturing	18,010	113,067
Serrano (2005)	1983–2002	U.S.	small business patentees	17,361	47,456
Putnam (1996)	1974	U.S.	also filed abroad		188,355
			all (imputed)		78,800
Ocean Tomo (2006)		U.S.	auctioned		23,278
European Studies					
Baudry and Dumont (2006)	2002	France	all		1,656
Gustafsson (2005)	1970–89	Finland	all	27,704	30,833
Lanjouw (1998)	1975	Germany	computers	7,235	13,027
			textiles	4,721	9,695
			engines	18,390	27,571
	1967–80		pharmaceuticals	5,850	15,219
Schankerman (1998)	1970	France	pharmaceuticals	2,607	6,893
			chemicals	2,548	7,942
			mechanical	4,683	24,165
			electronics*	5,049	31,704
Pakes (1986)	1951–79	France	all	853	9,000
	1950–74	U.K.	all	2,424	11,758
	1952–72	Germany	all	9,993	25,841
Pakes and Schankerman (1986)	1970	U.K.	all	2,974	11,128
		France	all	1,354	10,638
		Germany	all	9,126	30,564

* In Schankerman (1998) Japanese patents are excluded from the electronics group. In Pakes and Schankerman (1986) the values given are for patents in their fifth year.

grant runs between $50,000 and $80,000 in 1992 dollars. The median value is closer to $10,000.

The four available studies (five estimates) for the United States cover somewhat different samples. Barney (2002) studied all patents issued in 1986. Bessen (2006) used one sample of all patents obtained by domestic patentees and another sample of patents assigned to publicly traded manufacturing firms; the latter sample consists of larger firms and has significantly greater patent values. As will be seen below, larger patentees consistently have more valuable patents. Serrano (2005) used a sample that excludes individuals (and unassigned patents), including only patentees that acquire small numbers of patents. Putnam (1996) used a sample of patents that were also filed in one or more other countries. Using data on international filings (in a model similar to the renewal model), he estimated that patents that were successfully filed in the United States in 1974 that were also filed abroad were worth $188,000 in 1992 dollars. In general, patents that are filed in multiple countries tend to be much more valuable than patents that are not, so it is not surprising that Putnam's mean estimate is substantially higher than the others. Using Putnam's data it is possible to impute the mean value of all United States patents, including those only filed domestically. This figure is about $79,000.[7] Thus these estimates are roughly consistent. As a check, we included the mean value of patents sold at the well-publicized Ocean Tomo auction in April 2006. The traded values of these patents was quite a bit less, as will be discussed in greater depth in chapter 8.

Most of the research using renewal values had been done for European nations and the bottom portion of table 5.1 presents these results. The European patent value estimates are, in general, much smaller. The reported mean patent values range from $2,000 to $32,000, with an average of about $16,000. Although these estimates are not directly comparable to the estimates of United States patent values, they do provide a check on the United States estimates. A rough calculation suggests that United States patent values should be about four times larger than patent values in Germany, France and the United Kingdom, and they are.[8] The estimates based on United States renewal data thus appear to be broadly consistent with the larger literature using renewal data.

Throughout table 5.1, median values are much less than the mean values because the distribution is highly skewed. The median is a reasonable measure of what the "typical" patent is worth.[9] In fact, the median patent is not worth very much and might be worth less than the sum of the legal costs and administrative fees needed to obtain a patent. This means that patentees are, to some extent, gamblers. Each patent is like a lottery ticket. Inventors are willing to lose money on many patents for the chance of a big win on one patent. The mean value, on the other hand, is a better measure of what an inventor might be willing to pay for such a lottery ticket before the inventor has information on the quality of the invention. It is an average that takes into account the small probabilities of the big wins as well as the more common low-value patents.

Whether the mean or median better represents the reward that patents promise inventors depends on the inventors' attitudes to risk. The mean value will be the more appropriate measure for a large firm that diversifies by acquiring a portfolio of many patents. The median value might be more representative for a cash-constrained independent inventor with only a few patents. In what follows, however, we stake out a conservative path and use the mean value as the representative average so as to be consistent with our upper-bound rule.

Estimates of Worldwide Patent Value

The second method for estimating the value of patents relates the market value of public firms to their assets, including their stock of patents. In effect, investors reveal the value of a firm's patents by the amount they are willing to pay for a firm's shares. If we separate out that portion of a firm's value that can be attributed to the rents earned on patents from other sources of value, such as physical assets, goodwill, and so forth, then we will measure the value of those patents. We cannot do this if we only have data for an individual firm, but if we statistically compare a large number of firms (multiple regression), we can obtain a measure of the contribution that patent rents make to firm value.

This measure provides an upper-bound estimate of mean patent value; that is, it is larger than true patent value by some unknown amount.[10] Nevertheless, even though this estimate is biased upwards, it does serve as a check on the estimates derived using renewal data. The renewal estimates have their own shortcomings;[11] however, a comparison with estimates

Table 5.2.
Worldwide Patent Values

Study	Sample	Sample period	Value per patent (1,000s, $U.S. 1992)
Estimates from Market Value Regressions			
Cockburn and Griliches (1988)	Public manufacturing firms	1980	$213
Megna and Klock (1993)	U.S. public semiconductor firms	1972–90	$343
Hall et al. (2005)	Public manufacturing firms	1979–88	
	"(using means)		$119
	"(using medians)		$322
Bessen (2006b)	Public R&D performing firms	1979–97	$370
		MEAN	$275
Estimates Based on Patentee Filing Behavior			
Putnam (1994)	All patents applied for in 1974	1974	$230

derived from market value studies suggests that these shortcomings are not serious (see Bessen [2006b]).

Aside from issues of estimation methodology, there is an important difference in these estimates: the renewal method estimates the value of holding United States patents, but the market value regressions effectively estimate the value of *all* the patents taken out on an invention worldwide. That is, the market value estimate includes the value of the United States patent plus the values of the corresponding foreign patents. Although our primary focus is on the performance of the United States patent system, worldwide patent value estimates serve as a useful upper bound measure.

Estimates derived from the literature are displayed in table 5.2. The derivation of these estimates is described in Bessen (2006b). Estimates based on market value regressions range from $119,000 to $370,000, with an average of $275,000. Table 5.2 also displays the estimate of $230,000 arrived at by Putnam (1996) for the worldwide value corresponding to patents held in the United States. These estimates are derived from data on the number of countries in which patents are filed using a model similar to the renewal model (each additional country incurs additional fees). This estimate seems similar.

Recall that the estimate for United States patent value for manufacturing firms (table 5.1) is $113,000. Worldwide patent values appear to be about 2 to 3 times as large, a reasonable correspondence. These estimates, it must be remembered, derive from models that do not take into account differences in patent value between technologies or other patent characteristics. We now look at some of those differences.

Patent Value Across Groups and Time

Technology and Size Differences

The previous chapter documented the variation in performance of the patent system across time, country, and type of inventor. For this reason, we want to estimate patent values, and, later, patent costs, for different subgroups. Here and below, we look at two different groupings of inventors, classed by the type of their technology and by their size. These are not the only groupings we studied, but previous literature shows they are significant; we confirm and extend previous results.

First, we consider differences in technology. The evidence indicates important differences between industries and these appear to be related to how easily property rights can be defined for different technologies. In surveys, R&D managers in the chemical and pharmaceutical industries rank the effectiveness of patents substantially higher than do managers in other major industries. Only in the pharmaceutical industry did a majority of managers rate patents as more effective than other means of profiting from innovation. And only managers in the pharmaceutical and chemical industries considered patents as essential to developing and marketing 30 percent or more of inventions. Researchers have attributed this sharp difference to the comparatively clear boundaries of chemical (including pharmaceutical) patents:

> The most probable explanation for the robust finding that patents are particularly effective in chemical industries is that comparatively clear standards can be applied to assess a chemical patent's validity and to defend against infringement. The uniqueness of a specific molecule is more easily demonstrated than the novelty of, for example, a new component of a complex electrical or mechanical system. Similarly, it is easy to determine whether an allegedly infringing molecule is physically identical to a patented molecule; it is more difficult to determine whether comparable components of two complex systems "do the same work in substantially the same way." (Levin et al. 1987)

If, in fact, the boundaries of patents that claim chemicals are more clearly defined than the boundaries of patents claiming complex technologies, then patents on chemicals might be more valuable than patents on complex or other technologies; that is, chemical patents might provide stronger exclusion because they might be more likely to be successfully enforced. Conversely, patents on components of complex systems—technologies where many different inventions are combined into a system—might be less valuable because complex interactions between components might make the boundaries of each component less clear. Also, many more patents might be necessary to protect a single product.

To explore this conjecture, we used the Patent Office's technology classification system to categorize chemical patents and patents that covered components of complex systems. We identified the chemical patents as those that primarily claim chemical compositions or molecules.[12] Not surprisingly, these patents are primarily held by firms in the chemical and pharmaceutical industries. The top of table 5.3 shows the median and mean values of these patents for 1991, along with the values for a number of other subgroups, obtained using the renewal method. Chemical compositions are, indeed, substantially more valuable than other patents overall.

We identified patents on components of complex technologies as those from technology classes where litigation tended to involve multiple

Table 5.3.
Patent Value at Issue, by Subgroups

Value of U.S. Patents Issued in 1991	Median Value (Thousands $U.S. 1992)	Mean Value (Thousands $U.S. 1992)
Technology Groups		
Chemical Compositions	27.5	332.8
Complex (not Chemical)	10.2	52.0
Other	7.6	79.6
Size		
Small Entities	2.9	70.1
Large Entities	14.3	105.9
U.S. Individual (or Unassigned)	2.6	25.6
U.S. Non-Gov't Organization	14.8	115.8
Value of Worldwide Patents, by Industry		
Chemical and Pharmaceutical		1,465
Large Pharmaceutical Firms		7,177
Other Industries		260

patents.[13] This captures the idea that a complex product is likely to infringe multiple, interrelated patents and innovators are likely to obtain multiple, possibly overlapping, patents to better protect their inventions. We find that the computer and electronics industries hold the largest share of these patents, corresponding to intuitions about complex technologies. We then estimated the value of these patents for 1991. The mean value is significantly less than the mean value of other patents, although the median value is a bit higher. So, generally, our estimates of patent value across different technology types correspond to the intuitions about the effectiveness of patents.

These differences between technology groups correspond loosely to differences between industries. The lower part of table 5.3, above, looks at industry differences in the worldwide values associated with United States patents held by United States public firms.[14] As we might expect, the patents held by chemical firms are much more valuable than those held by other firms. This is especially true for a small number of large pharmaceutical firms (about twenty-five).[15]

The other main division among patents that we explore is between those patents granted to small and large inventors. It is often argued that small inventors play a special role in the patent system, a subject we explore in greater depth in chapter 8. Here, however, we simply report the results in table 5.3: patents granted to small inventors are much less valuable. The first comparison is between patents granted to large and small "entities." According to Patent Office regulations, individuals, nonprofit organizations (NPOs), and corporations with fewer than five hundred employees qualify as small entities and are charged lower fees. Large-entity patents are about five times more valuable in the median, and about 50 percent more valuable in the mean. Comparing individuals to organizations (mostly corporations), the contrast is even greater. In chapter 8 we explain that this large difference has important implications for our understanding of markets for patents.

The large differences in patent value across technologies/industries have important implications for the comparison we want to make between the benefits of patents and the costs incurred by the patent system. In particular, these estimates suggest that the economic benefits of patents are very highly concentrated among a small number of firms. Over one-half of the value of worldwide patents accrues to a small number of large pharmaceutical firms; over two-thirds accrues to firms in the chemical and pharmaceutical industries. When we compare benefits and costs (as we will in the next chapter), we will be careful to treat this group separately.

Are Patents Becoming More Valuable?

An important question for our inquiry is whether patent values are increasing over time. Jaffe and Lerner (2004), among others, argue that patents have gotten "stronger" in recent decades, meaning that it has become more attractive to patentees to enforce their patents through litigation. If patents

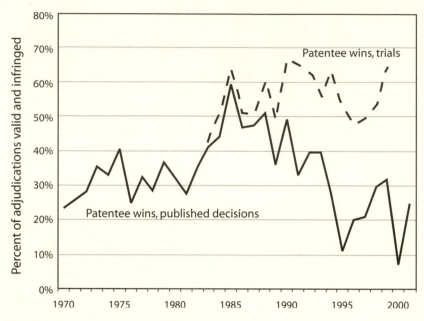

Figure 5.2. Time Trends in Patentee Win Rates
Sources: Henry and Turner (2006); Moore (2000)

have indeed become stronger since 1991, then estimates made for this year and earlier years might understate the value of patents.

The best available evidence indicates that this is not the case, however. Estimates based on market value regressions show that worldwide patent values were modestly lower during the 1990s than during the 1980s.[16] Moreover, the evidence suggests that patent enforcement did not become significantly more profitable to patent holders during the 1990s (as will be discussed further in chapter 7).

This evidence might seem to contradict Jaffe and Lerner, but, in fact, almost all of Jaffe and Lerner's evidence concerns the 1980s. One piece of evidence that they use is the percent of lawsuits "won" by patentees. By "won" they mean a lawsuit that was decided by a judge or jury (rather than settled) where at least one patent claim was found to have been valid and infringed upon (defendants in an infringement suit can challenge the validity of patent claims; an invalid claim cannot be enforced). The solid line in figure 5.2 shows this win rate for cases with published court decisions.

The win rate did, indeed, rise sharply after the creation of the Court of Appeals for the Federal Circuit (CAFC) in 1982, but it has fallen since then.[17]

Jaffe and Lerner advance two other arguments that patents have become stronger. First, they note that juries are pro-patentee compared to judges, and the use of jury trials has increased. These observations are correct, but even a series of win rates for jury trials does not show any increase after the mid-1980s (Moore 2000); see the dashed line in figure 5.2. Second, they argue that patent law has grown more favorable to patentees by providing stronger remedies and a decreased risk of invalidation. This argument is based on their reading of the case law, but all of the case law cited regarding stronger remedies occurred during the 1980s. Additional evidence suggests that patent litigation has not become more profitable to patentees during the 1990s.[18] And although some recent cases made it more difficult to find a patent invalid for reasons of obviousness, evidence from court decisions shows that the risk of patent invalidation decreased sharply during the 1980s, but has not decreased since then (Henry and Turner 2006).[19] At least one legal scholar (Lunney 2004) argues that during the early 1980s the courts exhibited a pro-patentee shift, especially regarding invalidation, but that during the 1990s the courts have acted to narrow the scope of patent rights, favoring the alleged infringer.[20]

To summarize, there is good evidence of a pro-patentee shift that might be associated with an increase in patent value during the early and mid-1980s. Although some legal decisions since then have favored patentees, there is, however, little evidence of an overall pro-patentee shift during the 1990s. We conclude that there is no evidence to suggest that mean patent values were greater during the 1990s than they were in 1991 and limited empirical evidence suggests that they might have been less.

SIGNIFICANCE: HOW BIG IS BIG?

Are these estimates of patent value large or small? The next chapter presents the crucial comparison of the private value of patents to the costs imposed on innovators by the patent system. Nevertheless, it is interesting to compare our estimates of patent value to a variety of yardsticks in order to appreciate the magnitude of the gross incentives patents provide. This is especially important because various commentators have circulated extravagant claims about the value of patent assets and the profits they produce. These commentators will likely feel that our estimates of value are too low. As we shall see, however, our estimates are not only internally consistent, but they also correspond reasonably well with information from examples where the profits from patents are known.

The Value of Patent Assets

Using our upper-bound mean estimate of $78,000, the aggregate value of United States patents granted to private U.S. parties in 1991 was about $4.4 billion in 1992 dollars—patents matter. This sum substantially exceeds the legal and administrative costs of obtaining those patents (those costs ran a bit under $1 billion, assuming patent prosecution cost about $15,000 per patent).[21] On average, patents deliver real value and inventors get their money's worth for the fees they pay their patent lawyers.

This is especially true for chemical patents, including pharmaceuticals. Although these make up only about 15 percent of patents granted in 1991, using the renewal estimates they account for about 45 percent of the value of those patents. Using the market value estimates of worldwide patent value in table 5.3, chemical and pharmaceutical patents account for over three-quarters of all patent value.

Using these same estimates of worldwide patent value, the global patents held by United States public firms in 1999 were worth $122 billion in 1992 dollars. This figure is based on our highest estimate of patent value and it seems quite substantial, but it is still quite small compared to the claims made about patent value by some commentators. It is widely argued, for example, that intangible assets have become a central part of the New Economy:

> In recent years intellectual property has received a lot more attention
> because ideas and innovations have become the most important

resource, replacing land, energy and raw materials. As much as three-quarters of the value of publicly traded companies in America comes from intangible assets, up from around 40 percent in the early 1980s. "The economic product of the United States", says Alan Greenspan, the chairman of America's Federal Reserve, has become "predominantly conceptual." Intellectual property forms part of those conceptual assets. (Cukier 2005)

But some, such as Shapiro and Hassett (2005), go further, contending that intellectual property constitutes 33 percent of corporate assets, amounting to about $5 trillion. They obtain this estimate by assuming that all corporate expenditures on R&D, software, and databases constitute intellectual property.[22] They use this analysis to propose that the United States take "aggressive measures to strengthen global enforcement of intellectual property rights."

More careful calculations suggest a rather more modest magnitude, at least as far as patents go. As we discussed in the previous chapter, firms rely on other means to earn returns on their R&D than patents (the case is similar for software investment). For this reason, the value of patents might be far less than the value of the knowledge related to the associated inventions. Comparing the value of United States patents held by public firms to their R&D, United States patent value is only about 3 percent of the value of the corresponding R&D investment. Comparing the worldwide value of patents held by public firms to their R&D, total patent value is 9–18 percent of the value of the corresponding R&D investment.[23] This means, roughly, that 85 percent of the value of the intangible assets is *not* captured via patents and can only very loosely be described as intellectual property.

Similarly, using firm-level data, the worldwide value of patent stocks of United States firms is only about 1 percent of their market value, much less than the 33 percent figure advanced by Shapiro and Hassett (2005). Moreover, the majority of this value is owned by a small number of large pharmaceutical firms. Shapiro and Hassett might (or might not) be right about the need for aggressive global enforcement of intellectual property rights, but the case cannot be made on the basis of such fantastical figures.

The Value of Patent Rents

In the next chapter, we compare the litigation costs of patents to the incremental profits that can be attributed to patents per se. These profits are what economists call "rents"—above-normal returns—and patent rents are the incremental rents beyond other rents that a firm earns. These rents can be compared to firm profits and licensing revenues as a check on our value estimates.

We impute patent rents by assuming a rate of return of 15 percent on the stock of patent assets net of depreciation.[24] Using our highest estimates of worldwide patent value from table 5.3, above, United States public firms in the chemical and pharmaceutical industries earned patent rents of about \$15.2 billion in 1999 and firms in other industries earned rents of about \$3.2 billion in 1999, both in 1992 dollars.

Are these numbers too low? One way of checking is to compare these rents to actual net income for a select group of firms. One industry where profits are supposed to depend heavily on patents is pharmaceuticals. Comparing patent rents to net income for large pharmaceutical firms from 1990 through 1997, we find that patent rents were 62 percent of net income. Assuming that firms earn a 5 percent profit margin under competitive conditions, we find that estimated patent rents accounted for 93 percent of total rents for these firms.[25] Patents do not account for all of the rents of these firms, but then they very likely earn substantial rents aside from their patents. First, they earn returns on their marketing investments, which exceed their investment in R&D. Second, they earn abnormal returns because they are in a highly regulated industry with restricted entry. Note that *generic* pharmaceutical manufacturers also earn abnormally high profits. So based on this rough calculation, our estimate of patent rents is certainly in the right ballpark.

Some readers might wonder why our figures pale in comparison to high estimates of licensing profits. Rivette and Kline (2000) and many others tout patent licensing as a great new source of profit. Apparently their enthusiasm was stoked by the widely circulated claim that IBM alone earned \$1.5 billion from patent licensing in 1999. How could our estimate of \$3.2 billion be right if IBM alone accounted for nearly one-half of these rents?

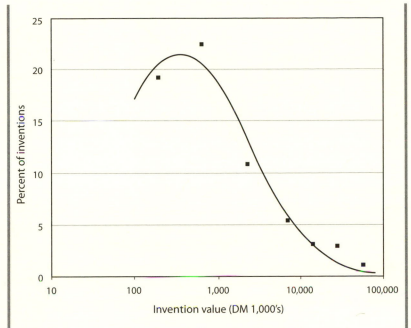

Figure 5.3. Percentage of Inventions of a Given Value (log x-axis)

Sidebar 5.1. Estimating Renewal Values

To estimate the distribution, we need to choose a family of distributions and "fit" one to the data by choosing the parameters that determine the specific distribution from that family (for example, the mean and standard deviation determine the particular distribution from among the family of normal distributions). To see how this can be done, figure 5.3 shows an alternative representation of the same data as appears in figure 5.1. Figure 5.3 is the same as figure 5.1, except that the x-axis representing value is now shown in logarithmic form, compressing the upper tail. In this form and in the range shown, the data approximate a normal distribution, the well-known "bell curve." This means that the data approximately fit a "lognormal" distribution. There is other evidence that invention and patent values in general fit a lognormal distribution reasonably well, and this distribution is what

(Continued)

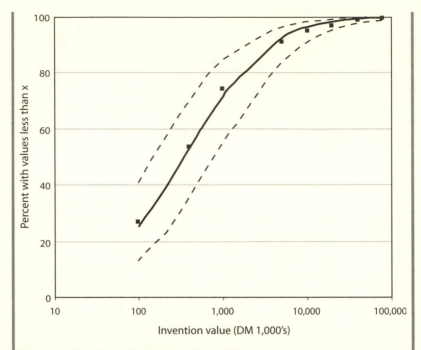

Figure 5.4. Cumulative Distribution of Patent Values

most of the patent renewal studies use, although a few use other distributions while obtaining similar results.

To see how renewal data can be fit to a distribution, figure 5.4 shows the same German invention data again, but now in the form of a cumulative distribution. That is, the first point indicates that 27 percent of the inventions had value of 100,000 DM or less, the second point indicates that 54 percent had value of 400,000 DM or less, et cetera.

The solid line shown represents a distribution that fits the data well. The dashed lines represent other lognormal distributions with different means. We estimate the distribution by choosing the combination of mean and standard deviation that fits the data best.

Note that the renewal data in the unnumbered table on page 100, above, can be described in a similar way to the data in figure 5.4: for 20 percent of the patents it is not worth $814 to keep them in force from years 4–8, for 41 percent of the patents it is not worth $1,562 to keep

> them in force from years 8–12, and so forth. Given a full set of renewal data, we can find the lognormal distribution with the parameters (mean and standard deviation) that best fit the observed cumulative expiration percentages. Once we have these best-fit parameters, we can generate estimates of the mean patent value, median patent value, and other averages.

The answer is simple. The $1.5 billion figure is an "urban legend" based on window-dressing in IBM's annual financial reports.[26] Beginning in 2000, IBM began listing "IP and licensing royalties" and this figure exceeded $1 billion ($1.5 billion in 1999, $1.7 billion in 2000, and a bit less in recent years). The majority of this $1.5 billion figure represented the value of intellectual property that was sold off, including the IP held by divisions that were sold off, as well as custom-development revenues. The actual amount of revenues from their patent licensing program was far less, about $200 million in 1999, in 1992 dollars.[27] Moreover, that figure is gross of the cost of IBM's several hundred patent lawyers and it has fallen to nearly one-half that level since then.

Looking at these data another way, IBM earned gross patent licensing revenues of about $7,600 per patent in 1999, plus whatever patent rents it earned by excluding competitors from the market, less the costs of its patent program. Our estimates of patent rents correspond to annual rents per patent in 1999 of about $531,000 in the chemical and pharmaceutical industries and about $39,000 per patent in other industries. IBM's licensing revenues correspond quite well with this latter figure, especially considering the exceptional nature of IBM's licensing program and the exceptional returns IBM received in 1999.

University patents, which include some of the most valuable technologies, provide another point of comparison. Based on the 2003 AUTM survey, universities earned licensing revenues of about $28,000 per patent, in 1992 dollars; this figure is also gross of costs, which consume a substantial share of this gross revenue (Thursby and Thursby 2003). Considering the importance of biotech-pharmaceutical patents in university licensing, this number seems quite modest compared to our estimates of rents.

These benchmarks provide assurance that our estimates of patent value and patent rents are realistic. Critics who want to contend that we substantially undervalue patents need to explain why large pharmaceutical firms do not have much larger profits and why IBM and universities do not earn much larger licensing revenues.

In summary, the picture that emerges from these comparisons is that patents are neither the only nor even the most important means of encouraging innovation. On average, patents make a rather small contribution in this regard. Claims that the U.S. patent system is responsible for current U.S. technological leadership are exaggerated, as are claims of huge profits and huge asset values for patents. Nevertheless, certain groups of innovators do receive large rewards from patents, and patents might nonetheless provide an important incentive for some innovators. Next we turn to the costs imposed by the patent system on innovators, so that we can estimate the *net* subsidy that patents provide.

Sidebar 5.2. Estimating Patent Value Using Firm Market Value

In a competitive market where firms can enter freely, the market value of a firm should roughly equal, on average and over time (in long-run equilibrium), the current value of the assets of the firm. If the market value were larger than the value of the assets, then the firm could profitably increase its assets by investing more. Also, other firms could profitably enter, driving prices down until the firm market values roughly equaled their assets.[28] Conversely, if firm market value is less than firm asset value, the firm can profitably sell off assets. This approximate equality between market value and assets just means that those assets earn normal returns. The market value of the firm should also equal the discounted value of future profits, so if the profit rate equals a normal return, the investment will equal the discounted returns.

Note that this approximate equality between market value and asset value assumes competitive markets with free entry. If, on the other hand, a firm has some market power—an ability to exclude others from the market to some degree—then firm value would persistently exceed

(Continued)

(Continued)

the current value of assets. In this case, the assets of the firm earn above-normal profits; that is, the firm earns rents.

The ratio of firm market value to the current value of the firm's assets (replacement value) is known as "Tobin's Q" after Nobel Prize–winning economist James Tobin, who used this ratio to study investment. Economists have also used average values of this ratio over time to measure rents. Hayashi (1982) identified the relationship between rents and market value, and we use his equation to estimate the portion of rents that can be attributed to patents (Bessen 2006b). But careful analysis shows that this correlation between patents and firm value involves more than the direct contribution of patent rents to firm value; firms also tend to obtain more patents when their R&D investments are more successful, so patents are also a proxy for the quality of the firm's technology. This means that estimates obtained by this method are larger than the value of the patent rents; that is, they are upper-bound estimates.

6   The Cost of Disputes

The private value of patents represents the incremental reward that inventors receive via patents. Innovators invest in research, development, and commercialization and their patents provide them rents either directly, if they market a product using or made with patented technology, or indirectly, if they license or sell the patents to others who use the patents to obtain rents in the marketplace. But every dollar an inventor or innovator invests in research, development, or commercialization can increase the risk of infringing upon someone else's patent. This risk—the expected cost of patent disputes—acts to reduce the profits inventors or innovators make on their investments. This means that patents can reduce the incentives to invest as well as increase them. This chapter estimates the expected costs of disputes for publicly listed firms and compares these costs to the benefits realized by the same firms in their capacity as patent holders. We explore the incentives for other inventors in chapter 8.

We make two major findings: first, the net incentives provided by the patent system vary significantly across industries and other groupings. For example, the chemical and pharmaceutical industries show substantially more positive incentives than do other industries. Second, although firms in the chemical and pharmaceutical industries have positive incentives, by the late 1990s the net incentives of the patent system became significantly negative outside of these industries. This provides strong evidence that the current patent system is broken.

THE PROBLEM OF PATENT LITIGATION

Are Defendants in Patent Lawsuits Thieves?

In a well-functioning property rights system, property boundaries are easily and inexpensively ascertained, and infringement can be avoided by "clearing" rights: that is, by either making sure trespass does not occur or by obtaining a license to use the property ex ante. For this reason, few real property disputes arise from people building houses on land owned by others (although disputes do arise more frequently when land rights are divided in complex ways). Clearance is efficient.

In contrast, a significant and growing number of very expensive lawsuits occur each year because firms have invested millions of dollars on the research, development, and commercialization of technology that is allegedly owned by others. Figure 6.1 shows the patent litigation "explosion." If this increase in litigation corresponds to an increasing burden on investments in new technology, then this tripling of the litigation rate is troubling.

But what if most alleged infringers have *not* invested in R&D? What if they are "cheaters" who steal others' technology *instead* of investing in R&D? Then the increase in litigation is not so worrisome. Every property system has some cheaters and incurs social costs in combating cheating, but such costs in the patent system do not necessarily impose a burden on genuine innovators. If, on the other hand, most disputes arise from inadvertent infringement, then a high and increasing level of disputes does represent a burden on innovation.

This distinction is important because some people argue that litigation is mainly about cheaters who get caught. Some people argue that alleged infringers are thieves and that concerns about excessive litigation are just a cover for attempts to weaken the patent system. George Jerome voiced such a view in a letter to the *Los Angeles Times*. The *Times* had just run an

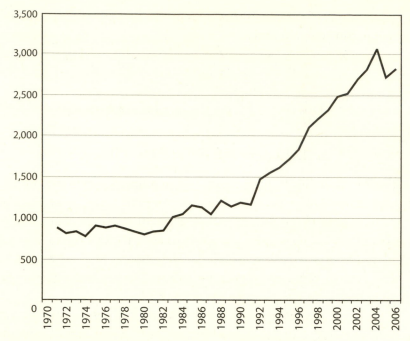

Figure 6.1. U.S. Patent Lawsuits Filed in District Courts
Sources: Administrative Office of the U.S. Courts; John L. Turner

editorial calling for patent reform. It referenced the recent lawsuit that NTP, a patent holder, filed against Research in Motion (RIM), the maker of the popular BlackBerry personal digital assistant. Mr. Jerome wrote:

Letter: Patent System Is Protection Against Theft

Like many large companies, *The Times* takes the position that patents are simply a thorn in the side of big business—not a means for the small inventor to make a mark on the world. This editorial points out the recent fight over the BlackBerry, citing the more than $600 million paid to the patent holder. Had Research in Motion Ltd. properly licensed the technology in the first place, or taken legal steps to prove the underlying patents to be invalid, the issue would have been a nonstarter. Instead, it did as it pleased, took what it wanted, and assumed lawyers would muck up the works enough to get away with it.

The patent system does not need an overhaul. The standard of business ethics needs a major overhaul. It is time that large companies are held accountable for stealing the property of others.

George Jerome

Is patent litigation just evidence that large businesses lack ethics or, instead, does the surge in patent litigation provide evidence that the patent system is broken? We argue that placing the blame on business ethics is just a smokescreen. Although some businesses surely cheat, such cheating is not a major cause of litigation, especially not a cause of *costly* litigation. If litigation were mainly about cheating, we contend, then there would not be so much litigation and what litigation did occur would be settled quickly. Instead, we argue that the very substantial costs of litigation are borne mainly by inadvertent infringers and that this is indeed a real problem.

A careful examination of the RIM story reveals some of the problems of Mr. Jerome's argument. Moreover, the RIM example illustrates aspects of patent litigation that contradict the cheating story of litigation more generally. It must first be noted that Research in Motion (RIM) is not a very good example of an unethical big business. RIM was started by a small inventor and until recently, RIM was a small company.[1] So, this is really an example of a small start-up being punished by a small patenter (Thomas J. Campana, the co-founder of NTP) who did not himself make the investments to commercialize the innovation.

More generally, large firms are not disproportionately alleged infringers. Mr. Jerome implies that large companies have the finances to hire the lawyers to "muck up the works" and get away with piracy, but small companies do not. This seems to suggest that litigation should mainly be about small inventors suing large firms. But large firms are not sued disproportionately by small firms.[2] Moreover, small firms have a substantially greater probability of being sued relative to their R&D spending than do large firms (Bessen and Meurer 2006). Further, RIM did not infringe to avoid investing in R&D. RIM has invested nearly half a billion dollars in R&D, much of it before RIM ever heard of NTP's patents.

Alleged infringers are not typically copyists who avoid spending R&D. Among public firms, alleged infringers actually spend *more* on R&D on average than do plaintiffs in infringement suits (Bessen and Meurer 2006).

Moreover, even after controlling for a wide range of variables, the more a firm spends on R&D, all else being equal, the *more* likely it is to be sued for infringement. This is inconsistent with the notion that infringers cheat to avoid R&D. We would expect cheaters to spend less on R&D, all things again being equal. And to the extent that R&D expenditures can be used to hide infringing technology, we would also expect greater R&D spending to be associated with a lower risk of detection. Instead, this pattern is entirely consistent with the inadvertent-infringement explanation—the more a firm invests in technology, the more it inadvertently exposes itself to patents of which it is not aware.[3]

The idea that patent infringers are large R&D spenders also seems to be at odds with the picture of pirates we hold from other areas of law. Copyright and trademark pirates are often small-time operators such as street vendors. They hope to "fly under the radar" of the property owners' monitoring efforts. Large retailers, on the other hand, take great pains to make sure that they are not selling counterfeit goods because any infractions would likely come to the notice of the property owners and their customers. We would expect large technology companies to take great pains to avoid infringement (as Kodak did) precisely because they are so visible.

This raises yet another point: if RIM consciously stole NTP's property, then one would expect RIM to at least make some effort to hide its crime. Instead, RIM *publicized* its allegedly infringing technology. RIM came to NTP's attention because of a press release that RIM put out—the functional description of RIM's product in the press release was sufficient for NTP to determine that an infringement lawsuit could be filed.

It would appear that actual evidence of hiding seems rather limited. Alleged infringers often act like RIM. For example, in lawsuits involving software, the alleged infringer typically has a publicly available product or service. Quite frequently patent holders claim that certain publicly observable product features are infringing. Moreover, the powerful reverse-engineering tools available for software mean that publicly available products can easily be checked for infringement. If most alleged infringers were cheaters, then we would expect relatively few lawsuits over publicly observable products— cheaters would avoid technologies where they could not hide their theft. But, in fact, most patent lawsuits involving software appear to involve publicly observable features and litigation rates on software patents are relatively high

(Allison et al. [2004]; see also chapter 9 in the present volume). And in general, firms report that they can detect infringement in most products, but not in most processes.[4] This does not seem to inhibit patent lawsuits over products relative to processes.

Additionally, if RIM's infringement were a simple story of a cheater who got caught, then we would expect RIM to settle quickly once it was caught, not to pursue extended and very costly litigation. Even after the suit was filed, it appears that, according to news reports, RIM could have settled for a few million dollars. Instead, it ultimately settled for over $600 million. Moreover, the suit also imposed substantial business losses on RIM. While the suit was ongoing, many customers delayed purchases or purchased from rivals. The market share of competitor Palm grew from 22 percent to 30 percent of the market, according to Palm financial reports.

Mr. Jerome in his letter tells us that RIM did not obtain a license up front because it assumed that its lawyers could "muck up the works enough to get away with it." Presumably, this is also why RIM did not settle once it was caught by NTP. Of course, lawyers can "muck up the works" in all areas of law (*disclosure*: one of us teaches law students the art of "Mucking Up Patent Litigation"; however, he covers both plaintiff- and defendant-related mucking).

But Mr. Jerome makes a really extraordinary argument. No one suggests that theft of real property occurs because thieves' lawyers can muck up the works. At the margin, thieves' lawyers might have the effect of softening penalties, making them a bit less of a deterrent. But in Mr. Jerome's tale, the ability of lawyers to muck up the works is central. In his view, RIM was so sure that it could get away with cheating that it ignored any need to license up front, was brazenly open about its theft, and felt no need to make amends, or even to settle quickly, so as to avoid costly litigation once its infringement was noticed. And, surprisingly, even though Mr. Jerome feels that patent lawyers are able to "muck things up" in such an extraordinary fashion, he does not see a need for patent reform.

And why are lawyers able to muck things up so much in patent litigation? Because patent litigation is uncertain. It is uncertain because the boundaries of patents are not clear and because the validity of litigated patents might be challenged. But it is this uncertainty *precisely* that is the major cause of inadvertent infringement. That is, if the boundaries and the validity of patents are not certain, even an honest innovator is forced to take bets about which technologies infringe and which do not. Sometimes he loses those bets and is sued for infringement. Despite what Mr. Jerome claims, one cannot, in good faith, observe the actions of an alleged infringer in these circumstances and tell whether that person is honest or a crook. Yet this very uncertainty is the linchpin of Mr. Jerome's argument.

There are, in fact, relatively few patent trials where the alleged infringers are found to have intentionally cheated. If a defendant in an infringement suit is found to have knowingly infringed upon a patented technology, then the patent holder can demand that the defendant pay enhanced damages and the plaintiff's attorney fees. Alleging "willful infringement" permits the plaintiff to conduct extensive discovery to turn up evidence of copying or other forms of misconduct. Only in about 4 percent of cases, however, are defendants found to have intentionally copied and obligated to pay enhanced damages.[5] Perhaps a larger number of cheaters escape penalties, but it does not seem likely that outright cheaters make up a large portion of the cases that go to trial. This does *not* mean that there are few cheaters—instead, as we suggested above, cheaters might just be more likely to settle early in the litigation process and not proceed through trial. Unless outcomes are uncertain, they have little reason to pursue costly litigation. Thus, these numbers do suggest that cheaters do not constitute a significant portion of the more costly lawsuits. And this is our primary concern here: the main costs of litigation fall largely on inadvertent infringers, not cheaters.

The focus of Mr. Jerome and others on infringers-as-cheaters is a smoke-screen. The ethics of businesspeople are largely irrelevant to questions of patent reform; or, put another way, the performance of the patent system is not about the ethics of its participants. Property systems should work even if the participants are cheaters at heart. Under a well-implemented property system, even the ethically deficient will rationally calculate that it is in their own narrow self-interest to obey the law and not trespass. A high level of ethics does reinforce property norms and helps make property self-policing, but patent policy should work despite businesspeople who might have the ethics of crooks, pirates, or worse. For this to happen, the boundaries and validity of patents need to be clear and the punishment relatively certain. Mr. Jerome's focus on business ethics hides the real problems posed by patent litigation, yet his argument relies on the uncertainty of patent litigation and this reveals the real reasons why patent policy *does* need to be changed.

It is appealing to place the blame on business ethics when many people believe that there is a decline in moral values, generally. It is likewise tempting to blame the lawyers when many people believe there has been an increase in abusive litigation. But, in fact, the rise in patent litigation is something quite distinct. If business ethics were in sharp decline or if there was a general rise in litigiousness, then this should affect *all or many* types of business-to-business litigation. Unethical or overly litigious businesspeople should welch on contracts, or abuse antitrust regulations, or go to court too frequently for all sorts of suits. The steady increase in patent litigation since the 1980s is, however, unique to patent litigation. Figure 6.2 shows rates of different types of lawsuit filings in Federal district courts normalized so that the rate for each type equals one in 1990. There is little to suggest a trend. The most common sort of business-to-business litigation—contract disputes—actually declined. Patent litigation exhibits an unparalleled steady and rapid increase, with the exception of a small decline in 2005. Only copyright litigation shows a greater rate of increase over this entire period, but that appears to be almost entirely due to a surge in copyright lawsuits involving music file-sharing during the last few years.

We thus conclude that patent litigation is a real problem for innovators and it does impose a cost on investment in innovation. We suspect that a certain amount of infringement is the work of firms that plainly cheat as an alternative to doing their own R&D. But once these firms are caught, they have little reason to pursue costly litigation, and thus they have little effect on our calculation of litigation costs. Given unclear patent boundaries and uncertain validity of patents, other firms that do invest in technology might be less than scrupulous in their use of possibly infringing technologies, or, perhaps more typically, they simply do not do exhaustive clearance searches because these are too costly and too uncertain. But in this case, their activity is not a substitute for investment in

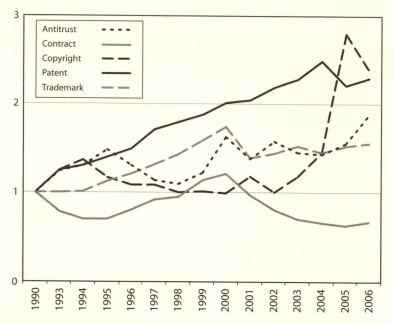

Figure 6.2. Relative Rates of Federal Litigation
Note: Normalized to 1 in 1990.
Source: Federal Judicial Center

innovation and the risk of litigation does provide a disincentive to invest in innovation.

Is the Patent Litigation "Explosion" a Hoax?

But how bad is patent litigation for innovators? One person who contends that it is not bad is Nathan Myhrvold, CEO of Intellectual Ventures, a firm that "invests in invention" and that some people describe as a "patent troll." Myhrvold contends that "there is no 'crisis' or 'explosion' in patent litigation."[6] Instead, he argues, large companies have exaggerated litigation problems so that they can weaken the patent system through legislative reform.

The truth, he contends, is that "the likelihood of a patent issued today being involved in litigation is smaller today than at any point since 1995." This might seem to vitiate our concern with the costs of patent litigation.

Figure 6.3. Probability that a Patent Is in One or More Lawsuits within Four Years of Issue Date
Note: Data adjusted for under-reporting.
Sources: Derwent LitAlert; USPTO PATSIC database

There are at least two problems with Myhrvold's argument. First, he is simply wrong—patent litigation probabilities are surging.[7] Figure 6.3 shows the upward trend in the probability that a patent granted in a given year will be involved in one or more lawsuits within four years of its issue date.[8]

Regardless of the trend, Myhrvold's favored statistic lacks clear economic significance. Patent litigation becomes a problem when it imposes social or private costs that are large in comparison to the benefits patents provide. Our focus is on how litigation costs affect innovators' incentives. The probability that a patent is in a lawsuit does not directly reflect on these incentives unless one makes some rather strong assumptions. A better approach is to actually compare estimates of the costs and benefits that do affect incentives. We turn to that comparison next. The results are quite different than the picture Nathan Myhrvold paints.

The Costs of Litigation for Public Firms

How does litigation affect innovators' incentives? Consider an innovator deciding whether to invest in an R&D project. The innovator weighs the cost of the investment against the total net profits the innovator expects to receive from that investment. Typically, those profits are not known with certainty, rather the innovator has some idea about what those profits will be if the innovation is successful and also some idea of the probability of success. Combined, these two estimates give the innovator some idea of *expected* profits. These provide the incentive to make the investment.

Litigation can affect this calculation in two ways. First, to the extent that the innovator expects to obtain profits through patents—recall that innovators obtain profits in many other ways, as well—then the innovator has to consider the difficulty she might run into in enforcing those patents. Costly enforcement will reduce the profits that the patentee can expect. Lower profits mean less incentive. They also mean that patents will be less valuable. In other words, our measures of patent value *already* reflect this effect of litigation on incentives. We do not need to perform any other estimates to capture this effect.

Patent litigation, however, also affects innovators in another way: an innovator might inadvertently infringe upon someone else's patent. This is true regardless of whether the innovator has patents of her own or not. Of course, an innovator who knows ahead of time that her technology will infringe upon someone's patent will seek to license that patent. But with unclear boundaries and clearance problems, she might lack specific knowledge of infringement possibilities before she proceeds. Nevertheless, she might still realize that someone might claim infringement in the future, giving rise to a possibly costly dispute. That is, she faces a *risk* that a dispute will arise.

How does this risk affect the calculation of expected profits? The innovator needs to incorporate some estimate of the expected payments and other costs associated with disputes that might arise (that is, the cost multiplied by the probability that a dispute will arise); this is the cost of insuring against infringement disputes. Note that these disputes are specifically associated with the innovator's use of new technology—patent lawsuits are rarely filed over old technology. For this reason, an innovator will look at this risk as a cost to weigh against the expected profits from the new technology. We noted in chapter 3 that infringement-defense insurance is not generally available; this calculation, however, effectively measures the cost of self-insuring. Below we elaborate a variety of different costs that disputes impose on innovators.

We only measure the risk of *litigated* infringement disputes.[9] Many disputes settle without a lawsuit filing. We do not observe these and so we cannot estimate their expected cost. This means that our estimates of infringement risk are understated—that is, they are lower-bound estimates. Our estimates do, however, include the lawsuits that settle without going to trial as well as the lawsuits that go to trial.

Also, we only explore litigation costs for publicly listed firms. Since most R&D is performed by public firms, this is the appropriate place to start our analysis. We defer a detailed analysis of patent-based incentives to innovate for small inventors until chapter 8.

Legal Costs

As a starting point, we present estimates of direct legal costs of patent litigation. We obtain these estimates from two sources. First, the American Intellectual Property Law Association (AIPLA) conducts a survey of its patent lawyer members. Second, in some cases, at the conclusion of a lawsuit, a judge might order one side to pay the other side's legal fees. From court documents we obtained these figures for eighty-nine patent lawsuits. Table 6.1 shows mean values in millions of 1992 dollars. The survey data does not distinguish between costs to the patentee-litigant and the alleged infringer, but the fee-shifting data does, and it indicates costs are high for both parties.

Legal costs naturally depend on how far the lawsuit has progressed. The earlier in the process, the less money will have been spent on lawyers. Some cases settle in a few weeks, typically at little cost. Others will go for months before they settle. In many of these cases, the firms proceed through discovery, which can be quite costly—costs through the discovery phase are about one-half the costs of cases that go through trial. Similarly, summary judgments (where a judge decides the outcome prior to a trial) cost less than trials. A case that is settled or terminated before too long

Table 6.1.
Estimated Legal Costs of Patent Lawsuits, from Survey of Patent Lawyers

a. Estimated legal costs from survey of patent lawyers

	Cost through Discovery (millions, $U.S. 1992)	Cost through Trial (millions, $U.S. 1992)
Amount at Stake		
Less than $1 million	$0.35	$0.61
$1–$25 million	$1.20	$2.10
More than $25 million	$2.59	$4.14

b. Mean legal costs from cases where fees were shifted

	Summary Judgment (millions, $U.S. 1992)	Trial (millions, $U.S. 1992)
Patentee	$1.10	$1.20
Alleged infringer	$0.66	$2.85

Sources: AIPLA (2005); Bessen and Meurer (2006)

might cost only one-half million to a million dollars. A case that goes to trial might cost one to several million. In extreme cases, legal costs can mount to tens of millions (for example, in *Bristol-Myers Squibb v. Rhone-Poulenc Rorer* the accused infringer, Bristol-Myers, was awarded over $25 million in attorneys' fees from Rhone-Poulenc Rorer).

Business Costs

But legal costs are not the only costs of litigation that affect innovating firms. Business costs of litigation can be much larger and can take many forms. Business can be disrupted as managers and researchers spend their time producing documents, testifying in depositions, strategizing with lawyers, and appearing in court. Litigation strains the relationship between the two parties and might jeopardize cooperative development of the patented technology or cooperation on some other front. Firms in a weak financial position might see their credit costs soar because of the bankruptcy risk possibly created by patent litigation. Preliminary injunctions

can shut down production and sales while the litigation pends. But even without a preliminary injunction, customers might stop buying a product that incorporates the disputed invention. Frequently, products require customers to make complementary investments; they might not be willing to make these investments if a lawsuit poses some risk that the product will be withdrawn from the market. Furthermore, patent owners can threaten customers and suppliers with patent lawsuits because patent infringement extends to every party who makes, uses, or sells a patented technology without permission, and sometimes to those who participate indirectly in the infringement.

Even simple delay can impose large business costs. Consider, for example, litigation against Cyrix, a start-up firm that introduced Intel-compatible microprocessors. Intel, the dominant maker of microprocessors, sued Cyrix and the litigation lasted four years (there were multiple suits). During much of that time Cyrix had difficulty selling microprocessors to computer manufacturers because most of them were also customers of Intel and they were reluctant to buy a product that might infringe. Cyrix also had difficulty finding fabricators willing to manufacture their chips—again, for fear of being sued themselves. In the meantime, Intel responded by accelerating its development of chips that would compete against Cyrix's offerings. In the end, Cyrix won the lawsuit, but lost the war, having lost much of its competitive advantage. In effect, Cyrix lost the window of opportunity to establish itself in the marketplace. Litigation exacted a heavy toll, indeed.

Given the varied and complicated nature of these costs, it might seem impossible to estimate them. This is not so, however. A number of researchers have used stock market "event studies" to estimate the costs of litigation and several have studied patent litigation specifically. The idea behind this approach is that investors reveal their implicit evaluation of the cost of litigation when they find out that a lawsuit has been filed. The filing or announcement of a lawsuit provides investors with news and they change their valuation of the stock price of the companies involved in accordance with their estimate of how this news will affect the firm's profits. The advantage of this approach is that it captures investors' evaluations of all the different costs and all the possible outcomes. Most lawsuits settle before trial or adjudication, and investors evaluate the effect of all of these outcomes on the value of the firm. Of course, even as a group, investors

Sidebar 6.1. Event Study Methodology

Economists have used event studies in thousands of papers, most frequently studying the reaction of the stock market to an event. Stock market event studies are typically based on a simple model of the stock market. The daily return from holding a particular stock is held to consist of two factors: an effect from overall market trends and an idiosyncratic effect for that stock. That is,

$$r_t = \alpha + \beta\, m_t + \varepsilon_t$$

where r_t is the return on a particular stock at time t, m_t is the return on a market portfolio, and ε_t is a stochastic error. If an event, such as a lawsuit filing, occurs on day T, then there might be an "abnormal return" to the particular stock on that day. This can be captured using a dummy variable,

$$r_t = \alpha + \beta\, m_t + \gamma\, \delta_t + \varepsilon_t$$

where δ_t equals 1 if $t = T$ and 0 otherwise. This equation is estimated over a sufficiently long pre-event window as well as the day of the event itself. The coefficient γ measures the "abnormal return." This model can be extended to cover an event window of multiple days in order to capture an extended reaction. In this case, one can calculate abnormal returns for each day as well as cumulative abnormal returns.

Everyone knows that daily stock returns capture a lot of random noise and "animal spirits." This noise is represented by our stochastic error term and when an event study is performed on an individual stock, the noise will often drown out any meaningful statistical result. Our estimates of cumulative abnormal returns are conducted on thousands of patent lawsuit filings, however, and this works to diminish the relative noise. Statistical tests show that our estimates are reasonably precise.

These cumulative abnormal returns might differ from our concept of "cost of litigation" in several ways. First, to the extent that information leaks out before or after the event window, this measure understates the cost. Second, the news of a lawsuit might also reveal information about the prospects of the firm aside from the impact of the litigation itself. For example, a firm might be more likely to be sued when its technology

(Continued)

(Continued)

is particularly successful. Then, the news of a lawsuit might be taken as a sign of success. In that case, the firm's loss of market value might understate the costs of litigation. As we discuss in Bessen and Meurer (2007), losses are not likely to be overstated for lawsuit defendants. Finally, the loss of firm wealth might be larger than the penalty that litigation imposes on investment if markets are not at their long-run equilibrium— for example, during a stock market "bubble." We correct our estimates for such effects.

are not necessarily fully informed, so any particular stock market reaction might contain a substantial random element. This "noise" can be reduced by averaging over a number of lawsuits. In addition, the overall fluctuation of the stock market influences stock price changes. Event study techniques adjust the stock market returns for overall market changes. See sidebar 6.1, "Event Study Methodology," which provides more details on this technique and some possible qualifications.

Figure 6.4, from Bessen and Meurer (2007), shows the mean change in stock market value for ninety-six pairs of firms on or around the day that the lawsuit was announced in the *Wall Street Journal*. These figures have been adjusted for the overall fluctuation of the stock market. The mean market value of the plaintiffs drops a bit, but the defendants' mean value drops almost 3 percent on the day the announcement is published, reflecting a very substantial expected loss.

Note that these losses reflect investors' calculations of all aspects of the lawsuit that might affect future profits. Thus it reflects the prospect that the alleged infringer might be forced to switch technologies and thereby incur substantial adjustment costs. It also reflects the possibility that the firms might settle instead of going to trial; in that case it reflects any unanticipated royalties that the alleged infringer might have to pay.[10]

Table 6.2 displays the relative and absolute cost of patent lawsuits from our study and three others. Bhagat, Bizjak, and Coles (1998), Bhagat, Brickley, and Coles (1994), and Lerner (1995) all use lawsuit announcements from the *Wall Street Journal* or news wire services and their estimates for the combined loss of plaintiffs and defendants is 2–3 percent, similar to the results shown in figure 6.4 (p. 136). For our sample of lawsuits that were announced in the *Wall Street Journal* (shown in figure 6.4) we

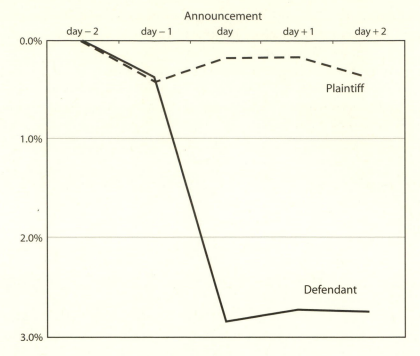

Figure 6.4. Change in Stock Value around the Day of Lawsuit Announcement in the *Wall Street Journal*

found a mean loss of 2.6 percent for alleged infringers and zero loss/gain for the patentees, yielding a combined loss also of 2.6 percent.

But most suits are *not* announced in the *Wall Street Journal.* To explore overall magnitude of litigation losses, we studied the effect of lawsuit filings on all alleged infringers that we could match to stock market data (the events had to meet certain technical criteria) from 1984–1999. This sample included 2,640 lawsuits where only one public firm was alleged to have infringed.[11] Losses for the latter group, also shown in this table, are only 0.61 percent.[12] Consistent with our upper-bound-value/lower-bound-cost estimation strategy, below we will use the smaller estimated losses.

We also explored possible differences in this loss rate across different groups of firms. The most important difference concerned firm size. Firms with fewer than five hundred employees had substantially larger relative losses: 2.08 percent vs. 0.56 percent. Relative losses do not appear to decrease

Table 6.2.

Change in Firm Value on Lawsuit Filing

	Alleged Infringer		Patentee + Alleged Infringer, Combined	
Mean Proportional Change				
Bhagat et al. (1998)	−1.50%	[33]	−3.1%	[20]
Lerner (1995)	−2.00%	[26]		
Bessen and Meurer (2007)				
Wall Street Journal sample	−2.60%	[82]	−2.6%	[80]
Alleged infringers, all public	−0.61%	[2,460]		
Alleged infringers, emp. > 500	−0.56%	[2,020]		
Alleged infringers, emp. < 500	−2.08%	[346]		
Both parties public	−0.62%	[661]	−1.0%	[661]
Absolute Change in Firm Value (Millions)				
Lerner (1995)				
Mean			−$67.9	
Median			−$20.0	
Bessen and Meurer (2007)				
Mean	−$28.7			
Median	−$2.9			

Note: Number of observations in brackets.

further among firms with more than five hundred employees. There was also some evidence that during the 1990s relative losses increased modestly, although this effect is weaker and only of marginal statistical significance.

The bottom of table 6.2, above, shows the absolute magnitude of these losses.[13] The median defendant has a total litigation cost of $2.9 million ($92), not much greater than the direct legal costs of litigation. The mean defendant, however, loses $28.7 million in total value, a much larger figure. Nevertheless, these estimates are substantially smaller than Lerner's (1995) estimates of the combined losses from his sample.

Finally, note that one persistent result across all of these studies is that patent litigation does *not* simply transfer wealth from the defendant to the patentee. The combined wealth of the two sides to the lawsuit decreases, as shown in the right-hand column of table 6.2, above. Economists have advanced several reasons why this might be so (see, for example, Cutler and Summers [1988]). Some wealth might be transferred to the patentee on average (showing up as part of the value of patents), some is transferred to consumers, some might be transferred to rival firms, and some is simply social loss from various sources, including nonproductive work by managers and lawyers. For example, when NTP sued RIM, RIM lost substantial market share. Although there was a transfer of wealth to NTP, there might have also been a transfer of wealth to RIM's competitors and to consumers who benefited from increased competition. This means that losses to the defendant do not necessarily reappear as patent profits realized by plaintiff firms.

THE BENEFITS AND COSTS OF PATENTS FOR PUBLIC FIRMS

Time Trends

We can take this analysis further by adding up the aggregate litigation losses incurred by our sample of public firms as alleged infringers from 1984 through 1999. These are shown as the heavy, solid lines in figure 6.5.[14] We show the performance of the chemical/pharmaceutical industry separately from other industries. Aggregate litigation costs for public chemical and pharmaceutical firms remained stable until the mid-1990s. For other firms, aggregate litigation costs increased beginning in the early 1990s, accelerating after 1994. Note that these estimates, based as they are on the common stock prices of firms, have been corrected to remove any effects of the stock market "bubble" of the late 1990s. These aggregate losses represent the aggregate infringement risk that was incurred each year, excluding the risk from disputes that were settled without lawsuit filings.

This aggregate cost of litigation can be compared to the aggregate incremental profits ("rents") derived from patents by public firms. We could compare the cost of United States litigation to the profits derived from United States patents. Using the value of United States patents from table 5.1, above, of \$113,000 and assuming an annual profit flow equal to 15 percent of the stock of patents, this yields an aggregate profit flow of less than \$4 billion, substantially less than the litigation costs shown in figure 6.5.

This might not be the right comparison, however, because litigation in the United States might affect profits that firms realize overseas, and these

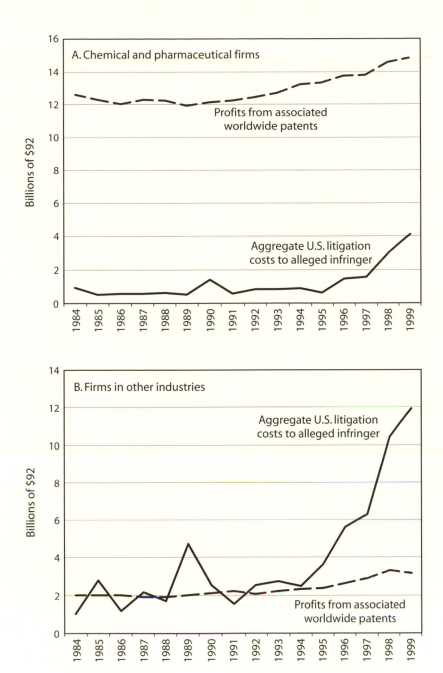

Figure 6.5. Aggregate Profits from Patents and Aggregate Litigation Costs for U.S. Public firms

include profits from foreign patents; that is, a lawsuit filed in the United States might result in a settlement that covers worldwide business. If the United States were the only venue in the world where patent lawsuits were filed, then we would want to compare the costs of United States litigation to the profits derived from worldwide patents. The dashed lines in figure 6.5, above, show estimates of the worldwide incremental profits from patents associated with United States patents. These are based on the highest estimate of worldwide patent values shown in the lower portion of table 5.3, above, again at an assumed 15 percent per annum net profit flow from stock of patents. The patent values in table 5.3 are higher than those in table 5.2, above, and they are higher than values of United States patents alone in table 5.1, above—by using the highest estimates of patent value, we weight the evidence in favor of the patent system, although we might possibly exaggerate the profits from patents.

Nevertheless, by the late 1990s litigation costs clearly exceeded the profits from patents outside the chemical and pharmaceutical industries. Moreover, this comparison understates the relative costs of patents for a number of reasons, including:

- To the extent that lawsuits and opposition proceedings are filed overseas, United States litigation costs will understate the costs of litigation that should be compared to the profits from worldwide patents. Moreover, as discussed in chapter 5, the estimates of worldwide patent value (based on market value regressions) are biased upwards.

- Many disputes are settled prior to filing a lawsuit, and the costs of these disputes to alleged infringers are not counted.

- These calculations ignore the costs of patent prosecution and clearance. Lemley (2001) estimates that the legal costs of patent prosecution run about $20,000 per patent application. This would add another $5.4 billion to the costs of the United States patent system in 1999 in total and about $1.3 billion to the public firms in our sample. In addition there are business costs of patent prosecution (for example, engineering time) and both legal and business costs of patent search and clearance, including legal-opinion letters.

- There is evidence that the value of patents declined somewhat during the 1990s while the losses associated with litigation increased somewhat. We have ignored these trends.

- For a variety of reasons, our estimates of litigation costs are understated.[15] In particular, our source of lawsuit information (Derwent's LitAlert) is known to miss about one-third of all lawsuits (Bessen and Meurer 2005a, b; Lanjouw and Schankerman 2001).

Thus we can safely conclude that during the late 1990s, the aggregate costs of patents exceeded the aggregate private benefits of patents for United States public firms outside the chemical and pharmaceutical industries. This implies that patents very likely provided a net *dis*incentive for innovation. On the one hand, the profits associated with patents might overstate the actual direct incentive to innovate to the extent that patenting might reduce other sorts of innovation incentives. For example, patenting might reduce the incentives provided through trade secrecy because patents disclose some information that might otherwise remain private.[16] The *net* incentive from patenting (relative to the alternative situation of not patenting, but receiving the full incentives from trade secrecy) will then be less than the profits realized through patents. In addition, the incentives that patents provide are not necessarily *innovation* incentives; they might be incentives to engage in opportunistic behavior (for example, trolling), especially if the patent system can be gamed.

On the other hand, aggregate litigation cost is a reasonable estimate of the aggregate risk firms face, which is a disincentive. It is true that relatively few firms are sued for patent infringement each year. What matters for incentives, however, is not whether a firm actually gets hit with a patent lawsuit or not. Instead, incentives are affected by the *risk* of a lawsuit. That is, when a firm decides ex ante how much to invest in R&D, the risk of a lawsuit will inhibit investment, regardless of whether the firm is unlucky enough to actually get hit with a lawsuit ex post. Aggregate litigation costs are equivalent to the cost of insuring against this risk. If alleged infringers were not mainly innovators themselves, then litigation costs might overstate the innovation disincentive. As we discussed at the beginning of the chapter, however, the evidence suggests that most of the cost of patent litigation falls on innovators, constituting a disincentive to innovate.[17]

It is true that some portion of litigation costs represent a transfer of wealth from the alleged infringer to patentee, and therefore represents a benefit to the patentee. It should be noted, however, that these expected transfers are already included in the estimate of profits from patents. Moreover, as was seen above, the evidence from event studies suggests that patent litigation might not produce a substantial gain in net wealth to patentees.

Thus, the evidence suggests that during the late 1990s, patents provided a net disincentive to innovation outside the chemical and pharmaceutical industries. For the firms outside of these two industries, litigation costs are several times larger than the profits from patents. There are two important caveats to consider when interpreting this result. First, public firms constitute only one group of patentees. United States public firms obtain only about 45 percent of the patents granted to United States residents. Public firms, however, perform the lion's share of R&D. In 1999 United States public firms spent $150 billion on R&D. Total company spending on United States industrial R&D was $160 billion.[18] So, to the extent that we want to measure the effect of patents on R&D incentives specifically, results obtained for this group of public firms are broadly representative. Nevertheless, in chapter 8 we look further at the incentives that patents provide to individuals and small firms.

Second, this is an aggregate result. Among public firms, there are inevitably winners and losers. One can easily find examples of firms that benefit from patents, such as Qualcomm, and others who are injured by patents, such as Cyrix. As above, *predictable* benefits and risks are what matter for incentives (and for the evaluation of policy) and some groups of firms face predictably greater benefits and/or predictably lower risks than others. The next section explores some of these differences.

Group Differences

The two panels of figure 6.5, above, show the significance of industry/technology differences. Table 6.3 explores some other differences. It shows the aggregate annual United States litigation cost and the aggregate annual United States patent profits for groups of public firms from 1996 through

Table 6.3.
Aggregate Annual Patent Profits and Costs by Group, 1996–99

	Annual U.S. litigation costs (billion $92)	*Annual U.S. patent profits (billion $92)*
Small firms (employees <500)	0.07	0.06
Large firms (employees ≥ 500)	10.80	2.52
Chemical patents	0.75	1.49
Complex patents	4.48	0.52
Other patents	5.09	0.79
Software patents	3.88	0.10
Business method patents	0.39	
Biotech patents	0.49	

1999.[19] For reasons of reliability, this table uses the profits from United States patents only, so litigation costs and profits shown are not directly comparable (to the extent that United States patent litigation serves to settle worldwide patent disputes). Nevertheless, the relative differences between groups is still informative.

The top two rows of table 6.3 explore firm size. Small firms make out relatively better than do large firms. During this period, large firms had litigation costs substantially exceeding United States patent profits. This was not so for small firms, whose profits on United States patents alone are about equal to their litigation costs. If we value small-firm global patents at $370,000, then their profit flow is $0.34 billion. Small firms make out better mainly because they are not sued as frequently. To the extent, however, that small firms make profits from patents that exceed their United States litigation costs, this net advantage was relatively small. By comparison, venture capital spending in the United States in 1996 was $10 billion. Small firms do not benefit much because they realize lower profits from their patents than do large firms and because when they are sued, small firms suffer larger relative losses. The lower portion of table 6.3 displays differences across technologies. As above, the clear winners are patents on chemicals, for which United States patent profits substantially exceed United States litigation costs. For other technologies, United

States litigation costs substantially exceed United States patent profits. Software patents are even bigger losers. Even valuing worldwide patents at $370,000,[20] annual worldwide profits from software patents are only $0.69 billion, far less than litigation costs.

Given this pattern of costs and benefits, it is hardly surprising that different groups currently have rather different agendas for patent reform. Indeed, some observers have noted that the pharmaceutical industry (chemical patents) and small firms are more favorable to the status quo, while the IT industries (complex and software patents) are more interested in deeper changes. We will explore the source and significance of these differences in the next chapter and we will look in depth at patents for small inventors and software development in chapters 8 and 9, respectively.

THE BOTTOM LINE

To summarize our major findings:

- The performance of the United States patent system deteriorated markedly during the 1990s as the private costs of patent litigation soared.

- By the late 1990s the risk of patent litigation for public firms outside of the chemical and pharmaceutical industries exceeded the profits derived from patents. This means that patents likely provided a net *dis*incentive for innovation for the firms who fund the lion's share of industrial R&D; that is, patents tax R&D.

- Small firms do better than large firms, despite lower patent values and higher relative costs of patent litigation. Nevertheless, the absolute benefits and costs are small.

- For chemical patents, the private benefits of patents still substantially exceed the costs of litigation, indicating a net positive incentive. On the other hand, for software, complex, and other patents the reverse is true, indicating a net disincentive.

These results provide strong evidence that for public firms patents no longer worked as a property system in general by the late 1990s. For these firms the patent system fails on its own terms. Chemical patents and patents held by small public firms are important exceptions. And other small firms and independent inventors constitute another important group, which we explore in chapter 8.

There *are* positive incentives to *patent*; that is, firms receive positive benefits from obtaining patents on their own inventions. Our results, however, show negative incentives on R&D; that is, the net effect of patents, including patents owned by others, reduces the returns from investing in innovation.

To gauge the significance of this disincentive, it is helpful to compare it to R&D spending by the observed group of firms. The ratio of the net profits from patents to the associated R&D spending can be thought of as an "equivalent subsidy rate" (or tax rate, if negative); that is, the effect of patents on R&D would be similar to the effect of a subsidy of this size paid by the government on R&D spending (see Schankerman [1998]). For our sample of public firms in 1995–1999, worldwide patent profits were about 71 percent of R&D in the chemical and pharmaceutical industries and litigation costs about 13 percent of R&D, leaving a net subsidy of about 58 percent, a strong incentive.[21] In other industries, however, worldwide patent profits were about 6 percent of R&D while litigation costs were also about 13 percent, leaving a net subsidy of about −7 percent; that is, patents acted as a net *tax* on R&D.[22] If we assume that patent prosecution costs, opinion letters, the effect of under-reporting, and so forth, add, say, 5 percent to the ratio of litigation costs to R&D, then the net patent "tax" is around 12 percent.

Hence it is important to emphasize that our results suggest that patents today constitute a *brake* on innovation, not a *roadblock*. This distinction is important because it is sometimes argued that the high rate of innovation in the United States provides evidence that the patent system is working. For example, after finding little empirical evidence that the "strengthening" of United States patents during the 1980s caused an increase in R&D or innovation, Jaffe (2000) argued, "If history concludes that the end of the twentieth century was a time of rapid and sustained technological progress, it is likely also to conclude that the patent policy transition ['strengthening' of patents] was a good thing."[23] But just because we live in a time of innovation and technological progress, it does not follow that patents spur innovation and technological progress. Innovation might occur *despite* the patent system. Nor does it follow that the policy changes of the 1980s (and 1990s) necessarily improved the performance of the patent system.

To the contrary, our evidence implies that patents place a drag on innovation. Without this drag, the rate of innovation and technological progress might have been even greater, perhaps much greater. Moreover, the performance of the patent system has deteriorated markedly since the late 1980s. Below we explore the role that policy changes might have played in this deterioration. But this deterioration should at least make us suspect that history will not look favorably on many of the policy changes of the 1990s despite the impressive scope and breadth of innovation during that decade.

And a deeper concern is that these policy changes might be only just beginning to affect innovation—after all, the rate of litigation has further increased substantially since 1999 (see figure 6.1, above). Indeed, the evidence available since 1999 suggests that things have gotten worse, not better. Not only has the total number of lawsuits increased, but the probability that a patent will be in a lawsuit has also gone up. In addition, legal costs have also risen (AIPLA 2005) and lawsuit damages have gone up somewhat (PricewaterhouseCoopers 2006). And no evidence suggests that the value of patents has increased commensurately, suggesting that the bill for these policy changes might not have come due yet.

7 How Important Is the Failure of Patent Notice?

INTRODUCTION

Chapter 3 shows that numerous legal and institutional features of the patent system undermine the notice function of property: the boundaries created by patents are hidden, unclear, or too costly to determine. This prevents patents from functioning efficiently as property. But how significant are these shortcomings? Are these minor failings or do they, in fact, explain much of the "tax" on R&D investment that we found in chapter 6?

This chapter links the tax created by patent litigation to inadvertent infringement caused by inadequate patent notice. We look at the quantitative evidence for clues about the cause of the surge in patent litigation that started in the 1990s. We also look at variations in patent litigation across technologies. We find that inadvertent infringement plays a crucial role in explaining the pattern of litigation over time and the pattern of litigation across technology. Simply put, notice failure and the resulting inadvertent infringement are central to the failure of patents to provide positive innovation incentives.

The Role of Measured Factors

The spike in litigation costs shown in the previous chapter is largely driven by a rapid increase in the hazard of litigation (the probability that a firm will be sued for patent infringement). Although we found some evidence that the relative cost of litigation might have increased during the 1990s, our calculations in chapter 6 were based on the conservative assumption that this cost did not increase.[1]

So our empirical research begins with a regression analysis to study the factors associated with the hazard that a firm will be sued for patent infringement (details of this study can be found in Bessen and Meurer [2005b]). Many of the factors associated with litigation can be measured and were included in our study. We find, however, that these measured factors only explain a limited portion of the increase in litigation hazards over time. We then consider several factors that cannot be directly measured, including the quality of patent notice. After accounting for measured factors, and eliminating several alternatives as inconsistent with the data, we conclude that notice failure and inadvertent infringement together provide the most substantive explanation for the surge in patent litigation.

Let us begin by exploring the extent to which measurable factors can explain the increase in patent litigation risk. In our sample of public firms, we included a variety of characteristics of the alleged infringer and rival firms. The factors we studied included: the size of the firm; the number of patents it holds; the characteristics of those patents; its R&D spending; its capital; its market value; its industry; the number of patents held by nearby firms (using a measure of technological similarity); the amount of R&D performed by nearby firms; and a time trend.

These factors correspond to many of the most obvious explanations for the increase in patent litigation:

- Larger firms (firm size) might be more likely to be sued because they are more lucrative targets and because they might be involved in more markets.

- Research-intensive firms (R&D) might be more likely to inadvertently infringe upon others' patents.

Table 7.1.
Contribution of Factors to Annual Growth in Firm in
Hazard of Being Sued, 1987–99 (Partial List)

	Annual growth
Firm size (employees)	0.6%
R&D/employee	0.6%
Market value/employee	0.9%
Capital/employee	−1.0%
Other firms' patents	0.2%
Time trend	6.3%
Total Growth Rate	7.9%

- Firms with better quality technology (market value) might also be more lucrative targets.

- Capital intensive firms (capital) might be sued less often because they are more willing to settle before a suit is filed. Their willingness to settle is greater because litigation that might idle their capital stock is especially costly.

- A firm might be more likely to be sued if its neighboring firms have many patents (other firms' patents).

These variables explain much of the variation in litigation rates between firms. They do *not*, however, explain much of the increase in litigation rates over time.

Between 1987 and 1999, firm litigation rates in our sample grew at an annual rate of 7.9 percent. Using our regression results, we can calculate the contribution each of these variables made to the total growth rate.[2] These contributions to the growth rate are shown in table 7.1. The measured variables account for less than one-quarter of the total growth rate in the litigation hazard. Most of the growth is explained by the simple time trend.

This means that most of the change in the litigation hazard is explained by factors that we did not include in the regression, but which changed over time. Likely candidates include related changes in law, institutions, and technology. We first look at the role of inadvertent infringement. We then look at several alternative explanations.

The Role of Notice Problems and Inadvertent Infringement

Two sorts of evidence suggest that notice problems might explain much of the residual increase in the litigation hazards: the pattern of change over time and the pattern across technologies.

Timing

The timing of many of the legal changes that eroded the notice function corresponds well with the surge in litigation hazards. Figure 7.1 shows two series that indicate the increase in litigation. The dashed line represents the aggregate ratio of lawsuits to deflated R&D. The solid line is the firm hazard of being an alleged infringer after controlling for measurable factors such as firm size, firm R&D, patent portfolio size of the firm and its rivals, and so forth. Both series show a marked increase beginning in 1992 with further increases in the late 1990s.

Indeed, there is significant reason to believe that patent notice problems became markedly worse during the 1990s:

- Court decisions changed the nature of claim construction (*Markman v. Westview Instruments*, 1996; *Vitronics v. Conceptronic, Inc.*, 1996); in addition, there has been significant internal controversy in the Federal Circuit over claim construction (Wagner and Petherbridge 2004).[3]

- The use of continuing patent applications and the duration of patent prosecution increased significantly during the 1990s, providing greater opportunities for strategic hiding of patent claims.

- Changes in the utility requirement for patentability allowed a substantial increase in early-stage inventions, especially in biotechnology

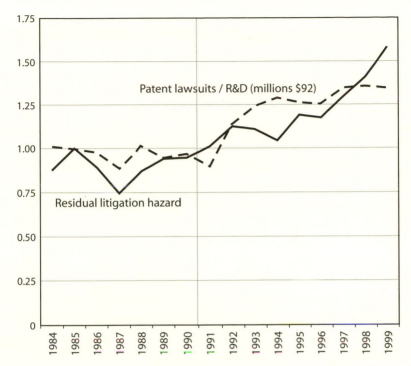

Figure 7.1. Time Trends: Firm Litigation Hazard and Aggregate Lawsuits/R&D
Sources: Bessen and Meurer (2006); Administrative Office of the U.S. Courts; NSF

(*In re Brana*, 1995). Changes in the treatment of software and business methods (*In re Alappat*, 1994; *State Street Bank and Trust v. Signature Financial Group*, 1998) permitted more patents with abstract claims. The effect of both was to increase the frequency of patents with putative claims on later-developed technology.

- The flood of patents and the increase in patent claims, although beginning during the 1980s, accelerated during the 1990s, increasing clearance costs.

Some of these changes affected all areas of technology; others affected just certain technologies, such as biotechnology or software. The evidence presented in chapter 3 suggests these changes in the 1990s degraded notice, increased inadvertent infringement, and could well explain the surge in litigation.

The Pattern of Patent Litigation across Technologies

The pattern of patent litigation across classes of technology shows striking variation and this, too, underlines the importance of the notice function. Patents on chemical compounds perform much more like property than other patents. Patents on complex technologies do not perform so well. Patents on software, business methods, and biotechnology are especially problematic.

Economists have long understood that the patent system works substantially better in the chemical and pharmaceutical industries than in most other industries. This difference also appears in our calculations of the net R&D incentive of patents in chapter 6. In the sample calculations shown there, chemical and pharmaceutical patents provided net positive incentives during the late 1990s.

The usual explanation for the superior performance of patents in these technologies is that the boundaries of chemical patents are clearer (see the discussion in chapter 5)—the structure of a molecule or the composition of a mixture can be defined with precision. It is straightforward to compare a patented molecule to the structure of a prospective infringing molecule. Chemical patents provide good notice.

The significance of these differences for litigation is illustrated in table 7.2. This table shows differences between patents in varying technology groups. The first three groups are mutually exclusive (the method of selection is described in chapter 5). The second three categories are overlapping subsets.[4] Column 1 of the table shows the probability that a patent will be involved in one or more lawsuits; the second column shows the expected number of lawsuits per patent.[5] Chemical patents are litigated at a rate that is roughly half the rate of that for other patents. On the other hand, in chapter 3 we identified several technologies that appeared to have particular problems with notice: biotechnology had problems with early-stage inventions, software and business methods had problems with abstract claims and a proliferation of large numbers. These technologies have very high litigation rates, especially with respect to business methods. Lerner (2006b) finds financial patents are twenty-seven times more likely to be litigated than other patents. As we saw in table 6.3, above, the performance of software patents generally was poor and contributed substantially to the overall cost of patent litigation.

Table 7.2.
Differences in Patents by Technology Group

	Probability Patent in Suit	Expected number of suits/patent	Relative Frequency of Claim Construction Appeal	Percent Invalid*	Mean U.S. Patent Value ($U.S. 1992)
Chemical	1.1%	0.026	0.84	46%	$332,790
Complex (excluding chemical)	2.0%	0.043	0.89	47%	$52,024
Other	2.2%	0.043	1.11	46%	$79,570
Software	4.6%	0.105	2.18	38%	$55,421
Business methods	13.7%	0.404	6.67		
Biotechnology	3.2%	0.072	2.37	44%	
All	2.0%	0.040	1.00	46%	$78,168

Source: Allison and Lemley (1998), "Empirical Evidence on the Validity of Litigated Patents."

Note that in chapter 5 we also found that chemical patents are more valuable than other patents. These estimates are reproduced in column 5 of table 7.2. Part of the reason for this is because chemical patents are litigated less. Patent litigation reduces the net profits that a patent owner can expect from a patent. A lower rate of litigation implies a higher patent value, all else being equal. This means that clear boundaries have a doubly positive effect on incentives, as we saw in table 6.3, above. Although chemical and pharmaceutical firms also obtain patents covering other technologies (for example, medical instruments), the clear boundaries provided by patents on chemical structures and compositions explain the overall superior performance of the patent system in these industries.

These boundaries might also explain an interesting pattern in patent-citation practice. The U.S. Patent Office recently began distinguishing whether references to prior patents come from the applicant or the examiner. The portion provided by the applicant provides a rough measure of the applicant's own awareness of the relevant prior art. Sampat (2004) studied data from 2001–2003 and found that in most fields, applicants contribute about 50 percent of references to U.S. patents, but they contribute 79 percent for drug (and other medical) patents and 67 percent for chemical patents (excluding drugs). This suggests that drug and other chemical inventors receive better notice of the prior patents in their fields. In other technologies, inventors themselves are apparently less aware of the relevant prior art, implying that they have not been put on notice of that art.

It is possible, of course, that characteristics other than notice problems might drive some of the differences across technologies seen in table 7.2, above. Column 3 shows the relative frequency with which each type of patent will have its claim construction reviewed on appeal by the Federal Circuit (normalized so the frequency for the average patent is 1).[6] Here again, the problematic technologies have much higher frequencies of claim-construction review, suggesting that claim clarity might indeed be worse for these technologies.[7] This implies that notice problems can explain a substantial part of the differences in litigation rates between technologies.

On the other hand, patent validity issues do not explain cross-technology differences, at least among those patents where validity challenges are pursued through trial. Column 4 shows the rates at which patents in different technology groups are found to be invalid when validity is challenged.[8] It does not seem that litigation rates are driven by major differences in patent validity, but interpretation of these differences is tricky, so we will discuss it further below.

It is also possible that these differences across technologies might just reflect different characteristics of the industries that use these technologies, not differences in the notice function. The pharmaceutical industry has a unique regulatory system and it also has industry-specific patent law (the Hatch-Waxman Act [1984], which controls the entry of generic drugs into the market). Pharmaceutical products often have much larger markets than the markets for many other industrial goods. But these differences do not explain the differences in litigation rates. Litigation rates for inorganic chemicals are also low, while biotechnology patents—which share much of the regulation of simple-molecule pharmaceuticals, but which have fuzzier boundaries—have high rates of litigation. So it seems

Table 7.3.
Match with Empirical Evidence

Hypothesis	Surge during 1990s	Surge Very Different across Industries	Differences across technologies		
			Litigation Rates	Claim Challenges	Invalidation Rates
Notice problems	**Yes**	**No**	**Yes**	**Yes**	**No**
Industry shakeout		*Yes*			
Stronger enforcement	*No*	**No**	*No*		
Litigiousness	*No*	**No**	*No*		
Trolls	*No**				
Patent examination quality (prior art search)	Maybe	**No**	**Yes**	*No*	*Yes*

Note: **Bold = consistent with evidence**; *italic = inconsistent with evidence*.
*For the troll hypothesis, we look at whether there has been a surge in the share of lawsuits from independent inventors.

that the differences in litigation rates are evidence of actual technological differences, not differences in industry characteristics.

In sum, notice problems explain a wide variety of evidence about litigation rates over time and across technologies. This makes the notice function a strong candidate to explain the large increase in litigation risk that remains after measurable factors have been taken into account.

ALTERNATIVE EXPLANATIONS

But are there other plausible explanations for the surge in patent litigation and the cross-technology litigation patterns? We consider five possibilities: industry factors, stronger enforcement, increasing litigiousness, increasing litigation from small inventors, and declines in patent examination quality. Table 7.3 reports how each of these explanations fares against the available evidence.

Industry Factors

It is possible that litigation norms changed in one or more large industries. Perhaps as industries matured, firms sought to obtain advantages in the courtroom that they could no longer obtain through technological advance. Perhaps industry shakeouts led firms to use their patents more aggressively. Or, perhaps, as firms failed, they sold their patents to "trolls" who in turn asserted them aggressively. Or, possibly, industry norms of mutual forbearance broke down, leading to a patent "arms race" with ensuing litigation. Or, it might be that the law remains unsettled in important new technologies, such as biotechnology or software, leading to increased litigation.

These explanations should lead to different patterns of change in litigation rates across industries and over time. If industry-specific factors are driving the increase in litigation hazards, then we would expect the growth in litigation to be largely confined to certain industries. On the other hand, if notice problems are driving the increase, this is not likely to be so. Although the notice function might partially explain some difference in litigation growth rates across industries (and differences in the *level* of litigation rates), for some of the reasons described above, deterioration in the notice function likely occurred in all industries. This suggests that if notice problems are driving the increase in litigation, *growth* in litigation rates should be seen in all industries, more or less.

Table 7.4 shows the litigation-hazard growth rate from 1987 to 1999 for eight industry groups. This is the rate of growth in the litigation hazard after all measurable variables have been taken into account. Although there are some differences between industries, all industries show relatively rapid growth in the litigation hazard after accounting for the measured variables. Thus explanations dependent on industry-specific factors are inconsistent with the evidence shown in table 7.4. We would hardly expect all industries to experience a shakeout or an arms race at the same time based purely on industry life-cycle dynamics.

There is some suggestion that software technology might be driving some of the growth in litigation. The two industries with the highest growth rates in litigation are both heavy users of software: namely, business

Table 7.4.
Time-Trend Contribution to Litigation Rate, by Industry

Chemicals/pharmaceuticals	7.4%
Machinery/computers	8.3%
Electronics	2.9%
Instruments	7.2%
Other manufacturing	7.7%
Business services/software	9.2%
Retail/wholesale	4.3%
Other non-manufacturing	6.8%

services/software and machinery/computers (but not, it should be noted, electronics). Using a broad definition of software patents developed by Bessen and Hunt (2007), we found that the share of lawsuits involving software patents grew from 2 percent in 1984 to 26 percent by 2002. In chapter 9 we argue that this increase is not so much due to unsettled law, but rather to the fact that both the law and the technology itself make software patents particularly prone to notice problems.[9]

So technology differences might generate some difference in litigation growth rates between industries, but overall there are not sharp differences in these rates, implying that industry-specific factors are not primarily responsible for the growth in litigation, although they likely contribute to that growth.

Stronger Enforcement

Another possible explanation for the litigation surge is that the rewards attendant upon litigation increased and/or that its costs decreased. Jaffe and Lerner (2004) argue that the rewards to patent plaintiffs have increased since the Federal Circuit was created in 1982, thus making it more attractive to file a lawsuit. Another variant, also related to the Federal Circuit, holds that the Federal Circuit reduced the likelihood that a patent would be invalidated at trial. When the risk of invalidation decreases, patent litigation is effectively less costly to the patent owner.

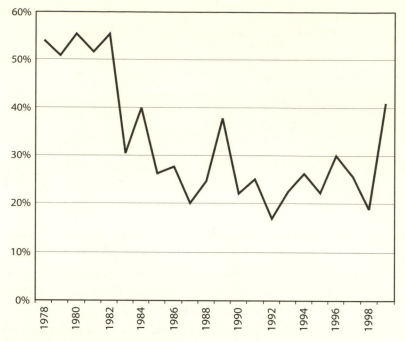

Figure 7.2. Percentage of Cases Finding Patent Invalid
Source: Henry and Turner (2006)

But these stories about stronger enforcement seem to have a timing problem. The decrease in court decisions finding patents invalid occurred during the early 1980s (figure 7.2). We would therefore expect litigation to increase mainly during the 1980s, if this were the main driving force. Similarly, as we discussed in chapter 5, the evidence that Jaffe and Lerner (2004) cite about stronger enforcement is confined to the 1980s.

Three sorts of evidence argue against an increase in the attractiveness of litigation to patent holders during the 1990s. First, as we saw in chapter 5, plaintiff win rates did not increase during the 1990s (see figure 5.2, above). Second, the event studies in chapter 6 do not find a significant increase in the returns to patentees on filing a lawsuit at that time;[10] that is, filing lawsuits did not become more profitable on average in that period. Finally, among the small number of lawsuits that proceeded to a favorable verdict for the patentees, damage awards have not been significantly increasing since 1990.[11] So, again, if enforcement were driving litigation, we would expect an increase in litigation hazards during the 1980s and little increase during the 1990s. Also, we would expect these factors to work more or less equally across all industries and technologies. While the growth rates are more or less equal, these factors do not explain the sharp differences in litigation rates by technology.

Increasing Litigiousness

Still another possibile explanation for the litigation explosion is that firms have simply become more willing to sue in general. Yet the litigiousness argument, too, has a timing problem. As we discussed in chapter 6, generally speaking other types of business-to-business lawsuits have not accelerated during the 1990s as patent lawsuits have (see figure 6.2, above). Nor does this hypothesis explain the sharp differences across technologies.

Small-Inventor Litigiousness

A related story holds that the increase in litigation comes from "trolls." "Patent trolls" are one of those great rhetorical confections that, unfortunately, mean different things to different people. In one version, patent trolls are patentees of any sort who opportunistically assert weak patents against the firms who actually develop the technology covered in the patent. In other versions, patent trolls are specifically small, nonproducing inventors who do not develop or commercialize new technology, who do not manufacture anything, but who do hope to snare other firms in their patent traps.

Of course, when patent notice is weak and patent quality low, it becomes impossible to distinguish between opportunists and true innovators. Opportunism is, to some degree, in the eye of the beholder. Moreover, even an honest innovator might assert a patent more broadly than justified if weaknesses in the law permit such behavior. Because of this indefiniteness, we choose a narrow and crude proxy for lawsuits by "trolls"—lawsuits by individual inventors.

There is reason to suspect that trolls (narrowly defined) might be responsible for an increase in litigation—perhaps lawyers working on contingency have made it easier for them to bring suit. There have certainly been a number of prominent lawsuits involving such trolls, often using lawyers on contingency fees, but does such anecdotal evidence represent the overall trend in litigation? The answer is no. Litigation data suggest that small inventors have not been the main driver of the increase in litigation, at least through 1999. We find that from 1984–1989, 24 percent of the lawsuits filed involved patents that had been awarded to individuals; from, 1990–1999, the comparable figure was 22 percent. Similarly, of the lawsuits against public firms, 29 percent were filed by other public firms during the 1980s; during the 1990s, 31 percent were filed by other public firms. So, the composition of litigants does not seem to have shifted between independent inventors and large firms.

If the surge in litigation is, in fact, driven by an increase in "bad actors," then it appears that this increase in bad actors occurred as much among public firms as it did among independent inventors. "Trolls" might still be responsible, but only in the broad sense of that term. This view is reinforced by the findings of Hall and Ziedonis (2007) on litigation in the semiconductor industry. They track the proportion of suits against semiconductor firms that originate from within the industry compared to the share of patentee plaintiffs who are not semiconductor manufacturers. Most of the increase in litigation through the year 2000 is from firms who are *within* the industry. The role of external plaintiffs increases at the very end of Hall and Ziedonis's sample period (year 2000), so nonmanufacturing plaintiffs might be growing in importance more recently.[12]

So while "troll-like" behavior is certainly a problem—one that is given opportunity to flourish thanks to poor patent notice—the surge in patent litigation is not primarily caused by small, independent inventors, although their contribution to litigation might be growing.

Patent Examination Quality

There has been much concern voiced about "patent quality." Perhaps, it is argued, patent quality has declined, provoking a surge in litigation. The term "patent quality," like "troll," also means different things to different people. Indeed, many of the concerns about the notice function of patents might be attributed to patent quality, broadly conceived. Here, however, we look at a particular, narrow definition of the term that is widely used: we address the quality of patent examination, specifically the ability of patent examiners to find invalidating prior art.

There are two stories about why patent quality in this sense might have declined. The first holds that the Patent Office has been slow to adapt to new technologies. Examiners might be unfamiliar with new technologies and lack the knowledge of where to look for prior art. This problem might have been exacerbated by the expansion of patent coverage to software, genes, and business methods. The second targets the management of the Patent Office. Jaffe and Lerner (2004) argue that management incentives changed in 1990 when the Patent Office became self-funded. The agency then had incentives to maximize revenues, so they provided examiners with incentives to process patent applications quickly, hurting examination quality.

As we argued above, a large number of invalid patents increases clearance costs, making inadvertent infringement more likely and litigation more frequent. So these stories about patent quality might be one particular variant of a more general inadvertent-infringement story. We suspect, however, that many commentators have overstated the specific role of prior art search during examination as a source of inadvertent infringement.

One challenge to this view comes from a study by Henry and Turner (2006) that documents the percentage of reported cases finding a patent invalid (reproduced as figure 7.2, above). Invalidity declined sharply after the Federal Circuit was established in 1982. This figure did not increase during the 1990s, however.[13] If patent search quality declined during the 1990s *and* the patents with missed prior art were litigated to a final decision, then there should have been an increase in cases finding patents invalid.

The lack of an increase in invalidation rates might simply mean that disputes over low-quality patents—that is, patents where the examiner failed to find existing prior art—settle quickly and do not proceed to trial. Indeed, if an alleged infringer has clear-cut evidence of invalidating prior art, there is little reason to expect extended litigation, which one would expect only if there existed significant uncertainty about the patent. In addition, the Federal Circuit has changed patent law to make it harder to invalidate a patent claim because the invention is obvious. But if disputes arising from insufficient examination do settle quickly, then a decline in patent examination quality would not lead to a rise in invalidation rates *nor* would it lead to an increase in costly litigation. So it is hard to conclude that the evidence on timing provides much support for the examination-quality hypothesis as an explanation for an increase in costly litigation. Of course, we suspect that there are plenty of invalid patents being issued, but they simply do not present themselves as being a major source of costly litigation.

The examination-quality hypothesis also suggests differences in litigation rates across technologies: in particular, new technologies should have higher litigation rates because patent examiners might need time to learn the prior art, terminology, and the like, of a new technology. Litigation rates are indeed higher in new technologies such as software and biotechnology.

But this evidence is not a perfect fit with the hypothesis either, for two reasons. First, if examiners need time to learn, then they should certainly show some evidence of learning. In particular, large numbers of software patents have been issued for over a decade, and the Patent Office has made special efforts to hire examiners with computer science degrees while issuing special guidelines for examining computer-related patents. Yet our estimates suggest that litigation rates for software patents have not declined in more recent cohorts (this will be discussed in greater depth in chapter 9). If examination quality is driving software-patent litigation, then it should show some improvement. It does not.

Second, one would expect new technologies to show high rates of invalidation. The evidence in table 7.2 (reproduced from Allison and Lemley [1998]), above, suggests, however, that biotechnology and computer-related patents have *lower* rates of invalidation than other patents. As noted above, this might simply mean that disputes involving poorly examined patents settle early. If so, this again means that low-quality patent examination does not appear to be generating extended, costly litigation.

On the other hand, some of this same evidence might provide support for the idea that patent quality has declined in other ways. For example, the decline in patent invalidations shown in figure 7.2, above, might be evidence that the courts have lowered patentability standards. Lunney (2001) and other legal scholars argue that the Federal Circuit has changed the rules used to determine whether an invention is obvious or not, resulting in fewer patent invalidations for reasons of obviousness. This change in standards might be responsible for many more patents that seem blatantly obvious to the layperson. Yet such a change in quality is not a change in patent examination quality per se; that is, it is not a change in the amount of missed prior art. Rather, this change in quality should be attributed to the weaker patentability standards set by the courts. In a number of cases, many involving software patents, the Patent Office has attempted to apply a rigorous standard of non-obviousness, only to be overruled by the Federal Circuit (for example, *In re Lee, In re Zurko*).

Thus we suspect that, in a broad sense, patent quality has declined. Poor prior art search necessitates that some patents will be awarded to someone other than the actual first inventor; this can cause problems for the true innovators. Obvious patents, another type of low-quality patent, are a problem because large numbers of obvious patents make clearance difficult and costly, leading indirectly to litigation. Patents that are of low quality because they are vaguely worded, overly abstract, of uncertain scope, or that contain strategically hidden claims can also directly induce litigation. All of these variants of low-quality patents, taken together, could certainly explain the surge in patent litigation. But patent quality involves much more than prior art search and the evidence does not support the view that a decline in the quality of Patent Office prior art search *by itself* has been a main driver of the spike in patent litigation.

The rows of table 7.3, above, summarize the correspondence between these various theories and the observed patterns of litigation over time and across technologies. The explanation based on notice problems corresponds rather well to this varied empirical evidence; by comparison, the other explanations do not fare so well.

In summary, the institutional and legal shortcomings of the patent system, many of them of recent origin, best explain the growth in litigation risk and the growing failure of patents to work as property. Relatively little of this growth can be attributed to levels of R&D spending, number of patents held, or the value or size of firms.

The evidence suggests, however, that the deterioration of the notice function might be the central factor fueling the growth in patent litigation. Changing incentives to litigate and declining patent quality might also contribute. But the general picture remains one where the performance of the patent system has declined as patents themselves have become less and less like property.

8   Small Inventors

In Chapter 6 we saw that today's patent system provides negative incentives for most public firms. It is true that the smallest public firms earn positive net rewards from the patent system and that this is also likely true for small, nonpublic companies, individuals, and other inventors not included in our analysis. Nevertheless, since our analysis covers those firms that perform the lion's share of R&D, our results do indicate that the patent system does not provide positive incentives for R&D in most industries.

But some would argue, among other things, that we have used the wrong yardstick. Further, some would contend that we have overlooked the real benefit of the patent system—the crucial protection it provides to small inventors. Many would hold that the innovations made by small inventors are more important than the innovations derived from the billions of dollars spent by large firms on R&D, and, consequently, that the performance of the patent system should be judged by its ability to foster innovation among small inventors, not so much by its ability to provide incentives for R&D investment. Finally, some would conclude that the patent system works well for small inventors, so concerns about poor notice are misplaced, patent reform is not necessary and indeed might even be detrimental.

Consider the testimony of Dr. David L. Hill, President of the Patent Enforcement Fund (a group that "pursues licensing for infringed technological patents") before the Subcommittee on Courts and Intellectual Property of the United States Congress on November 1, 1995:

> [T]he vast majority of important inventions which create new products and lead to entirely new industries come from independent inventors working alone or in very small companies. . . . It is true that most of the R&D expenditures are by the major companies and it is also true that many inventions are made by them and are reflected in the many patents issued to them. However, the study of those patents and inventions shows that they are almost entirely improvements on existing products. Very rarely indeed does the breakthrough invention occur in work sponsored by a major corporation. It is those pioneering inventions which arise almost always with individual inventors and which are primarily responsible for the seeding and growth of our economy through the creation of new industries. Those are the inventions which we most value as a product of our Patent System.

Dr. Hill then went on to argue that proposed legislation would undermine small inventors in favor of large businesses and inventors in Japan.

We are rather sympathetic to the view that small inventors make special contributions. One of us was, in fact, a small inventor/innovator who wrote one of the first desktop publishing programs and started a small software company. Below we elaborate sound economic reasons why it is important to have a healthy mix of small and big inventors and innovators.

But the role of the small inventor is frequently hyped and distorted. There is little empirical evidence to support Dr. Hill's claim that big firms "very rarely" achieve "breakthroughs" or that individual inventors are "primarily responsible" for "pioneering inventions." The evidence does, however, suggest that the patent system "works" for small inventors in the sense of providing positive incentives. In chapter 6 we saw that small public firms likely make profits from their worldwide patents that exceed their infringement risk. Although we do not have data on the infringement risk of nonpublic small firms, independent inventors and university inventors, we suspect that many of these inventors face little risk of being sued for infringement; because their commercial application of technology is likely small or non-existent, they have little investment at risk of infringement.

But even recognizing that small inventors make a uniquely important contribution and even assuming that they receive net benefits from patents, we argue that small inventors would still benefit from improved patent notice for the following reason—the evidence shows that small inventors get substantially less value from their patents, on average, than do big inventors. Although small inventors fare better overall because they face much lower costs from inadvertent infringement, they are also harmed by the same notice problems that harm big inventors. Small inventors especially suffer because fuzzy boundaries mean that they realize less value from licensing or selling their patents. Thus, reforms that improve patent notice should help all inventors.

Do Small Inventors Make More Valuable Inventions?

We begin by looking at whether the inventions made by small inventors really are substantially more valuable to society than those made by inventors in large companies. In theory, there are several reasons why small inventors might be particularly important to innovation. First, an inventor working independently or in a small firm might have much stronger incentives (and perhaps nonpecuniary rewards) than an employee in the R&D department of a large firm (see Arora and Merges [2004]). Inventors at small firms are likely to receive a larger share of the profits from their inventions than do the R&D employees of large firms. As long as the independent inventor or small firm can *realize* comparable profits (which, as we shall see, is not necessarily true), then this means that the rewards for success will be greater for small inventors. Greater rewards mean greater effort, all else being equal, and thus possibly better-quality innovations or a greater likelihood of success.

Second, large, incumbent firms might be slow to develop innovations that threaten to "cannibalize" existing markets. Industry entrants and outsiders do not worry about displacing their existing product line and thus have stronger incentives to develop technologies that replace older technologies. The theoretical literature that has developed this point is inconclusive, though, because in some cases incumbent firms will innovate first to "preempt" innovation by potential entrants. Either way, the existence of potential entrants spurs innovation.

Third, even if the quality of innovations from small inventors is no different than the quality of large-company innovations on average, there might be an important advantage to having diverse sorts of innovators with different experience or technical knowledge. Breakthrough innovations are sometimes realized as combinations of previously known techniques. In these cases, the probability of a breakthrough will increase with the diversity of potential innovators. Often, historical accident plays an important role in the origins of this diverse technical knowledge, so that even a large, multiproduct firm cannot necessarily count on having experience with all the technologies needed to make a breakthrough. Theoretical models have shown that such "innovative complementarities" can dramatically increase the rate of innovation (Bessen and Maskin 2007), much as biodiversity can increase the rate of biological evolution. Empirical evidence we cited in chapter 3 suggests that industries are often most innovative when many firms enter the industry (Gort and Klepper 1982). In these cases, small inventors might add a critical element of technological diversity to the pool of potential innovators attacking a problem. This might then lead to breakthroughs.

But what does the empirical evidence say about the role of small inventors? By some measures it is vital and growing more important; by others it is declining, unimpressive, and even socially harmful. To a great extent the answer depends on what kind of small inventor we examine.

Individual Inventors

The iconic individual inventor plays a much smaller role today than he once did. Khan (2005) describes nineteenth-century America as a time of flourishing individual invention. Individual inventors got the vast majority of patents. Inventors would sometimes commercialize their inventions, but often they sold their rights; a robust patent market had developed by the middle of the century.

Toward the end of the century, the picture began to change. Lamoreaux and Sokoloff (1996, 1999) found that patent sales were increasingly dominated by specialized inventors, rather than ordinary mechanics or farmers who might obtain just one or two patents during their lifetimes. Increasingly, patent rights were sold before the patent was issued, a sign that corporate support was needed at an earlier stage. The authors attribute these changes to the increasing complexity of technology. Fisk (1998) describes how the law regarding employees' rights to patents changed slowly to recognize this reality:

> The notion of the inventor as a genius working alone in his shop became increasingly anachronistic as the complexity of technology required numerous machinists, chemists, or other skilled workers to contribute to the development of ever more sophisticated and complicated machines, compounds, and processes. Collective research and development had become the source of most inventions long before courts and the public finally realized it.

The relative decline of individual invention continued during the twentieth century. Figure 8.1 displays the share of U.S. patent grants from 1963–2003 dispensed to individuals.[1] By 2003 individual inventors accounted for only about 12 percent of patents.

Additionally, most of the recent inventions made by individuals are hardly breakthrough technologies. The most prolific patentee in U.S. history is Donald Weder, with 1,336 patents;[2] Thomas Edison only obtained 1,093. Weder's patents concern flower pots, bundling flowers, and other inventions relevant to florists. This is not atypical. Here are the top five technology classes of patents granted to individual inventors from 1996–99:

Rank	Technology class	Description
1	52	Static structures (e.g., buildings)
2	473	Games using tangible projectile
3	606	Surgery (surgical instruments)
4	280	Land vehicles
5	2	Apparel

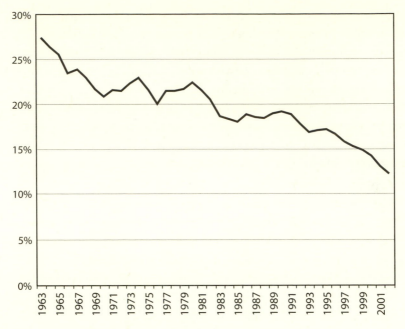

Figure 8.1. Share of Patents Granted to Individuals

With the exception of surgical instruments, these are not cutting-edge technologies. Most individual inventors appear to work, instead, in mature technologies.

More notable still is that some of the most successful individual inventors succeeded not because of their inventive contribution but because of their patents. Jerome Lemelson, a prolific inventor with close to 600 patents, is renowned among patent lawyers as the master of "submarine" patents—patents kept hidden for many years. Lemelson slowed the prosecution of his patents, sometimes for over twenty years.[3] He waited until his technologies were independently invented and commercialized, and then he brought his patent to the surface and negotiated royalties after the potential licensees were locked into the patented technology.[4] Although his patents covered breakthrough technologies such as bar-code scanning, he did *not* contribute these breakthroughs to society.

So most individual inventors patent in areas that are hardly high-tech and individual inventors no longer account for a major share of patents.

Despite this, however, it still might be true that a small subset of individual inventors account for a large share of breakthrough inventions.

To gauge the role of individual inventors in making important inventions, we looked at the inductees into the National Inventors Hall of Fame. This group seeks to honor "the women and men responsible for the great technological advances that make human, social, and economic progress possible." Each year, representatives from thirty-seven national technical and scientific organizations select inductees from among nominated inventors (who are required to be patentees). Through 2002, thirty-nine inventors had been inducted into the Hall of Fame for inventions patented after 1970. Of these, only 23 percent had made their inventions when they were independent inventors or were working for small companies. These numbers suggest that although individual inventors seem to be an important source for some breakthrough inventions, they are not the source for the majority of such inventions and, in fact, their contribution to breakthrough inventions is comparable to their overall share of patents. Most of the inventors in the Hall of Fame—59 percent—made their inventions while working for large companies.

The remaining 18 percent made their inventions while working for large universities or hospitals that provided research support. Clearly, this is an important group of inventors, especially for ground-breaking inventions— university/hospital inventors account for about 4 percent of U.S. patents assigned domestically, yet they have a substantially greater representation among Hall-of-Fame inventors.[5] Moreover, university/hospital inventors depend heavily on publicly funded research dollars. These inventors work in large-scale, R&D-intensive organizations and they depend relatively little on patents for funding.[6] The role of academic researchers does not change the basic picture: a majority of the Hall-of-Fame inventors worked for large, research-intensive organizations, most at large companies.

Small Firms

Many small inventors, perhaps most of the successful small inventors, work in start-up companies. Thus, we need to look at the effect of patents on start-ups and other small firms. A glance toward the many successful start-ups in biotechnology and IT industries suggests that small firms are important sources of invention and innovation. By some measures, small firms make more inventions relative to their size (Acs and Audretsch 1990). But the question here is whether small inventors make inventions that are substantially more *valuable* to society than those inventions made by large firms. Our calculations already take into account the *number* of innovations made by small firms. We only need to reconsider our conclusions if breakthrough inventions are predominantly the work of small inventors.

The evidence confirms that small firms are quite innovative but it does not establish that they are vastly more important than large firms. Lerner (1999) surveyed the literature on firm size and R&D and concluded, "Small businesses, in aggregate, do not appear to be particularly research-intensive or innovative." As we suggested, small firms do lead innovation in certain sectors. Lerner continues: "One of the relatively few empirical regularities . . . is the critical role . . . of entrants—typically de novo start-ups—in emerging industries." Biotechnology and the Internet were pioneered by small firms drawing on technology "developed with federal funds at academic institutions and research laboratories." So some small firms play important roles in emerging technologies and their patents (to the extent that they obtain patents, about which see below) might be particularly valuable, but this does not necessarily mean that most valuable patents come from small firms.

Patent-based data are also equivocal. Patent citations are sometimes used as a rough measure of "importance." Patents owned by firms with fewer than five hundred employees are only slightly more likely than patents owned by larger firms to be among the top 1 percent of the most frequently cited patents (CHI Research 2003). But, again, small firms do not receive the majority of patent citations.[7] Nor do small firms account for the majority of prolific patenters, defined as inventors who obtained ten or more patents in the last two years. In early 2000 about 70 percent of prolific inventors were in large firms and only 16 percent were in small firms (CHI Research 2004).

Christensen (1997) lauds small firms because they lead the way in achieving breakthroughs using *disruptive* technologies. But he is careful not to disparage the quality of inventions by large firms. In his case study of the disk drive industry, he notes that "the established firms were the leading innovators not just in developing risky, complex, and expensive component technologies . . . , but in *literally every other one of the sustain-*

ing innovations in the industry's history."[8] He explains that disruptive technologies initially tend to be cheaper, simpler, and lower in quality (in the
eyes of the leading customers of the established technology) than the established technology that they displace, but they have some attribute that
appeals to a new market niche.[9] "Not only are the market applications for
disruptive technologies *unknown* at the time of their development, they
are *unknowable*."[10] In Christensen's account, the small firms that pioneer
breakthrough technologies might not be inherently more important inventors than those in large firms, but, exploiting certain niches, they just happen to develop technology that later turns out to be critical.

There is little doubt that individuals and small firms make many important inventions and that the patent system should seek to encourage their
activity. Scant evidence, however, supports the contention that the "vast
majority" of important inventions come from independent inventors or
that "very rarely" do major corporations make breakthrough inventions.

ARE PATENTS MORE VALUABLE TO SMALL INVENTORS?

Even if it *were* true that small inventors are overwhelmingly responsible for
technical breakthroughs, we would still hold that the patent system is broken. The system does provide an incentive to small inventors, but that
incentive is surprisingly small, and we think a more property-like patent
system would increase the incentives for small inventors.

Table 8.1 reports estimates of private patent value by the size of the patentee. These estimates are explained in chapter 5 and further details are
available in a study by Bessen (2006a). The first two rows show that small
entities—the Patent Office's classification for individual inventors, nonprofit organizations, and firms with fewer than five hundred employees—
earn substantially *less* value from their patents, both in the median and in
the mean; this group includes many high-tech firms. This finding is also
supported by other research.[11] Part of this gap occurs because individual
inventors earn much less than inventors at corporations and other organizations (rows three and four). As we have seen, most individual inventors

Table 8.1.
Patent Value, by size

	Median Value ($U.S. 1992)	Mean Value ($U.S. 1992)	Standard Deviation
Small Entities	2,943	70,100	1.93
Large Entities	14,310	105,916	1.88
U.S. Individual	2,589	25,598	1.79
U.S. Organization	14,812	115,846	1.90
Small entities*	7,204	84,024	1.79
Large entities*	40,482	133,130	1.95

*Depreciation rate constrained to be equal across size classes. Note that individual patents include those unassigned at issue.

work in low-tech fields, so their patents might be inherently less valuable. But even within patents granted to organizations, including small public firms, small entities earn substantially less.[12]

These estimates suggest that small inventors on average realize substantially less value from their patents than do inventors at the larger firms that are responsible for most R&D spending. Of course, some small-inventor patents are highly valuable. Nevertheless, considering the entire distribution of patent values, small inventors realize less value from their patents. It is possible that small inventors simply have inventions that are less valuable to society. Although this might be true for individuals inventing "games using tangible projectiles," based on the evidence from the National Inventors Hall of Fame we doubt that this is true for small firms in general. Instead, we think that small inventors—both individuals and small firms—*capture* a smaller share of the social value of their inventions than inventors at large firms. This finding might seem surprising because many people believe that patents are essential to start-up firms. There is a myth that a start-up David usually needs patents to protect itself from an incumbent Goliath. But if small firms realize so little value from their patents, then it seems that David has a feeble sling.

Indeed, the evidence shows that the majority of start-ups do not, in fact, rely on patents. Only in a few industries do most of the start-ups

Table 8.2.

Percentage of new public firms with patent applications

Industry	SIC Code	Number of New Firms	Percentage with Patents
Oil and gas extraction	13	118	11%
Chemicals and pharmaceuticals	28	450	53%
Machinery, including computers	35	478	55%
Electronics	36	477	58%
Instruments	38	470	67%
Communications	48	141	10%
Wholesale/retail	50–59	528	11%
Holding companies	67	106	26%
Business services, including software	73	846	21%
Health services	80	109	11%
Engineering, research, accounting, and other services	87	165	33%
ALL	——	5,163	35%
ALL, 1995–99	——	1,439	37%
ALL, R&D-performing	——	3,047	50%

apply for patents early on. In one study of 877 venture-financed software start-ups, only 24 percent had obtained any patents at all within five years of receiving financing (Mann and Sager 2005). For a sample of 212 venture-financed biotech start-ups, 56 percent had received one or more patents within five years of receiving financing. Patents might help certain new firms get financing, but it appears that patents are not always required for firms to receive venture capital financing.[13]

The patenting behavior of software and biotech start-ups carries over to the IPO stage. Table 8.2 lists the percentage of firms that had filed one or more successful patent applications by the time the firm was first listed in Compustat, a database of publicly listed firms.[14] This is for a sample of

5,163 firms that were first publicly listed from 1979–1999. Only 35 percent of these new firms had any patent applications at the time of their listing. For R&D-performing firms, 50 percent obtained patents and in some high-tech industries, such as instruments, electronics, computers, and chemicals/pharmaceuticals, the majority of new firms had patent applications.[15] But in other high-tech areas, such as software, engineering services, or communications, most firms did not. Note also that the share of newly public firms with patents did not increase substantially during the late 1990s. Despite the great increase in patenting in recent years, only 37 percent of the firms newly listed between 1995 and 1999 had any patent applications at the time they went public.[16]

One reason the metaphor of David and Goliath might not hold up is that important start-ups typically operate in nascent technologies and often do not compete directly with large incumbents. Clayton Christensen writes, "Perhaps the most powerful protection that small entrant firms enjoy as they build the emerging markets for disruptive technologies is that they are doing something that it simply does not make sense for the established leaders to do."[17] When start-ups do face incumbents they might be on the wrong end of a patent lawsuit. Patents can be used anticompetitively by incumbents to discourage entry by small inventors. Lanjouw and Lerner (2001) found some evidence of the anticompetitive use of preliminary injunctions in patent lawsuits.

But, perhaps more fundamentally, because patents do a relatively poor job of capturing value for small firms, these firms rely on a variety of methods other than patents to appropriate value from their innovations. Famous computer and software innovators like Apple and Microsoft used copyright and trade-secret law more than patent law to protect their respective technologies. Many high-tech start-ups market their innovations in conjunction with services. Others embed their technology into products or components and rely on lead-time and goodwill advantages to earn a profit. Indeed, the software industry grew up with little patent protection by selling technology products that were components of a larger system in arm's-length transactions.

A survey of small high-tech firms indicates that the high cost of getting and enforcing patents often leads them to choose trade-secret protection instead of patent protection (Cordes, Hertzfeld, and Vonortas 1999). This might explain why Lerner (2006a) found that small firms appear disproportionately often in trade-secret lawsuits.[18] In sum, small firms use a mix of strategies to appropriate value from their inventions.

Although patents might be critical to some small firms, they do not appear to be particularly important to most. Nevertheless, it is troubling that small inventors capture relatively little value from their patents. To the extent that patents do provide incentives for some small inventors, greater incentives to small inventors would be helpful. We next explore why patents fail to deliver more value to small inventors.

Why Don't Patents Deliver More Value to Small Inventors?

The complementary problems of barriers to innovation and poorly functioning technology markets explain why the patent renewal estimates of patent value are smaller for small inventors. Small inventors get less value than big firms from their patents because it is harder for them to profit from invention. The road from invention to commercialized technology is often long, costly, and uncertain. Big firms are often better equipped to develop and commercialize inventions. Also, big firms are often better able to appropriate value from new technology through means other than patents; for example, they might have already established a market for complementary products and services.

The disadvantages that small inventors face in development and commercialization would not be such a problem if the market for patent rights worked more smoothly. In idealized competitive markets with well-defined property rights, a small inventor could sell or license his patent to a large firm and capture a healthy return. But the market for patents and markets for technology transfer more generally often do not function quite so well. Moreover, poor patent notice decreases the value that small inventors can realize through the market. When patents suffer from notice problems, prospective licensees (or acquirers) might not be willing to pay the full value of the patent—after all, they might face a heightened risk of litigation if they adopt the technology covered by the patent. These problems help explain the small patent value captured by small firms.

Development and Commercialization by Small Inventors

Early in the history of the United States, inventors profited from their inventions by commercializing them. Khan and Sokoloff (1993) found that over 85 percent of the great inventors from 1790 to 1865 were directly involved in commercial exploitation of their inventions. Times have changed. Economic and technological shifts gradually have made it harder for inventors to act as innovators. Today, a small firm that is strapped for cash, for example, might be unable to develop and commercialize an innovative product to its full potential. Lacking an adequate cash flow, the firm might choose not to pay to renew a patent. The invention might nevertheless be highly valuable if it were combined with an appropriate production facility and distribution network. Lacking these complementary assets, small inventors typically do not realize as much value from their patents as big inventors.

Small firms might also be at a disadvantage when it comes to enforcing their patent rights. Big firms can spread the fixed cost of monitoring for infringement over a larger number of patents.[19] Small firms might face liquidity constraints that discourage them from filing lawsuits, and thus be less able to develop a reputation for aggressively enforcing their patents. To some extent, these disadvantages can be mitigated by the use of contingency lawyers and by patent litigation specialists such as REFAC.

The transition from invention to innovation is hard for small inventors who face greater per-patent costs of development, commercialization, monitoring, and enforcement. These greater costs alone do not explain, however, the observed disparity in patent values for two reasons. First, in theory, greater post-issue costs do *not* necessarily cause lower patent value. Small inventors facing greater post-issue costs should get patents only when expected patent revenues are greater. Indeed, there is evidence that small firms have a lower propensity to patent than large firms. When small inventors require a higher threshold before obtaining a patent, the patents actually obtained might be *more* valuable than those obtained by inventors facing a lower threshold. This might be true even after taking into account the extent to which these costs decrease the net value of the patent.[20] So, by themselves, these costs do not explain the observed disparity.

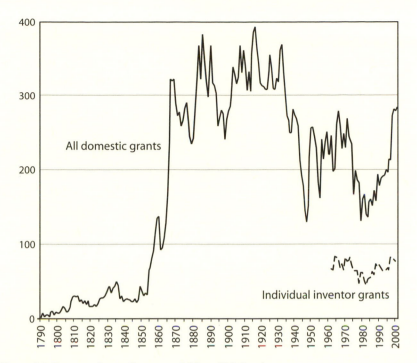

Figure 8.2. Domestic Patent Grants, per Million U.S. Residents

Second, markets might alleviate the difficulties that small inventors face in developing and commercializing inventions. If large firms have the complementary assets needed to develop and commercialize the invention, then they might be willing to license the patent or the technology; alternatively, they might buy the patent. In a competitive market with multiple large firms as potential licensees (purchasers), the small patentee should be able to realize something close to what a *large* firm could realize from the technology, leaving the licensee (purchaser) with a small profit.

The Markets for Patents and Technology

The latter half of the nineteenth century witnessed just such a market that began with a patenting boom in the 1850s. Figure 8.2 shows the ratio of patents granted to domestic inventors to the resident population of the

United States. Patenting as a popular activity soared beginning during the 1850s and it remained at high levels throughout the second half of the nineteenth century. This was an era that Khan (2005) calls a period of "Democratic Invention." Ordinary mechanics and farmers could create inventions, get them patented, and sell them to a manufacturer. Almost all invention was the activity of individual inventors. Although firms did sometimes hire multiple inventors, corporate R&D as we know it today did not really emerge until the twentieth century; further, nineteenth-century law gave employees broad rights to inventions they made on the job (Fisk 1998; Lamoreaux and Sokoloff 1999). When firms wanted to control a technology, they went into the market and purchased patents covering that technology, sometimes acquiring hundreds or even thousands of patents (Mass 1989).

But beginning in the late nineteenth or early twentieth century, this market went into decline. Figure 8.2 shows a steady decline in the patenting activity of the U.S. population. Although patenting has recently surged, this increase has not affected the patenting of individual inventors (shown in the figure by the dashed line).

More generally, the share of patents that are sold (reassigned) has dropped dramatically from nineteenth-century levels. Lamoreaux and Sokoloff (1996) estimated that during the 1870s the ratio of patent sales contracts to patents was 83 percent; almost all of these patents were granted to small inventors. By contrast, Serrano (2005) found that for patents granted to small inventors between 1983 and 2001, only 18 percent were ever traded. Not surprisingly, he found that the traded patents tend to be more valuable.

In recent years, technology licensing has been "a hit-or-miss process based largely on personal networking. Typically, it takes the average corporation 12 to 18 months to find a buyer for each available technology. As a result, the traditional practice yields only a few deals annually per large company."[21] For this reason, Rivette and Kline (2000) have argued that most firms have what they call "Rembrandts in the Attic"—that is, large numbers of unused technologies that might be profitably licensed.

The impression of weakness in the market for patents is supported by more methodical empirical data. First, survey data finds that patent holders are often not able to find licensees willing to pay the requested price. In a survey of holders of European patents, Gambardella, Giuri, and Luzzi (2006) found that only 61 percent of patentees who wanted to license their patents were able to do so. This suggests a significant market failure.

Second, licensors generally fail to capture much of the value of their inventions. Caves, Crookell, and Killing (1983) found that, on average, licensors only receive about 40 percent of the value of the rents earned on their technologies. In general, the gains from trade for small patentees are small; by one estimate, a patentee realizes only a 14 percent gain from the sale of a patent (Serrano 2005).

This dismal performance is at odds with some recent enthusiastic depictions of the new market for patents. Some entrepreneurs, anticipating a booming market, recently established patent brokerages and exchanges, patent auctions and investment banks, and even sophisticated financial instruments to securitize patents and manage IP risk.[22] They, and numerous press reports, cite the $33.7 billion trade in intellectual property and IBM's $1.7 billion in "patent licensing" as evidence of a veritable "gravy train" in patent licensing.[23]

Unfortunately, much of this seems to be hype. The statistics on trade and IBM's licensing have been misrepresented.[24] And most of the new crop of patent market start-ups have failed to generate many transactions.[25] Perhaps the most successful effort has been the Ocean Tomo patent auction. On April 6, 2006, Ocean Tomo, an "intellectual property merchant banc," held the first live patent auction. This effort generated widespread interest, and Ocean Tomo plans to hold these auctions twice per year. This auction offered a total of 394 patents. Of these, only 26 percent were sold at auction (a few additional patents were sold in private negotiations immediately after the auction). As one might expect, there were a few highly valuable patents and most of the others were not very valuable. Two sold for more than $1 million, but the mean value of a patent sold at the auction was only $29,000—substantially less than our estimates of average patent value in chapter 5.

Clearly, these results confirm, not contradict, our main point here: the poor state of technology markets makes it difficult for small inventors to realize as much value from their patents as large firms do.

Why Don't Technology Markets Work More Effectively?

Patent and technology markets that once worked well do not work so well today, mainly because technology has grown more complex. We noted earlier that growing technological complexity increased inventor specialization during the late nineteenth century. It also prompted firms to set up the first R&D labs. Interestingly, Lamoreaux and Sokoloff (1999) find that in the late nineteenth century some of the early corporate R&D departments were founded to help companies evaluate the technologies on the market; this was no longer a straightforward task that any ordinary mechanic could do.

Contemporary technologies are even more complex, and simple access to a patent is seldom sufficient to transfer all of the knowledge needed to commercialize the technology. A series of studies involving Darby and Zucker (2001a; Darby, Zucker, and Welch 2001; Zucker, Darby, and Armstrong 1998, 2001; Zucker, Darby, and Brewer 1998) show that in biotechnology and semiconductors, successful innovation depends on the ongoing participation of the initial inventors. For technologies developed at universities, ongoing participation is so important that universities increase licensing revenues by offering faculty inventors a larger share of the proceeds (Darby, Zucker, and Wang 2004; Lach and Schankerman 2004). In practice, faculty inventors use a wide variety of other means to supplement (or as an alternative to) patents to transfer knowledge to industry (Agrawal and Henderson 2002).

This, in turn, means that transacting over complex technologies might be considerably more complicated and difficult than transacting over patents. With a simple technology, the prospective purchaser can read the patent and get a pretty good idea of the potential value and quality of the technology. A nineteenth-century manufacturer of cotton spinning machines could read a patent on spinning machine spindles and know pretty much what that invention did and what it was worth. A potential purchaser of a more complex invention might not be so well informed. Typically, the inventor has important knowledge about the technology that is not communicated in the patent disclosure and, for this reason, she has a better idea about the technology's value than the potential purchaser. This gives rise to what economists call the "lemons" problem (lemons, as in unreliable used cars).[26] As the lemons problem grew, the market for patents declined at the end of the nineteenth century, and the problem continues to impede technology markets today.

In addition, the purchaser of a complex technology will often need to purchase more than just the patent. Some critical knowledge might not be patented, but kept instead as a trade secret. Other knowledge might be *tacit*; that is, people on the development team might have informal or experiential knowledge that is not easily communicated. It is not surprising, therefore, that technology-transfer contracts often involve complicated arrangements regarding trade secrets and the participation of personnel. Such terms, of course, are not likely to be resolved quickly on an auction floor or patent exchange.

In short, there is an important distinction between a market for *patents* and a market for *technology*. Most firms—excepting those forced to deal with patent trolls—want to purchase technologies, not mere patents. For this reason, patents are sold or licensed as part of the bundle of goods and services needed to implement a technology. But this sort of transaction is more complicated and costly than a mere patent license or assignment.

Given the lemons problem, tacit knowledge, and the importance of collaborative development, it is unrealistic to expect technology markets for today's complex inventions to function as well as the robust markets during the heyday of the individual inventor. Nevertheless, patents could better promote complex technology transactions if patent boundaries were better defined (see sidebar 8.1, "Do Patents Facilitate Technology Transactions?", at the end of this chapter). The limited available evidence suggests that poor patent notice undermines the ability of inventors to contract over technology, making it more difficult for them to realize profits through the market.

How Does Patent Notice Affect Small Inventors?

But there is another, more important way that patent notice affects the rewards small inventors realize from patents: poor patent boundaries might limit the amount that a prospective licensee is willing to pay. Naturally, licensees will not pay more on royalties than they expect to gain

Sidebar 8.1. Do Patents Facilitate Technology Transactions?

Patents can, under some circumstances, facilitate the licensing or sale of technology. But the available empirical evidence about technology licensing suggests that this is only true when patent boundaries are well defined. In theory patents might facilitate technology licensing by facilitating the disclosure of information about the technology. As we noted above, with complex technologies, the prospective licensee or purchaser often lacks information about the quality of the technology. The inventor wants to convey information about the technology in order to conclude the transaction. One way to do this is to reveal some technical details, but doing so might expose the inventor to a risk of expropriation (Arrow 1962); that is, the prospective licensee might use the revealed information to copy the technology rather than to license it. Economists have identified a variety of ways that contracting parties can get around this difficulty (see, for example, Anton and Yao [1994] and Gallini and Wright [1990]). But clearly, if patents can effectively prevent copying, then they can assist the safe disclosure of information in the negotiating process—the prospective expropriator will face a lawsuit. This can facilitate the licensing or sale transaction (Merges 2005).[27]

But this mechanism fails when patents have poor boundaries. First, the enforcement of the patent right might be uncertain, permitting some degree of expropriation. Second, when patent boundaries are unclear, a prospective licensee who decides, in the end, to use an alternative technology might nevertheless risk a lawsuit. Negotiations might reveal information helpful to the pursuit of the patent holder's case, such as information about the prospective licensee's technology and markets— that is, negotiations involve information leakage in *both* directions. This might make prospective licensees reluctant to enter into negotiations unless they are certain that they want to use the technology.

There is some limited evidence on licensing behavior and it suggests that patents can facilitate licensing transactions when they have clear boundaries, but not otherwise. Anand and Khanna (2000) found that a higher portion of interfirm alliances involve licensing in the chemical and pharmaceutical industries. Above, we have noted that clear boundaries

(Continued)

(Continued)

> on chemical patents play a unique role in these industries. Gans, Hsu, and Stern (2002) found that start-up firms are more likely to license (or be acquired) if they have one or more patents or if they rate patent protection as being relatively "effective." But the converse must also be true: when patent protection is ineffective, because, say, unclear patents make enforcement uncertain, then licensing is less likely to occur.[28]

in profits from access to a patent. Litigation risk attributable to weak patent notice reduces these profits. If, for example, a manufacturer expects profit erosion because of the risk of an infringement assertion by some other patent owner, then the manufacturer will revise downward the royalties it will pay the first patent owner. This means that although small inventors might not be exposed directly to significant litigation risk as alleged infringers, this risk reduces their incentives *indirectly*. A similar argument applies to small inventors who choose to bring their technology to market themselves—once they invest in substantial complementary production and distribution assets, they are at risk for significant litigation costs.

This brings our argument full circle. Small inventors might play a particularly important role in innovation. Although small inventors might not be the only, or even the major, source of important inventions, they do make important contributions. The good news is that small inventors receive positive incentives from the patent system; this might, in fact, be one of the strongest rationales for having a patent system. The economic impact of important inventions from small inventors depends, however, on the market for technology. For well-known reasons, contracting over technology is difficult and often incomplete.

These difficulties are particularly significant when patents have poor notice. First, when this happens, prospective licensees or purchasers make lower profits. Thus, they will only be willing to pay lower royalties or a lower purchase price. Second, the negotiation process is more costly and the risk of bargaining breakdown is elevated. Thus, fewer transactions are completed and inventors realize less profit from those that are completed.

Even though small inventors benefit from the current patent system, problems of poor patent boundaries affect them, perhaps even more so than inventors at large firms. Policy debate over patents has often pitted large firms against small inventors, as Dr. Hill's quotation earlier in the chapter suggests. Certainly some policy measures benefit one group of inventors at the expense of the other. Our analysis suggests, however, that small inventors and large firms might have more in common regarding patent policy than has been generally recognized, not least that they both suffer substantially from poor patent notice.

Of course, there are other self-proclaimed "small inventors" who are not in the business of developing new technologies; instead, they are in the business of using patents to extract rents from innovative firms. Unfortunately, poor patent boundaries with unclear patent claims and related troubles provide profit opportunities based on patents that do not represent real invention, but which nevertheless permit legal claims against innovators. These rent-seekers have little in common with real inventors, either large or small.

9   Abstract Patents and Software

Introduction

In Chapter 7 we noted that patents on software, and especially patents on business methods (which are largely software patents), stood out as being particularly problematic. These patents had high rates of litigation and high rates of claim-construction review on appeal. This chapter explores whether there really is something particularly awry with software patents and, if so, what it is.

We argue that there is, in fact, something crucially different about software: software is an *abstract* technology. This is a problem because at least since the eighteenth century, patent law has had difficulty dealing with patents that claimed abstract ideas or principles. In chapter 3 we observed that abstract patent claims can violate the "rule of first possession," allowing patent holders to lay claim to arguably broad ranges of technology that they have not invented. Such patents often have unclear boundaries and give rise to opportunistic litigation. Here, we explore how software can be considered "abstract" and how this affects patent notice.

Although not all software patents contain abstract claims, the technology facilitates abstract claiming. In addition, court decisions in the 1990s have undermined legal doctrines that restricted abstract claims in software patents in particular. Software also seems to be an area with large numbers of relatively obvious patents. For these reasons, it is not surprising that a substantial share of current patent litigation involves software patents.

Are Software Patents Different?

A number of commentators have argued that patents on software or business methods are no different from patents in other technology fields. The evidence from chapter 7, taken together with other evidence we present below, casts serious doubt on this assertion. The evidence supporting the assertion is quite limited. Allison and Tiller (2003) and Hunter (2003) argue that business-method patents are of comparable "quality" to other patents because they have a similar number of claims, citations, and so forth, as do other patents. This conception of patent "quality" is quite limited, however, and does not relate at all to how these patents function as a property right.

Others admit that there might be some difficulties with software patents, but contend that these difficulties are merely temporary. Campbell-Kelly (2005), a computer science professor, argues that "software patents are not radically different from those of other technologies; the patent system has adapted to the particular demands of new technologies over time, and the software patent system is already making such adaptations." He concludes:

> It is ten years since software patents have been issued in large numbers. The anxieties expressed in the early 1990s about the effect patents would have on the software industry have not been realized. History shows us that software patents are not so different from other patents in the information technology industries, and that the patent system is capable of adjusting to the particularities of individual industries. For example, early in the last century chemical processes were thought to be unpatentable, but the system soon adapted to a new reality and now it is difficult to imagine this issue was once controversial. With software and business method patents the United States Patent and Trademark Office is instituting changes that will make the system work better. For example, it has increased the number and quality of software patent

examiners, and in time the databases and searching mechanisms for prior art will improve.[1]

There are several things to take issue with in this argument. First, Campbell-Kelly gets his history wrong. Chemical processes have always been patentable and have never been controversial in the United States. The very first patent granted in 1793 was for a chemical process to make potash and many famous chemical processes were patented during the nineteenth and early twentieth centuries (for example, the Solvay process, the Haber process, et al.). Moreover, in United States history, no other technology has experienced anything like the broad industry opposition to software patents that arose during the 1960s. Major computer companies opposed patents on software in their input to a report by a presidential commission in 1966 and in amici briefs to the Supreme Court in *Gottschalk v. Benson* in 1972.[2] Major software firms opposed software patents through the mid-1990s (for example, in U.S. Patent Office hearings in 1994). Perhaps more surprising, software inventors themselves have mostly been opposed to patents on software. Surveys of software developers in 1992 and 1996 reported that most were opposed to patents (Oz 1998). Although other countries have witnessed general opposition to patents in the past (for example, some European countries abandoned the patent system during the nineteenth century) and although some countries have opposed patents on certain technologies in the past (for example, some countries permitted patents on manufacturing processes for pharmaceuticals, but not patents on the chemical structures themselves), such broad opposition from *within* the affected industry and among the affected inventors seems to be unprecedented in U.S. patent history.

Second, it is hardly clear that the "anxieties" expressed about software patents have not been realized. The principal "anxiety" Campbell-Kelly identifies concerns the development of so-called patent thickets. Citing an article written by Richard Stallman and Simson Garfinkel in 1992, Campbell-Kelly writes, "Opponents of software patents argue that patent 'thickets' will necessarily impede the flow of new software products." Campbell-Kelly is not alone in arguing that rumors of the death of the software industry due to the malign influence of patent thickets have been greatly exaggerated. Merges (2006) agrees that "the predictions of the software patent doubters in the early 1990s have been effectively refuted so far." He argues that the United States software industry has not become dominated by large firms nor has it shown signs that the entry of small firms has diminished.[3] Mann (2005) makes a similar argument based on interviews with small software firms.

Now credible evidence shows that software publishers have flourished so far despite the growth of software patents. Some preliminary studies suggest that although there is evidence of some detrimental effects of patents within the software industry, they have to date not been serious or widespread. Cockburn and MacGarvie (2006) found that patents deter entry in the software industry, all else being equal, but that this deterrent effect is muted because entrant firms can improve their odds of success by getting patents, too. Noel and Schankerman (2006) find that patent thickets reduce the market value of software firms, but this effect, too, is muted because software firms can counteract it by obtaining patents themselves.

But the arguments of Campbell-Kelly, Merges, and Mann seem to be largely directed at a carefully chosen straw man. The general concern is over software *patents*, not the software *industry* per se. This distinction is important because almost all software patents are obtained by firms *outside* the software industry. Bessen and Hunt (2007) found that the software-publishing industry only obtains 5 percent of all software patents granted; most are obtained by firms in the electronics, telecommunications, and computer industries. Software, of course, is a widely applied, general-purpose technology and only about one-third of all computer programmers and systems analysts are employed in the software-publishing and software-services industries.

To date patents have had little negative effect within the software-publishing industry because there are—despite the concerns of commentators—no substantial patent thickets within the industry. Cockburn and MacGarvie looked carefully at software industry market segments from 1994–2004 and found that in most segments, 80–95 percent of the incumbent firms have *no* patents related to that segment. This does not mean, however, that software patents do not contribute to patent thickets in *other* industries. Indeed, many of the industries that obtain the lion's share of software patents, such as the semiconductor and computer industries, have been identified by multiple researchers as having patent thickets.[4] Nor does this

Table 9.1.
Litigation characteristics by patent technology

	Probability of patent in suit	*Relative frequency of claim construction appeal*	*Percentage of lawsuits (2002)*
All	**2.0%**	**1.00**	——
Chemical	1.1%	0.84	13%
Complex (excluding chemical)	2.0%	0.89	34%
Other	2.2%	1.11	
Software	4.6%	2.18	26%
Business methods	13.7%	6.67	4%
Biotechnology	3.2%	2.37	3%

Note: Probability of suit adjusted for truncation bias and under-reporting.

mean that software patents might not create a thicket in the software industry in the *future*, as software firms have been accelerating the pace at which they obtain patents. All of which is to say, concerns about thickets in the software industry might simply be premature.

More generally, Campbell-Kelly, Merges, and others focus heavily on this one "anxiety" about patent thickets when, in fact, a wide variety of other concerns have been raised about software patents since the 1960s, including some during the early 1990s (see, for example, the comments by software firms at the U.S. Patent Office hearings held in San Jose, California, in 1994).[5] Many of these anxieties concerned the ability of the patent system to properly handle software patents, including worries about how well patent boundaries could be defined.

The empirical evidence suggests, in fact, that some of these concerns might be quite valid. Software patents play a major role in the rise of litigation that we have identified as central to the deteriorating performance of the patent system. Table 9.1 shows several characteristics of patent by technology type. The first two columns, repeated from tables in chapter 7, show the probability that a patent is in a lawsuit and the relative frequency with which claim construction is reviewed on appeal. Recall, the second column measures the uncertainty of claim construction. The last column

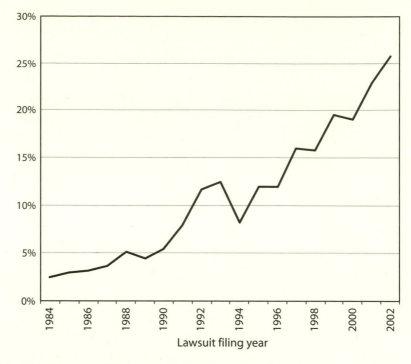

Figure 9.1. Percentage of Patent Lawsuits Involving Software Patents

shows the (non-exclusive) percent of lawsuits filed in 2002 that involve a patent of the given technology type. Over one-quarter of all patent lawsuits involve software patents. Moreover, that share has been growing rapidly. Figure 9.1 shows the percentage of lawsuits involving software patents over time.

Clearly, software and business-method patents are different from most other patents, both in their litigation rates and frequency of claim-construction problems. And a very major part of the poor performance of the patent system can be attributed to lawsuits involving these patents. It is therefore hardly surprising that major IT firms have become very vocal in their advocacy of patent reform. Although many of these firms support the use of software patents, one can hardly argue that the use of software patents has been without "anxieties."

Campbell-Kelly further argues that whatever problems exist, the patent system is already adapting to solve them. Indeed, the Patent Office issued

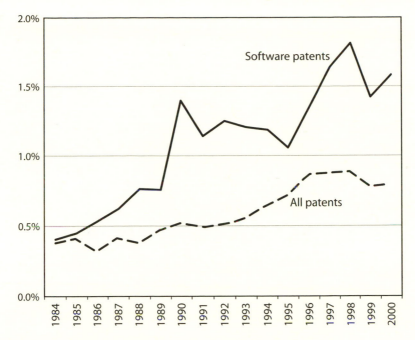

Figure 9.2. Probability that a Patent Is in Lawsuit within Four Years of Issue
Note: Data adjusted for under-reporting.

new guidelines in 1996 for examining software patents, has begun hiring large numbers of electrical engineers and computer scientists, while a vast body of patent prior art has developed for the software industry (over 150,000 patents). Significant numbers of software patents have been issued since the 1980s, so if the problems of software patents just require adaptation to this new technology, then we would expect the adaptation to be well underway, as Campbell-Kelly suggests.

The empirical evidence suggests otherwise, however. The problems of software patents are not diminishing; if anything, they are getting worse. Figure 9.2 shows the probability that a patent will be in one or more lawsuits within four years of the patent's issue date (adjusted for under-reporting).[6] Software patents issued in more recent years are much *more* likely to be litigated, not less. The adaptations made by by the patent system do not seem to be have produced a net positive effect on litigation rates. This suggests that something more persistent is at work here than the adaptation of patent examination procedures to a new technology.

Software Patents/Abstract Patents

Some Problematic Software Patents

We believe that, on average, software patents suffer notice problems more acutely than patents drawn from most other areas of technology. There also seem to be large numbers of obvious software patents, which aggravate these notice problems. Taken together, these factors probably explain why software patents impose higher litigation costs than other types of patents. The following disputes illustrate some of the reasons why software patents have unpredictable boundaries.

U.S. Patent No. 4,528,643: "System for Reproducing Information in Material Objects at a Point of Sale Location"

(Interactive Gift Express, Inc. v. Compuserve Inc., 256 F.3d 1323)

This is the widely litigated E-Data patent discussed in chapter 1. On appeal, five different claim terms were disputed.[7] E-Data's actual invention was a kiosk or vending machine to be used in retail locations for producing digital music tapes or other digital reproductions. One of the disputed claim terms was "point of sale location." The district court judge interpreted this limitation to mean that the patent did not cover transactions that occurred in private homes—that is, in the manner associated with consumer digital e-commerce. In industry jargon, this term refers to the location within a retail store where items are checked out and transactions take place. This jargon was first used during the 1970s when electronic terminals began replacing cash registers. On appeal, however, the Federal Circuit interpreted this term more broadly to cover transactions that occurred within private homes. This meant that the patent could cover a wide range of e-commerce applications far beyond E-Data's original invention, and the owner of this patent (E-Data) has asserted it against companies ranging from the New York Times Companies to Compuserve to McGraw-Hill.

Another disputed claim term was "material object." The district court interpreted this to mean that the technology had to produce a digital reproduction in something separate from the computer itself;

the computer's internal hard drive did not count as a "material object" for the purposes of this patent. In this case, the Federal Circuit supported the district court's narrower interpretation. Nevertheless, even with the narrow interpretation of this term, the patent still appeared to cover a wide range of activities far beyond the original invention, activities that merely shared a functional similarity to the original invention.

The practice of using vague, expansive terms such as "material object" is by no means limited to software technology. But software might be particularly susceptible to the use of abstract terms because many of the standard terms of art are themselves abstract ideas that are meant to apply to a wide variety of possible applications; that is, software is *itself* an abstract technology.

The abstract use of standard terms is well illustrated by the following patent.

U.S. Patent No. 4,751,669: "Videotex Frame Processing"

(Wang Lab., Inc. v. America Online, Inc., 197 F.3d 1377)

Videotex was a 1970s-vintage online service that was a precursor to the modern Internet. Individual users could log on to a centralized server and display a variety of different types of information on a local terminal or (later) personal computer. Compuserve and Prodigy were popular videotex systems in the United States.

Wang Labs entered this market in the early 1980s with a system that used Wang PCs connected to servers over telephone lines. The software running on the personal computers used an interface modeled after the graphical user interface developed at Xerox PARC during the 1970s and early 1980s that was used in the Smalltalk and Xerox Star products. In particular, the Wang software displayed information in "frames," overlapping rectangles each containing different information. Frames are, of course, quite familiar to users of windowed operating systems such as the Apple Macintosh operating systems and Microsoft Windows. In contrast to the Xerox Star and the later systems, however, Wang offered a "poor man's" implementation: the low-resolution monitor on the Wang PC was not capable of displaying the high resolution bit-mapped graphics used on these other systems, but only displayed text characters and crude graphic characters.

Nevertheless, Wang obtained a patent in 1988 that claimed, among other things, the general use of frames to display different kinds of information retrieved from servers.[8] This patent putatively covered a broad range of possible technologies that might use a graphical user interface far beyond Wang's actual product. The Internet browser was one of these later-developed uses. Accordingly, Wang sued Netscape and America Online in 1997. This immediately caused great concern among Internet companies.[9]

The judges, however, interpreted the claim term "frame" narrowly. Since Wang's actual system, as described in detail in the patent, only used a character-based display, the court concluded that the term "frame" as used in the patent only pertained to character-based displays, despite the origin of the term and its industry usage. Because the Netscape browser used a higher resolution bit-mapped display, it was found not to infringe.

This meant that a wide range of Internet and other applications were not subject to this patent. Although industry participants were relieved by this decision, they could hardly have expected it, given the industry usage of "frame." The unpredictable nature of claim construction meant that the boundaries of the patent were surely uncertain for many years. Wang was certainly not unreasonable in attempting to assert what it thought was a legitimately broad patent, even though Wang did not itself invent the Internet browser.

Indeed, because of the abstract nature of software, claims made in one field might affect technologies in very different fields. The following example illustrates this situation.

U.S. Patent No. 5,758,257: "System Method for Scheduling Broadcast of and Access to Video Programs and Other Data Using Customer Profiles"

(*Pinpoint, Inc. v. Amazon.com, Inc.*, 369 F. Supp. 2d 995)

A common set of programming techniques match objects in one list to objects in another. How broadly should claims to matching programs be interpreted? In 2003, Pinpoint, a company whose only business is patent licensing, sued Amazon, the online bookseller, because Amazon's website provided personalized book and movie recommendations to customers. Pinpoint had obtained a patent that claimed a system for recommending TV programs to viewers based on past choices.[10] But the patent claimed a more general procedure, often called "collaborative filtering," for matching "customer profiles" (information on customer preferences—for example, customer likes romance novels) to "content profiles" (information on content—for example, book is a romance novel). Pinpoint felt that its TV technology was claimed broadly enough to cover Amazon's book-recommendation technology.

Amazon argued, among other things,[11] that the method Pinpoint actually described used a numeric comparison to do the matching, even though the patent claim did not limit the comparison to a comparison of numeric quantities. Amazon claimed that its technology did matching instead by comparing categorical descriptions—for example, romance novels, mystery novels, et cetera. The first judge (there were multiple hearings) disagreed with this interpretation. The second judge, instead, agreed with Amazon, arguing that Pinpoint's patent did not cover Amazon's technology because Pinpoint's patent only covered matching "based on mathematically comparing mathematically expressed customer preferences with mathematically expressed program contents." This was deemed not to cover matching based on categorical descriptions.

This broad interpretation, which might have covered a wide range of matching and collaborative filtering applications, was thus narrowed. The second judge in this case (Judge Richard Posner) seems to have made a pragmatic decision that this patent did not deserve such broad coverage of applications very different from the original invention. Arguably, the broad interpretation matched the *plain meaning* of the claim. No computer programmer reading this claim prior to Judge Posner's decision would distinguish between matching routines based on mathematical expressions and matching routines based on categorical descriptions. Indeed, any programmer would see this is as a distinction without a difference: in a computer, matching based on categories *is* a mathematical routine; the software simply translates verbal descriptions into mathematical expressions.[12]

Of course we do not point this out to cast stones at Judge Posner or to question the mathematical competence of judges generally. First, Judge Posner's decision was based on more than this distinction. More important, this example is really a simple illustration of a basic problem: defining the boundaries of software patents precisely can be difficult, perhaps impossible. As we shall see below, even the best computer scientists and mathematicians in the world might not be able to unambiguously define the boundaries of software-patent claims.

We argue that the patents in the disputes outlined above share a common characteristic: they feature abstract claims. Of course abstract patent claims are not limited to software patents. We now turn our attention to abstract patents, explaining what they are, what is wrong with them, and how the law restricts them (or not).

The Problem of Abstract Patent Claims

It is often stated that patents are not granted for abstract ideas or principles, but only for practical inventions that might be based on such ideas or principles. The patent statute itself contains no such explicit restriction; the courts, however, have interpreted various provisions to imply such a limitation. As we noted in chapter 4, courts have resisted patents on abstract "principles of manufacture" since the eighteenth century in Britain and a similar restriction has been part of patent law in the United States at least since the first half of the nineteenth century. For example, faced with a patent that claimed "the art of cutting ice by means of any power, other than human power," Justice Story in 1840 argued, "Such a claim is utterly unmaintainable in point of law. It is a claim for an art or principle in the abstract, and not for any particular method or machinery, by which ice is to be cut. No man can have a right to cut ice by all means or methods, or by all or any sort of apparatus, although he is not the inventor of any or all of such means, methods, or apparatus" (*Wyeth v. Stone*, 30 F. Cas. 723).

This language evokes the fox-hunting case discussed in chapter 3, *Pierson v. Post*, and affirms the principle that possession is a key feature of property rights. Abstract claims like this tend to be problematic because they stray too far from the invention the inventor actually possessed. It is doubtful the inventor knew "any or all of such means, methods, or apparatus" to cut ice. The distinguishing feature of an abstract patent claim is not that it covers a broad range of technologies, although that is often the case, but rather that it claims technologies unknown to the inventor.

The patents in the lawsuits above fit this description. Freeny did not anticipate or know about Internet e-commerce when he filed his patent application. Nevertheless, the company (E-Data) that owned his patent subsequently and plausibly read the words in his patent to cover e-commerce. Wang did not conceive of the general Internet browser, but Wang interpreted the language in its patent to cover the operation of such browsers after they emerged.

The process of interpreting patent claims is one of mapping the words in a patent to a range of technologies, much as a surveyor maps the words in a deed to demarcations on the ground. With abstract patent claims, however, the words cover unknown territory, claiming technologies that are unknown at the time the patent is filed and that might change over time, especially in the fast-moving fields of technology.

There are two inter-related problems with such abstract claims. First, these claims reward patentees for inventions they do not invent. This means that the actual, future inventors face *reduced* incentives because they have to obtain a license from the patentee to develop or to commercialize their inventions. Clearly this counters the social benefit of the patent system. Second, it might be difficult to determine the boundaries of such claims and thus also to provide notice, to conduct clearance searches, or even to determine the content of the prior art. The problem of mapping words to technology is difficult and it is made more so if the claims are not tethered to a specific device or to a specific physical or chemical process. Patent lawyers use the phrase "the embodiments of the invention" to describe the specific devices and processes disclosed in the patent document. Courts often interpret the meaning of the words in a claim in light of the specific embodiments of the invention. The mere idea of, say, cutting ice cannot provide the same important information about patent boundaries that concrete embodiments provide.

The E-Data, Wang, and Pinpoint patents illustrate several notice problems caused by abstract claims in software patents. First, the words in an abstract claim map to an uncertain set of technologies when they are not limited to distinct embodiments. This was the problem with the term "frame" in the Wang claim and with "matching" in the Pinpoint claim. Sometimes, the progress of technology will render this mapping increasingly uncertain over time.

Second, software patents might be particularly prone to strategic use of vague language by applicants to gain undeserved scope. This was the problem with claim terms "point of sale location," "material object," and "information manufacturing machine." Although clever lawyers can use vague language with any technology, abstract technologies particularly lend themselves to such abuses because they are inherently described in abstract terms.

Third, notice problems can also arise with abstract claims even when the words themselves seem quite clear. This might seem counterintuitive, but it often happens when a patent claims all techniques for achieving a desired result, as in the case of the claim to "the art of cutting ice by means of any power, other than human power." Judge Story, recognizing that this patent claimed far more than the technology actually invented, narrowed the patent scope to correspond more closely to the actual embodiment of the invention. Arguably, the judges in the Wang and Pinpoint cases also narrowed patent scope for similar reasons—that is, they recognized that such broad claims are *inequitable* and they undermine the purpose of the patent system by penalizing the actual inventors of later-developed technologies. Sometimes, it is quite clear up front that claims will be interpreted narrowly—the patent statute provides for such narrowing when the claim only describes a general means for achieving a function. Nevertheless, in a broad range of cases, significant uncertainty remains as to whether abstract claims would be upheld, and, if so, how they would be interpreted if challenged in court. This means that these claims have uncertain boundaries, giving rise to opportunistic disputes and litigation. Even though judges might often (but not always!) take a pragmatic approach and interpret such claims narrowly—as they seem to do often with software patents—the uncertainty about boundaries makes clearance difficult and subjects inventors to the risk of inadvertent infringement.

WHY SOFTWARE PATENTS ARE DIFFERENT

These problems of abstract patent claims clearly apply to a broad range of technologies in addition to software. Why should software have a particular problem with abstract patents? We argue that the abstractness of software technology inherently makes it more difficult to place limits on abstract claims in software patents. To make things worse, the courts have undermined the legal doctrines that might be used to contain this problem. Finally, the nature of software technology in combination with the courts' relaxation of patentability standards has led to the proliferation of trivial, seemingly obvious software patents that make clearance infeasible.

Can We Know the Boundaries of Software Inventions?

Patent law depends on comparisons between technologies. Determining whether a technology is novel requires a comparison to prior technologies. To ascertain whether a technology infringes on a patent necessitates a comparison to a patented technology.[13] These comparisons determine the effective boundaries of the patent.

In the examples given above, this determination was difficult or uncertain. In part this was because clever lawyers drafted patent claims using vague, expansive terms such as "material object." In other cases, lawyers argued for interpretations of claim terms that affected the range of covered technologies. Such lawyering exists for all patented technologies. Nevertheless, patent law assumes that once the words are mapped to a specific set of technologies, one can readily determine which technologies are equivalent and which distinct.

In the case of software, however, this assumption is not always true. Computer algorithms might be equivalent, but computer scientists might not *know* that they are equivalent. In many cases, it has taken years for them to discover that different techniques are equivalent. For example, it has been shown that the "traveling-salesman" problem, which is used for routing delivery trucks among other things, is more or less equivalent to the "map-coloring" problem and a whole range of other problems. This means that an algorithm for solving the traveling-salesman problem is also, if worded broadly enough, an algorithm for doing map coloring. In other cases, computer scientists suspect that algorithms are equivalent, but they are unable to prove the equivalence.

Other observers have also noted the disparate representations of computer algorithms and their possible significance for patent law (de Laat 2000; Klemens 2006; Newell 1986). Our point here is that these different representations of the same technology create critically difficult problems for the notice function of the patent system.

Consider, by way of example, the Karmarkar patent on an algorithm for linear programming (U.S. Patent No. 4,744,028). Linear programming is a method used to optimize the operation of petroleum refineries, to schedule airline flights, and to route long-distance telephone calls. A method was developed to solve these problems on computers during the 1940s, but this method becomes very slow as the size of the problem (for example, the number of telephone switches) grows. Narendra Karmarkar, a researcher at Bell Labs, developed a new, faster algorithm for linear programming in 1984, which AT&T touted as a "breakthrough."[14] AT&T filed a patent on this algorithm in 1984 and obtained a patent in 1988. AT&T also developed a product (KORBX), bundling the software with a high-performance computer. Although AT&T did make a small number of sales and also apparently licensed the patent, this effort was not a significant commercial success.

This patent is sometimes cited as an example of what a software patent should be: a highly specific, nontrivial contribution to practical knowledge. Yet serious questions exist as to the boundaries of even this patent, questions as to whether its claims are truly novel, and whether Karmarkar actually "possessed" all the technologies claimed. One problem is that Karmarkar's algorithm seemed similar to technologies developed during the 1960s. In 1986, computer scientists demonstrated, in fact, that Karmarkar's algorithm is equivalent to a class of techniques that was known and applied to linear problems during the 1960s (Gill et al. 1986). Moreover, after this equivalence was demonstrated, computer scientists began applying algorithms based on these older techniques to linear-programming problems—some of these algorithms appeared to work better than the Karmarkar-AT&T approach (Marsten et al. 1990).

The reason that the older technology had not been widely applied to linear-programming problems during the 1960s was that a critical complementary technology had not been developed— namely, techniques for efficiently performing calculations for sparsely populated matrices (Marsten et al. 1990). The new wave of linear-programming applications following Karmarkar—including AT&T's own offering—depended on these new matrix-calculation techniques. Indeed, without these techniques, Karmarkar's algorithm by itself was not particularly efficient compared to the linear-programming techniques of the 1940s. These matrix techniques were neither claimed nor mentioned in Karmarkar's patent.

Given these facts, consider the difficulty of determining the boundaries of this patent. Would anyone have seen Karmarkar's algorithm as novel in light of the techniques used in the 1960s? Certainly not after 1986, when their equivalence was proved. But even in 1984, computer scientists might well have had doubts, yet they would have been unable to make a certain comparison (see, for instance, the account of one operations researcher in Saltzman [1994]). Similarly, would AT&T have been able to assert its patent successfully against people who used linear-programming techniques based on those used in the 1960s? Apparently, AT&T was able to obtain a cross-license from IBM, which had used these older techniques.

The abstractness of the patented algorithm means that these determinations cannot be made with certainty. Patent law assumes that two technologies can be unambiguously determined to be equivalent or distinct; this sets the patent boundaries. Yet for software, this assumption simply does not hold. Although this assumption works for most other technologies, it distinctly does not—or does so insufficiently well—for software algorithms. And if computer scientists cannot make these determinations with any certainty, how can we expect judges and juries to do so?

Of course, not all software patents cover algorithms. Some are quite specific and limited in what they claim. Yet others, as in the examples above, use abstract terms that are either inherently subject to expansive interpretations or they use aggressive patent drafting to extend the reach of their claims. But in these cases as well as those involving algorithms such as Karmarkar's, the abstractness of the technology means that, taken as a whole, software patents are more prone to unclear notice than are many other technologies.

Patent Law and Software

Patent law has developed several different doctrines to grapple with the treatment of abstract patent claims (these doctrines are discussed further in sidebar 9.1, "Abstraction and Related Doctrines"). Since 1990, however, the Court of Appeals for the Federal Circuit has significantly undercut these doctrines as applied to software inventions.

In general, patent law restricts abstract patents with three doctrines:

1. *Subject matter.* Various decisions have excluded certain abstract subject matter, such as mathematics and natural laws. Some decisions require a physical or chemical transformation or structure, another way to exclude claims that are too abstract.

2. *Enablement.* The disclosure principles of patent law require that the patent should provide sufficient information to enable a person skilled in the art to make and use all of the inventions claimed. For example, in a famous case, Samuel F. B. Morse included the following claim to his patent on the telegraph:

> Eighth. I do not propose to limit myself to the specific machinery, or parts of machinery, described in the foregoing specifications and claims; the essence of my invention being the use of the motive power of the electric or galvanic current, which I call electro-magnetism, however developed, for making or printing intelligible characters, letters, or signs, at any distances, being a new application of that power, of which I claim to be the first inventor or discoverer.

The Supreme Court feared that future inventions were likely covered by Morse's eighth claim and therefore the Court invalidated it. Although the Morse opinion is sometimes read as concerning patentable subject matter, the Court argued that the patent failed to document the processes or machinery these future inventions would use, nor could it, because Morse did not know them.

3. *Limits on functional claims.* The patent statute directly authorizes and regulates one style of abstract claim language called "means-plus-function" language. When a claim term recites only a general means of performing a function (as opposed to actually describing the specific

Sidebar 9.1. Abstraction and Related Doctrines

Morse's telegraph illustrates the problem of abstract patents and the use of patent law doctrines to restrict abstract claims. This invention falls into a variety of classes of technology that we list here in order of decreasing abstraction:

1. *Telegraphy.* Telegraphy is the transmission of information over distances without physical transport. Telegraphy is an ancient idea and ancient telegraphic inventions included communication by lights, smoke signals, and semaphores.

2. *Electrical Telegraphy*—the communication of information by electrical signals. The idea of electrical telegraphy dates back at least to 1753. An invention using electrostatic means (sparks) was demonstrated in 1795. Inventions using electrochemical means (generation of bubbles or discoloring impregnated paper) were demonstrated as early as 1809.

3. *Electromagnetic Telegraphy.* In 1820, Hans Christian Oersted demonstrated that electric current through a wire caused a magnetized needle to deflect. Based on the testimony of the eminent scientist Joseph Henry, the court in *O'Reilly v. Morse* (56 U.S. 62) concluded, "[I]t was believed by men of science that this newly-discovered power might be used to communicate intelligence to distant places. And before the year 1823, Ampere of Paris, one of the most successful cultivators of physical science, proposed to the French Academy a plan for that purpose." There were, however, a number of technical obstacles to developing a practical invention based on this principle. Scientists soon found that the signal became weaker with distance and would not work at distances over two hundred feet. In 1831 Joseph Henry devised a method for using higher voltage and winding multiple coils on an electromagnet. This permitted him to demonstrate a system to his class at Princeton over greater distances. In 1835 Henry also devised the relay, so that multiple circuits could be combined to extend the range of the total system indefinitely. Pavel Schilling developed the first binary system of transmission (a code designated by whether the current was

(Continued)

(Continued)

flowing or not) in Russia in 1832. Another electromagnetic telegraph was developed by the mathematicians Gauss and Weber in Germany in 1833. And the first commercial telegraph system was introduced by Wheatstone and Cooke in England in 1837. This system used five wires, allowing thirty-two different characters to be designated by the state of each circuit.

4. *Morse's Specific Invention* (described in patents granted in 1840, 1846, and reissued in 1848). Morse's invention combined features developed by others and added some of his own. Morse used electromagnets with coils and relays, both developed by Henry. Morse used a single wire, rather than five wires. He did this by developing a code that designated alphanumeric characters by combinations of binary signals of different duration. Also, Morse developed an elaborate printing device (which was later largely abandoned in favor of sound).

In this hierarchy, the more abstract classifications are broader; that is, they include a larger range of inventions—the more specific classes are subsets of the more abstract classes. In addition—and this is an important point—abstract classes might include many potential inventions that were not known at the time. For example, the term "electromagnetic telegraphy" might reasonably be interpreted to include the use of electricity and magnetism to transmit images, not just text. This was likely seen as a desirable application of the technology at the time of Morse's application in 1838 and earlier, but it was not until 1843 that Alexander Bain invented the first primitive facsimile machine. So an abstract principle or an abstract inventive idea describes some general characteristics of the function or structure of a class of inventions that might include some potential applications, for which specific means of realizing the desired results have not yet been invented.

What, then, is wrong with granting patents on such abstract principles? What is wrong, say, with having a patent that claims to cover telegraphy by electromagnetism? In theory such patents might seem an attractive way to provide incentives to scientists like Oersted.[23] This ignores, however, the requirements of an efficient property system:

(Continued)

property requires clear notice. Lacking a tangible manifestation of the "invention," courts might find it difficult to determine priority or infringement. For example, who first conceived the idea of electromagnetic telegraphy? It was certainly not Morse. There is documentation that André-Marie Ampere had arrived at the idea as early as 1823, but he, too, might not have been the first. The idea of electromagnetic telegraphy might well have occurred to many people—including Oersted himself— more or less simultaneously upon hearing of Oersted's accidental discovery. Clearly it is much easier for a court to determine priority when the act of invention requires a tangible demonstration or a working scale model (as was the case during much of the nineteenth century).

But even if priority is determined by a concrete physical invention, it is still possible to claim abstract ideas that might have obscure boundaries. Indeed, when Morse obtained a reissue of his patent in 1848 he added just such an abstract claim to the seven specific claims that described his actual telegraph:

> Eighth. I do not propose to limit myself to the specific machinery, or parts of machinery, described in the foregoing specifications and claims; the essence of my invention being the use of the motive power of the electric or galvanic current, which I call electro-magnetism, however developed, for making or printing intelligible characters, letters, or signs, at any distances, being a new application of that power, of which I claim to be the first inventor or discoverer.

There are two problems with such an abstract claim. First, such a claim rewards Morse for inventions he did not invent. As the Supreme Court wrote,

> For aught that we now know some future inventor, in the onward march of science, might discover a mode of writing or printing at a distance by means of the electric or galvanic current, without using any part of the process or combination set forth in the plaintiff's specification. His invention might be less complicated—less liable

to get out of order—less expensive in construction, and in its operation. But yet if it is covered by this patent the inventor could not use it, nor the public have the benefit of it without the permission of this patentee.

Such future inventors would face *reduced* incentives because they would have to obtain a license from Morse to develop their inventions.

Second, it might be difficult to determine the boundaries of such a claim and thus it might be difficult to provide notice, to conduct clearance searches, or to even determine what the prior art is. For example, Morse's first seven claims describe his actual invention and the words in those claims are given meaning by reference to the description of that invention. Given this description, one can readily understand how to make and use Morse's telegraph and this specific knowledge can be compared to the ways other technologies are made and used. But no such information is provided for the eighth claim. No information is provided on how to make and use all of the inventions covered by this claim because, in fact, Morse himself did not know all of these inventions or how they work. Consequently, this claim lacks clear boundaries.

What technologies are included in "making intelligible signs at any distance"? Does this include signs made with pointing needles (discovered before Morse)? Does it include handwritten signs used in Bain's facsimile machine? Does it include video images (cathode ray tubes work by exerting electromagnetic force on electrons)? Does it include signs made with electromagnetic radiation—for example, beacons or semaphores using light (an interpretation Morse could not have been expected to know)? Does it matter how electromagnetism is used? For example, Bain patented a facsimile machine that used electromagnets, but only to synchronize a timing mechanism (which he had patented earlier) at two locations. Does this count as electromagnetism, "however developed"? Similarly, does Morse's eighth claim cover wireless electromagnetic communication, as in radio telegraphy? Indeed, is there any limitation on how the information is communicated to the distant location? Although some technologies clearly fall within the scope of this claim, in other cases the boundaries are not so clear.

(Contined)

Abstract words that provide only a partial functional description of a technology class are simply insufficient to provide clear notice in many cases.

The Morse decision is often described as based on a lack of an adequate disclosure. This is a specific case, however, where the disclosure was inadequate because the claim was abstract and therefore involved unknown and uninvented technologies. It might be helpful to distinguish this doctrine from several closely related doctrines in patent law. Sometimes *O'Reilly v. Morse* is discussed as an example of the "enablement" doctrine of "undue experimentation" discussed in the case of Sawyer and Man in chapter 3 (Merges and Nelson 1990). There is an important difference, however, between these cases. With Sawyer and Man, the class of claimed inventions was identifiable and the court could therefore consider the amount of experimentation needed to find an effective fiber for electric lighting. In Morse, however, the class of claimed inventions was not known. The Court could not determine the amount of experimentation needed to find, make, and use the claimed inventions, because these inventions were not identified. Instead, the Court had to make a judgment about the abstractness of the claim— their reasoning was that the claim was so abstract that there would *likely* be inventions covered by the claims that were not described in the patent. This is clearly a more difficult and less fact-based inquiry.

A related issue is the balance between the incentives to pioneer inventors and the incentives to commercialize their inventions. Some scholars advocate granting broad patents to pioneers to encourage them to commercialize their inventions (see the "prospect" theory of Kitch [1977] as well as Kieff [2001]). More generally, the Morse decision is sometimes described as primarily about setting the breadth of the patent in order to adjust the balance between pioneer inventors and subsequent commercializers or other inventors. Although the decision in Morse did affect the scope of the patent, it had little to do with this balance. Because the inventions covered by Morse's eighth claim were not known, the grant of a broad patent covering them to Morse could hardly provide any incentive for him, or for anyone else, to commercialize these inventions. The problem with Morse's eighth claim was

(Continued)

not so much that it was broad, but that the range of inventions it covered was not known.

Two other distinctions are also worth noting. Although some abstract patents use vague words such as "material object," others do not, as in the Wang patent. Sometimes the "indefiniteness" requirement discussed in chapter 3 is interpreted to relate to the vagueness of words used in claims. The point about abstract patents is not so much that they use vague words (although they lend themselves to that abuse), but that the words circumscribe a set of technologies that is not known. Finally, abstraction is sometimes considered opposite to the practical (as in *Alappat* case). Morse's patent, however, clearly had practical value, yet the eighth claim was also abstract.

means), the term is limited to the specific structures described in the patent document and their equivalents. This provision facilitates patent notice; interested observers interpret the otherwise abstract term by locating concrete technology described in the patent.

Patent law appears to take a belt-plus-suspenders approach to dealing with abstract patent claims. Perhaps this is because it is difficult to pin down exactly what sort of abstract claiming is impermissible. How well do these legal doctrines limit abstract claims in software patents? Unfortunately, the Federal Circuit has made several decisions specific to software patents that undermine the performance of these doctrines.

The Morse case teaches that a high-level, functional description of electronic communications technology was not adequate to serve as an enabling disclosure for his eighth claim. Beginning in 1990, however, a series of decisions by the Federal Circuit allowed similar high-level, functional descriptions of software inventions to satisfy this requirement.[15] Software patents do not, in general, need to include the computer code nor detailed flowcharts nor any other detailed description of specific operation. In practice, this has meant that the disclosure requirement is rarely a sufficient ground upon which to invalidate software patents, despite widespread use of claims that are every bit as abstract as Morse's eighth claim.[16]

The evolution of subject-matter restrictions for software is a bit more complicated (for an overview, see Samuelson [1990]). In its 1972 decision in *Gottschalk v. Benson*, the Supreme Court recognized that patents on mathematical algorithms might run afoul of the problems raised by Morse's eighth claim and the common law restrictions against patenting laws of mathematics. Despite popular misconceptions, the Court did not prohibit patents on software. Instead, the decision had the effect of subjecting patents involving software to an additional two-step test designed to limit abstract claims: the first step was to determine whether the patent recited a mathematical algorithm; if so, the second step asked whether the patent would preempt all uses of the algorithm. Such claims would be impermissible.

The application of these rules was controversial and confused, in part because the appellate courts saw things rather differently than did the Supreme Court. The law evolved until 1994 when, in *In re Alappat*, the Federal Circuit effectively discarded this subject-matter test and replaced it with the simple criterion that inventions involving software are patentable as long as they are "useful, concrete, and tangible." By this, the court apparently means that an invention is not abstract as long as it has some practical—that is, useful—application (the words "concrete" and "tangible" are apparently superfluous).[17]

Although this is one meaning of the word "abstract," it is not the meaning favored by the Supreme Court in *Benson*,[18] which we have identified as having caused notice problems. In that case, as well as in Morse's eighth claim and the ice-cutting claim, abstract language allowed the patent to claim all means of achieving a result or all technologies with similar functional form. The tests based on *Benson* recognized that the abstract language of software algorithms might be particularly problematic in this regard. With *Alappat* those concerns are ignored. Indeed, in 1998 in *State Street Bank & Trust Co. v. Signature Financial Group, Inc.*, the Federal Circuit concluded that a software patent that claimed all means of calculating accounting ratios for certain kinds of mutual fund groups did, in fact, meet the "useful, concrete, and tangible" criterion. In effect, the use of any subject-matter test to limit abstract patent claims has been eliminated for software.

Until recently, the notice-enhancing restrictions on means-plus-function language have not had much effect on software patent claims. Beginning in 1999, however, the Federal Circuit has required that patents deemed to use such wording must disclose a specific algorithm.[19] This is a small step in the right direction. Its value might be limited, though, because of the broad and uncertain range of mathematical equivalents to algorithms, and because patent applicants can always avoid means-plus-function language and find another way to craft abstract claims.

Judging from our reading of Federal Circuit cases, the net effect of these changes is that there are few limits to abstract software patent claims. Software patents that make broad, abstract claims are, in general, held to be valid.[20] For software patents, the court has made specific exceptions to general principles of patent law. This does *not* mean, however, that these patents are always construed broadly. As in with the Wang and Pinpoint patents discussed above, the Federal Circuit often interprets the claims narrowly. Often—but not always (for example, the E-Data case)!—the judges seem to take a pragmatic approach and narrow these broad patents. Although this practice might save defendants in many of these trials, it only serves to further undermine the notice function: now, not only are there claims with uncertain boundaries, but the court has inserted additional unpredictability over how these claims will be interpreted if brought to trial and appeal. In effect, the enablement clause and *Alappat* decision let the abstraction genie out of the bottle; the Federal Circuit appears to be attempting to stuff it back in the bottle using "creative claim construction" on a case-by-case basis. This situation cannot last.

Obvious Software Patents

Problems of abstraction are severely aggravated by the proliferation of patents on trivial inventions. Arguably, the Wang and Pinpoint patents (and possibly the E-Data patent) noted above are at best trivial improvements on existing knowledge; at worst, they are blatantly obvious. The potential combination of large numbers of trivial patents with abstract claims creates enormous notice problems for software patents.

As we discussed in chapter 3, patent proliferation is a general problem, one not restricted to software patents. Changes in the non-obviousness requirement for patentability have affected all types of patents. It is possible, however, that features of software technology make it particularly susceptible to the patenting of obvious ideas, especially given the legal doctrines of non-obviousness developed by the Federal Circuit. For one thing, the general-purpose nature of software technology—again, because the technology is abstract, similar techniques can be used in a wide range of applications—makes it inevitable that techniques known in one realm might be applied in another, yet the documentary evidence that the Federal Circuit requires for a demonstration of obviousness might not be published. For example, a large number of patents cover well-known business processes updated with a software implementation. It might not be a coincidence that several of the precedents where the Federal Circuit has weakened the non-obviousness requirement involve software (*In re Lee, In re Zurko*). Whatever the cause, the combination of large numbers of software patents that are both trivial and abstract produces significant problems with respect to patent notice.

The effect of this flood is apparent in e-commerce patents. As noted above, David M. Martin has estimated that "if you're selling online, at the most recent count there are 4,319 patents you could be violating. If you also planned to advertise, receive payments for or plan shipments of your goods, you would need to be concerned with approximately 11,000."[21] One software executive estimates that checking clearance costs about $5,000 per patent.[22] It is no accident that most software users do not clear rights. Checking thousands of patents is clearly infeasible for almost any software product. Consequently, firms do not clear their technologies; instead, they inadvertently infringe and costly litigation is the result.

In sum, patents on software are *not* just like other patents. The evidence shows that software patents are particularly prone to litigation and to disputes over patent boundaries, a concern that has been raised about them since the 1960s. We attribute these problems to the abstract nature of software technology; too many software patents claim all technologies with similar form or all means of achieving a result, when the actual invention is much more limited and often trivial.

Patent law has developed a number of doctrines to circumscribe abstract patent claims. Unfortunately, the Federal Circuit has set software-specific precedents that essentially remove most restrictions on abstract claims in software. Perhaps the court acted out of a desire to promote patents in this field of technology that has historically not used patents. The result has been both a proliferation of software patents *and* lawsuits.

Software patents are not the only patents to suffer problems of abstract claims. Any technology can be claimed abstractly and, to make matters worse, the Federal Circuit has recently eroded limits on abstract patents for nonsoftware business processes and even basic scientific ideas (for example, *Laboratory Corp. of America v. Metabolite Laboratories*). But overall, software patents likely have a far greater influence on the performance of the patent system than do nonsoftware business processes.

Software patents are, in fact, responsible for a major share of patent lawsuits. They thus play a central role in the failure of the patent system as a whole. Any serious effort at patent reform must address these problems and the failure to deal with the problems of software patents—either with software-specific measures or general reforms—will likely doom any reform effort. We turn to possible changes in patent policy in the next chapter.

10 Making Patents Work as Property

In 2002, the Federal Trade Commission (FTC) and the Department of Justice (DOJ) held joint hearings on the patent system and its relationship to competition policy. According to the FTC/DOJ report, "The hearings took place over 24 days, and involved more than 300 panelists, including business representatives from large and small firms, and the independent inventor community; leading patent and antitrust organizations; leading antitrust and patent practitioners; and leading scholars in economics and antitrust and patent law." Based on these extensive hearings, the FTC/DOJ concluded that "questionable patents are a significant competitive concern and can harm innovation"; they recommended a series of changes in patent policy. They were joined in making patent reform recommendations by the National Academy of Sciences (NAS), the American Intellectual Property Law Association (AIPLA), and others. Congress began holding its own hearings in 2005. It revisited the topic in 2006 and 2007, but so far, no coalition has emerged that is capable of pushing through significant reform.

These policy recommendations come from some very smart people, many of whom have much more practical experience with the patent system than do we. Nevertheless, we think we still have something to contribute to the discussion. Because our quantitative analysis is comprehensive and because we evaluate reform proposals against measurable performance objectives, our analysis might help avoid policies that are ad hoc, unbalanced, or partial. For example, many people have focused solely on patent examination quality as the objective of reform, based largely on anecdotal evidence of trivial, obvious, or otherwise invalid patents. Although we support efforts to improve patent examination quality (large numbers of questionable patents create conditions in which poor patent notice is unavoidable), our analysis suggests that this is only part of the problem and the patent system cannot likely be fixed by addressing only this issue.

Of course, the notice problems that we find central to the poor performance of the patent system are not the only ones looking for a remedy. We argue, however, that many proposed reforms, including reforms directed toward improving patent examination quality, are unlikely to be effective unless patent notice is improved generally. In this chapter we look at what might be involved in making patents an effective policy instrument generally, and in improving patent notice specifically. In the next chapter, we look at some specific ideas to improve notice.

Can Patents Be an Effective Policy Instrument for Innovation?

In economic theory, patents can play a critical role by providing incentives for inventors to invest in R&D and other innovative effort. Markets alone do not necessarily provide a socially optimal level of incentives (Arrow 1962), and so patents are seen as an important policy instrument to remedy this market failure. Innovation incentive is not the only possible social benefit of patents, but most economists see it as the most important one. For completeness, below we will discuss another possible benefit, the diffusion of information.

Our empirical analysis indicates that the patent system provides little innovation incentive to most public firms; these are the firms that perform the lion's share of R&D. So it seems unlikely that patents today are an effective policy instrument to encourage innovation overall. On the other hand, our empirical analysis also suggests that patents might have worked reasonably well as a property system as recently as the 1980s; that is, on average the patent system delivered positive incentives to public firms. This suggests that patent reform might be feasible.

This is hardly a foregone conclusion, however. First, as we elaborate upon below, we think that successful patent reform might be surprisingly difficult, in part because so much of the new technology is being developed in areas like software, where clear property rights might be inherently difficult to define, and in part because we think that many of the current problems of the patent system stem from institutional inadequacies and, therefore, require difficult institutional reform. Second, to be an *effective* policy instrument, patents need to do more than to merely provide positive incentives. They need to provide incentives that are sufficiently large. They also need to do so efficiently—that is, with relatively little cost to society—and their effectiveness needs to be judged relative to other policy instruments that can be used to increase investment in R&D and other innovative effort.

Economists have long recognized that there are alternative policy instruments to encourage innovation. One is procurement: the federal and state governments directly contract for industrial research. In 1991, direct federal spending on industrial R&D was $26.4 billion. This sum is much larger than the value of patents granted to United States entities in 1991— $4.4 billion, as we estimated in chapter 4.

Another policy instrument is subsidies. One government innovation program that some economists see as very successful is the Advanced Technology Program (ATP) of the National Institute of Standards and Technology (NIST), which provides subsidies to firms to develop promising new technologies. Other subsidies are in the form of tax deductions and credits. The United States tax code provides an implicit subsidy to R&D by allowing all R&D to be directly expensed rather than to be treated as a capital expenditure; this means that tax deductions might be taken more quickly, providing an implicit subsidy. In addition, since 1980, there has been a Federal Research and Experimentation Tax Credit. In 1991, firms claimed $1.6 billion in tax credits under this provision (NSF 2005).[1] This figure has increased to over $6 billion and, in addition, many states have added similar tax credits of substantial value (Wilson 2005). So it is clear that the incentives provided by procurement, subsidies and tax credits might be substantially larger than the gross subsidy provided by patents.[2]

But each of these policy instruments, including patents, comes with different offsetting social costs. Procurement programs tend to reflect the idiosyncratic needs of government agencies, especially the military, rather than the needs of society at large. Direct-subsidy programs, such as the ATP, might have difficulty "picking the winners" because government agencies might lack knowledge about the technology that private firms have. Although the well-managed ATP program has been quite successful in this regard (Darby, Zucker, and Wang 2004; Feldman and Kelley 2003), this is a relatively small program that might not scale up easily. Tax credits reward low-quality R&D (and, to some extent, other activities relabeled "R&D") as well as high-quality R&D. In addition, tax credits are of limited value to cash-strapped small inventors.

Patents also might be of limited value to liquidity-constrained inventors in comparison to direct subsidies, which provide up-front rewards. Perhaps more significant, the costs of the patent system, as we have emphasized above, are quite substantial. In addition to the costs of litigation and disputes resolved prior to litigation, the costs of obtaining patents are large, and often prohibitive. The cost of obtaining the patents granted to domestic entities in 1991 was about $1–1.5 billion, compared to a gross value of $4.4 billion.[3] Even if patent reform succeeded in reducing litigation costs by billions of dollars, most of the gross value of patents might still be consumed by the costs of litigation and application. In comparison to many other innovation policy instruments, patents might be rather costly. If a dollar spent on the ATP program generates greater R&D investment than a comparable dollar spent on expected patent costs, then patents might be inefficient as a policy instrument; that is, they have high opportunity costs for social policy.[4]

We do not have the necessary information to perform such a complete comparison of the costs and benefits of patents relative to other policy instruments.[5] Our point here is simply that the patent system has relatively high social costs. In order for patents to constitute an effective economic policy instrument, patent reform will likely have to do much better than to merely provide positive incentives. Nevertheless, we will proceed upon the assumption that patent reform is a worthwhile and feasible endeavor and explore what reforms to improve patent notice might entail.

IS IT WORTH FIXING THE NOTICE FUNCTION?

There are a couple general arguments that might be raised against reforms that improve the notice function of the patent system. First, some have contended that many efforts to improve patent notice will decrease inventors' incentives and are therefore undesirable. Second, the notice function involves costs to society and many hold that it is more efficient to incur those costs during litigation rather than at the time of patent application. We consider each argument in turn.

Many efforts to improve patent notice are indeed likely to affect the rewards patentees can realize from their patents. For example, a more robust prohibition of vague language in patents (indefiniteness) will reduce the scope of some patents. Put another way, some patents will be construed to cover smaller sets of technologies, and therefore the potential rewards to patentees will be reduced. Such a reform might improve patent notice, but it reduces the inventors' incentives to obtain a patent. For this reason, it has been argued, such a reform is undesirable, or, at the very least, any purported benefits of patent notice have to be weighed against the corresponding loss of incentives.

But this argument takes too narrow a view of incentives. Patent policy seeks to "promote the progress of science and useful arts." The activities that patent policy should encourage are inventing, innovating, and trading technology, *not* patenting itself. Our empirical analysis has shown that poor patent notice has reduced the incentives to invent. This is because these incentives depend not only on the value realized through patents, but also on the costs of disputes and litigation—it is the *net* reward that matters, not the reward from patents alone. Undoubtedly, some reforms that improve notice might reduce patent value more than others. But patent reform should aim to increase total net incentives both by reducing litigation and dispute costs and by keeping patent value as large as possible at the same time. See sidebar 10.1, "Do Inventors Really Need to Hide Their Claims in Order to 'Protect Their Property?'" for an example of this argument.

A second, related argument holds that early, clear notice is simply too expensive to achieve. Improving notice in the Patent Office imposes costs

Sidebar 10.1. Do Inventors Really Need to Hide Their Claims in Order to "Protect Their Property"?

Recently, the Patent Office proposed a reform to the application process that would increase transparency by making it harder to hide claim language. Specifically, among other changes, the Patent Office proposed a limit to the number of "continuing applications" available to a patent applicant. Continuing applications extend the length of patent prosecution and they can be used to hide claims from the public. The American Intellectual Property Law Association (AIPLA), the patent lawyers' lobby, protested vociferously that with this very modest reform, "Inventors would be far less able to adequately protect their property" (AIPLA 2006). Moreover, they argued that

> Most practitioners who engage in these strategies [of continuing applications] are not trying to game the system, but are simply trying to protect the interests of the creative people who make and disclose inventions to the public, and of the entities that convert ideas to reality and bring tangible benefits to the public. While there is little doubt that continuing prosecution abuses occur, we believe that most continuing prosecution applications are filed for legitimate reasons, not simply to delay prosecution. (AIPLA 2006)

This reform should not be seen as punitive, as it is not merely intended to punish those who game the system. We recognize that new technology might be difficult to understand, and it might take a while for a prosecutor and an examiner to negotiate acceptable claim language. But even if there were no strategic abuses of the continuation process, reform is still warranted. AIPLA understandably worries about marginal declines in patent value that might occur if a little more discipline were imposed on the prosecution process, but an impartial observer concerned about innovation would also worry about behavior that undermines clear, public patent boundaries, and adds to the risk of inadvertent infringement.

A "legitimate reason" to use continuing applications under current law is to modify claims to cover a competitor's technology. This practice

(Continued)

(Continued)

is permitted regardless of whether the competitor independently invented the technology, and of whether the competitor consulted a published patented application and invented around the original claims. When such amended claims are granted, the competitor finds they are infringing upon a patent claim that was hidden during the often lengthy prosecution. Not surprisingly, such behavior leads to costly litigation. The evidence suggests that patents that have continuation applications are *much* more likely to be litigated. And this litigation places a burden on those "creative people" attempting to "bring tangible benefits to the public."

So, the AIPLA argument takes a peculiarly narrow view of inventors' property, one that conveniently forgets that the value of inventors' property depends on that property having clear public boundaries to avoid unnecessary disputes. The rhetoric about "protecting inventors' property" appears to be no more than a cover to support short-sighted policy that will undermine that very property in the long run. During the 1980s, when the patent system performed better, use of continuing applications was far less frequent (see chapter 3), yet the evidence suggests the patent system seemed to do a better job of providing innovation incentives at that time.

on most patent applicants; perhaps, as some argue, it would be better to wait until litigation to resolve patent boundaries. Lichtman (2004) makes just this argument in defense of a generous doctrine of equivalents; recall that this doctrine expands patent scope at trial beyond the literal claim language.[6] Therein, he critiques Meurer and Nard (2005a, b), who, for their part, argue in favor of better patent notice and stringent restrictions upon the doctrine of equivalents. Lichtman counters that "because patents are both rarely asserted and rarely read, it is probably inefficient to expend significant resources improving patent clarity across the board." Put otherwise, most patents turn out to be of little value, so why impose a cost on all patent applicants? For to do so will only reduce their incentives. On the other hand, "to whatever extent the notice problem is relevant, it is not as important as it might at first seem, because someone skilled in the relevant art can often correctly interpret a patent claim despite some number of literal imperfections." In addition, Lichtman holds that judges might be better able to interpret claims later in the life of the technology, at which point they will have better information about how the technology at issue has evolved.

This argument fails because it misjudges the cost of notice problems. Lichtman guesses that as the doctrine of equivalents is restricted, the increased costs of obtaining patents will swamp the savings in litigation costs. Our empirical analysis shows, however, that the total business costs of litigation are much larger than attorneys' fees from litigation or prosecution costs. Policies that delay the clarification of patent boundaries exact a heavy toll on technology investors by opening them up to the risk of costly inadvertent infringement. Our estimates show that, at present, these risks are simply much more significant than the concerns raised by Lichtman.

Lichtman further contends that decisions about patent boundaries are "better" if made later, when more information is likely to be available. But how are they "better"? If boundaries set at trial (or on appeal) often depend on newly available information, then it necessarily follows that boundaries will be unclear at an earlier date when the given technology is adopted. Neither the patentee nor potential infringers will have the information required to know exactly how the boundaries will be construed at trial. This is precisely the sort of feature of our current patent system that discourages investment in innovation—with patent boundaries hard to predict, innovators risk inadvertent infringement and/or prospective licensees risk inadvertent infringement, reducing potential licensing revenues.[7]

Lichtman apparently means that decisions made at trial are "better" because judges will more often decide boundaries so as to reward the more-deserving party. But the genius of a property rights system is that it relies on such judicial discretion as *little* as possible. Clear boundaries permit property holders to earn their own rewards (or not) with little intervention from judicial decision makers or any other centralized authority. Without clear notice, no property system can work well and the result is excessive disputes. It is scant consolation if, in a system with poor notice, judges often reward the more-deserving party in the small percentage of disputes that actually proceed through trial.

Indeed, Duffy (2000) writes, "The quality of an authoritative claim interpretation depends not on its fidelity to some abstract ideal of interpretation, but on its *predictability*." The arguments that improving patent notice will harm inventor incentives or incur excessive social costs might seem plausible in the abstract. Both arguments, however, ignore the practical reality that predictable property rights are needed to avoid incentive-destroying risk; our empirical results underline the magnitude of that risk.

Finally, notice that although these arguments are couched in terms of the doctrine of equivalents, they are really more general.[8] A critic like Lichtman could object to many of the notice-improving reform proposals we will put forth in the next chapter because they might impose excessive costs on patent applicants. Again, our response would be that the benefits from reducing inadvertent infringement are likely to be larger.

PATENT NOTICE OR PATENT QUALITY?

The FTC's 2003 report, "To Promote Innovation: The Proper Balance of Competition and Patent Law and Policy" concluded that "questionable" patents block competition and harm innovation. Based on this conclusion, the FTC proposed, among other things, a post-grant administrative procedure where third parties could challenge the validity of patents. For example, a third party who is aware of some prior art that might invalidate the patent would have an opportunity to present that evidence in a Patent Office hearing. Similar proposals have been advanced by other organizations and post-grant opposition has been featured in proposed legislation. Also, some groups have advocated other methods for weeding out invalid patents, such as providing the Patent Office peer-review information on patent applications, a program the Patent Office has embraced.

We agree that questionable patents are a problem—they are *part* of the patent notice problem—and we look favorably on reforms to reduce their numbers. Reducing the number of such patents would reduce the cost of clearance searches and improve the ability of innovators to determine whether their technology potentially infringes upon others' patents. If efforts to weed out trivial or invalid patents reduce search costs dramatically, then this can have a very positive effect on patent notice.

Patent invalidity, however, is only one part of the broader problem of patent notice. A narrow focus on validity might derail other critical reforms to improve notice. Moreover, without changes in other aspects of patent notice, efforts to improve patent quality through post-grant opposition and the like would be of dubious efficacy. This is because determination of the relevant prior art *depends* on how the claims are defined. If the claims have uncertain boundaries (or if the appeals court will interpret the boundaries in unpredictable ways), then efforts to improve patent examination will not be effective at improving patent quality.

Consider, for example, the E-Data patent we discussed in chapter 1. The invention in this patent was for a kiosk for producing music tapes and other digital products, but the patent's owner interpreted the patent to cover most digital e-commerce. Some people (Aharonian 2000) argue that there is prior art that makes this patent invalid: videotex and online bulletin boards were used to sell downloadable software over networks well before this patent was filed in 1983. These technologies were clear examples of digital e-commerce. Would a more diligent patent examiner or an opposition proceeding or peer review have brought this evidence to light and prevented this patent from being issued? We doubt it. Prior to the Federal Circuit's initial ruling in 2000, just about everybody involved except the patent owner thought that this patent only concerned sales at retail locations or vending machines. None of these parties would have seen this evidence as relevant to the claims in the E-Data patent, given the way the patent examiner and others interpreted the claims. Until patents have clear, easily determined, predictably interpreted boundaries, improvements in patent quality can only have a limited effect.

Some careful economic analyses (Graham and Harhoff 2006; Hall and Harhoff 2004) suggest a European-style post-grant opposition procedure could weed out many invalid American patents and raise social welfare. We believe this argument is correct; however, we suspect that the effect on costly litigation might be limited. As noted above, most patent litigation that proceeds to adjudication does not concern patent validity challenges.[9] Moreover, we saw that the most litigious technology areas do not have higher rates of patent invalidation. Conversely, the European experience suggests that opposition proceedings are not a simple substitute for litigation. Opposition rates for EPO patents are three times higher for chemical patents than they are for semiconductor/software patents (Graham et al. 2002), just the reverse of litigation rates. Moreover, opposition rates declined sharply over the 1990s, just as litigation rates exploded in the United States.

In a nutshell, our enthusiasm for oppositions is tempered by recognition that poor patent notice limits the effectiveness of an opposition proceeding. When patents offer poor notice, few firms will have an incentive to analyze patents and oppose weak patents as a strategy for clearing a path to the market. Perhaps, firms will oppose patents that are asserted against them, but even then, notice problems will discourage opposition. Many patents are weak not because they are invalid, but because the patent owner stretches the scope too far. A potential infringer might see little to gain by appearing at an opposition hearing when its best defense is not invalidity but noninfringement. Furthermore, oppositions might be quite expensive if it is necessary to replicate the claim-construction process that occurs in a regular patent trial—claim construction is necessary before validity can be determined. And it is easy to envision most of the problems that district courts have with claim construction recurring at oppositions. Anyone familiar with the cost of interference proceedings conducted by the Patent Office would not rest easy with the assumption that U.S. oppositions could be relatively as inexpensive as their European counterparts.

Consider, by way of contrast to the situation with the E-Data patent, the likely effectiveness of an opposition involving a pharmaceutical patent of questionable validity. Anecdotal evidence suggests that certain generic drug companies already pursue a strategy of testing the validity of patents on commercially significant drugs. If a U.S. opposition procedure were introduced,[10] a generic drug maker planning to make a drug that is bioequivalent to the patented drug would have clear notice of the patent rights. Similarly, the panel hearing the opposition would generally have little doubt about the scope of the relevant claim.[11] Many of the problems discussed above would be avoided. The drug company would have a strong incentive to bring forward its evidence of invalidity via opposition instead of at a patent trial as long as the opposition was relatively cheap and effective.

We suspect that much of the focus on patent validity has arisen because it is relatively easy to demonstrate examples of patented inventions that lack novelty or seem obvious. Indeed, anecdotes about silly patents have been a staple of press coverage of patent issues. Abundant evidence of questionable patents does not, however, necessarily mean that these constitute the main reason the patent system performs poorly today ("the drunk-looking-for-his-keys-under-the-lamppost" fallacy). MacLeod (1988) reminds us that trivial, worthless, and fanciful patents have been around for at least two centuries. So, although we favor a post-grant opposition system, we think much more is needed in the way of reform. And this will not be easy.

NOTICE AND INSTITUTIONAL REFORM

Since the patent system provided positive incentives as recently as the 1980s, it might seem straightforward to restore incentives by reversing a few legal precedents or by correcting a few deficiencies in the law. Indeed, many patent-reform proposals are directed at technical features of the law, such as the way infringement damages are calculated for complex products or products that are shipped overseas. We suspect that many of these changes would be beneficial; however, we doubt that these changes, by themselves, will be effective at restoring positive net incentives to the patent system. We take this position because we think that effective reform requires fundamental change in the structure and functioning of the key institutions of the patent system.

Reform requires basic institutional changes in the Patent Office and in the courts. As we saw in chapter 3, patent institutions fail to perform some of the fundamental functions needed for an effective property system. Clear notice requires that boundaries can be determined and verified early in the technology-development cycle. In practice, this means that the Patent Office needs to play a role similar to the role played by surveyors and registries in determining land boundaries. Patent examiners need to record the interpretation of claims that they use to decide patent validity and courts need to defer to these interpretations unless they are in clear error. In addition, both courts and third parties need to be able to obtain expert opinions on whether technologies fall within the claims, as interpreted by the patent examiners. Thus, the Patent Office needs to play a fundamentally different role in order for reforms to be effective. In the next chapter we sketch out some notice-improving Patent Office reforms.

Some readers might rightly question the wisdom of reforms that place greater responsibility in the hands of the Patent Office. Many see the Patent Office as a dysfunctional institution that contributes significantly to the poor state of the patent system.[12] But critics have faulted the Patent Office for issuing patents on inventions that are obvious or lack novelty or are not enabled; the agency, it should be noted, has not been criticized for doing a bad job of interpreting patent claims. We agree with Duffy (2000), who argues that on the whole the Patent Office handles this task effectively.

Duffy proposes "the use of administrative opinions [from the Patent Office] to assist federal courts in claim interpretation."[13] He observes that this sort of practice is common in other areas of administrative law.[14] Some measure of deference to the Patent Office makes sense because examiners are likely to be just the sort of technical specialists who are the intended audience for patent claims; judges are not, and they would likely benefit from some assistance from the Patent Office. We think it is not surprising that the patent courts in Japan, Germany, and the United Kingdom all rely to some extent on their respective patent offices for help in claim interpretation.

Their experience provides some hope that the function of the Patent Office and its role in the litigation process can be changed. But there are also clear obstacles to institutional reform. One is a view, held by some (see, for example, the view of the Federal Circuit in *In re Zurko*), that the operation of the Patent Office is "exceptional" and the management practices of other administrative agencies are not relevant. Interest groups who are relatively content with the current patent system, such as patent lawyers and the pharmaceutical industry, might also resist reform.[15]

Institutional reform must target the courts as well as the Patent Office. We fear the structure of the patent courts has actually contributed to the deterioration of patent notice. In particular, the courts have not responded well to notice problems posed by new technologies. The Court of Appeals for the Federal Circuit is a major source of the growing patent notice problem. In 1982 this court was established in an institutional experiment: patent appeals would be heard by this single court, an arrangement that is unique among all areas of the law (Dreyfuss 1989). Part of the rationale for this experiment was that it would increase the predictability of patent law by making its application more uniform. Several years earlier, in 1975, a congressional commission, the Hruska Commission, reported that patent law was applied differently in different circuits. This conclusion was based on a survey of patent lawyers who noted a tendency toward "forum shopping"—plaintiffs would seek to file in a court in a circuit with a pro-patent reputation; defendants would seek to transfer the trial to an anti-patent court. According to the Hruska Commission, this lack of uniformity made patent enforcement unpredictable and a centralized appellate court would increase uniformity and predictability.

Forum shopping persists despite the creation of the Federal Circuit (Moore 2001), though Atkinson, Marco, and Turner (2006) show that the practice declined in the late 1970s, perhaps in anticipation of the creation of the Federal Circuit (see also Quillen [1993]). But a decline in forum shopping does not mean much if the parties shop less because they will face equally uncertain patent law in every possible forum. The important question is whether the Federal Circuit made patent law more predictable. Certainly, claim interpretation has not been predictable (Wagner and Petherbridge 2004) and its predictability appears to be declining still—as we noted in chapter 3, the rate at which the Federal Circuit reverses district court claim construction is rising (Moore 2005).

One explanation attributes this failure to a particular weakness of a centralized appellate court, which, unchecked by competition from other circuits, might, it is held, tend to make decisions that expand its influence by widening its own discretion. This appears to be true of the development of claim interpretation law, where, on appeal, the Federal Circuit discards the factfinding and expertise of the Patent Office and district courts in favor of a fresh interpretation based largely on its reading of the patent document. Such a new interpretation, coming on appeal after trial, surely increases the unpredictability of patent boundaries. This viewpoint was expressed forcefully by Federal Circuit Judge Mayer, joined by Judge

Newman in a dissent in *Phillips v. AWH* (Federal Circuit *en banc*, July 12, 2005):

> This court was created for the purpose of bringing consistency to the patent field. See H.R. Rep. No. 312, 97th Cong., 1st Sess. 20-23 (1981). Instead, we have taken this noble mandate, to reinvigorate the patent and introduce predictability to the field, and focused inappropriate power in this court. In our quest to elevate our importance, we have, however, disregarded our role as an appellate court; the resulting mayhem has seriously undermined the legitimacy of the process, if not the integrity of the institution. In the name of uniformity, *Cybor Corp. v. FAS Technologies, Inc.*, 138 F.3d 1448 (Fed. Cir. 1998) (*en banc*), held that claim construction does not involve subsidiary or underlying questions of fact and that we are, therefore, unbridled by either the expertise or efforts of the district court. What we have wrought, instead, is the substitution of a black box, as it so pejoratively has been said of the jury, with the black hole of this court.

As we have discussed above, greater discretion by the appeals court implies the lower predictability of patent boundaries, leading to poor notice and a greater risk of litigation.

These difficulties are compounded by the emergence of new technologies that pose particular problems for patent notice. As we noted in chapter 3, the flood of early-stage patents (partly the result of the Bayh-Dole Act, which encourages universities to patent early-stage technologies) makes it more difficult to define clear boundaries with regard to later-developed technologies, especially in biotechnology. And as we discussed in the previous chapter, abstract claims in software patents might be especially difficult to translate into well-defined property boundaries.

Patent law needs to adapt to these new technologies, yet, as several legal scholars have emphasized, a single centralized appeals court might be a poor institutional arrangement to develop new law (Duffy and Nard 2006; Rai 2003). In other areas of law, where there are multiple appellate courts, different courts adopt different policy innovations and there is some degree of competition between them. Each gains experience with different doctrines, allowing the Supreme Court (or the appellate courts themselves) to select the best approach based on this experience. In addition, as Scherer (2006) points out, the Hruska Commission warned against the creation of a single appeals court, concerned that it would become subject to "tunnel vision," lacking the insights to be gained from exposure to a wide variety of fields.

The process of developing new law is more difficult with a single appellate court. Although different judges on the Federal Circuit sometimes have very different views on newly developed doctrines,[16] it has been difficult for the court to resolve these differences. For example, the Federal Circuit attempted to settle differences on claim construction in an *en banc* hearing (meaning that all twelve judges participated in the hearing) in *Phillips v. AWH Corp.*; however, the scathing dissent by Judges Mayer and Newman in this case quoted above suggests that this attempt failed to achieve harmony.[17] Moreover, lacking distinct, well-developed doctrines evolved by competing courts, the Supreme Court cannot easily intervene (the Supreme Court declined the opportunity to hear *Phillips*).

Whatever the reasons, the Federal Circuit has not done a good job of managing the notice problems posed by patents on software and biotechnology inventions. We noted in earlier chapters that the Federal Circuit has relaxed or eliminated doctrines that restrict abstract claims in software, business methods, and other areas (see the previous chapter). Besides opening the gates to a flood of new patents, the court increasingly has allowed abstract patent claims that are inherently uncertain. Further, the Federal Circuit has encouraged patents on early-stage inventions in biotechnology and, at the same time, has produced conflicting decisions on how these patents cover later-developed technology (see chapter 3).

The court's poor response to new technologies suggests that a single, centralized appeals court is not an effective institutional arrangement. This structural deficiency is no doubt exacerbated by the tendency of such institutions to expand their own role and by the expansionist ideology of some judges, who seek to expand patent coverage to "everything under the sun made by man"—a phrase that is popular with the Federal Circuit and appears in *Diamond v. Chakrabarty*, the Supreme Court opinion that extended the reach of the patent system to genetically engineered organisms.[18]

Some readers might be troubled that multiple appellate courts would create different versions of patent law in different circuits and thereby create harmful uncertainty. It is certainly true that appeals courts had different interpretations of patent law before the Federal Circuit was created, but that uncertainty must be weighed against the benefit of better-quality patent law that would likely result from intercircuit competition. A reasonable hope is that patent law would ultimately become more predictable.

Moreover, there is an important difference between notice and certainty of the law. Although uncertainty is not desirable, all else being equal, the legal system can tolerate a certain amount of it, especially if the institutions exist to resolve the uncertainty. Making patent boundaries clearer is of paramount importance. When parties know they have moved onto a (possibly valid) patent right and that they will need to negotiate, they often will reach an agreement that can successfully manage uncertainty about the validity of the patent.

In sum, fundamental institutional deficiencies call for fundamental institutional change. We doubt that subtle tweaks to the provisions of the patent statute can really effect much change without basic institutional reform.

PATENT NOTICE AND SOCIAL WELFARE

We have asserted that if patents perform more like property that it will be good for society. But is that really true? We have kept a narrow focus on the costs and benefits of patents to innovative firms. What, then, about consumers? Have we missed something? We now take a few moments to argue, once again, that reforms that improve patent notice are apt to improve social welfare overall.

Whether consumers benefit from patents is a hard empirical question that we do not attempt to answer in this book. The impact of notice based patent reform on consumers is, perhaps, an easier question. Admittedly, our empirical evidence does not directly address this issue, but on theoretical grounds we *do* think that consumers will benefit from the kinds of reform we support. Consumers benefit from *good* patents that hasten innovations that would otherwise come too late or would not have happened at all in their absence. Consumers suffer from *bad* patents that give market power to firms that are not truly innovative, thus leading to unnecessarily high prices, as also from patents awarded to firms that would have innovated regardless of patents and from patents that claim technologies far beyond what the patentee actually invented.

Reforms that increase claim precision and trim back overly broad claims should benefit consumers by reducing the number of bad patents issued. Consumers are harmed by these reforms only when the reforms misfire and trim back the claims of true innovators who depend on patent-based incentives. Similarly, reforms that stem the patent flood harm consumers only to the extent that they make patent applications too expensive for true innovators. Since our reform proposals reduce or have no effect on the market power of patentees, they pose little danger of greater patent-induced output restrictions.

Perhaps notice-based reforms threaten pioneering inventors. If pioneers tend to produce more abstract inventions, or if clear claims are especially hard to write for pioneering inventions, then our hostility to abstract inventions and imprecise claim language could harm pioneers. Although this is a genuine concern, Meurer and Nard (2005a) show that the Federal Circuit was able to limit the doctrine of equivalents, improve patent notice, and avoid undue harm to pioneer inventors. The key point is that broad claims do not have to be vague claims. Furthermore, the Edison and Sawyer and Man light bulb saga, discussed in chapter 3, shows that a pioneer is not always first in time, and a pioneer can benefit from restrictions on abstract claim language.

A final concern is that our reform proposals will push many inventors into trade-secret protection of their inventions and society will lose the benefit of the patent disclosure. Trade secrecy is likely to grow more important as patents become more expensive, but the harm from lost disclosure is likely to be small. Trade secrecy is simply not feasible for many inventions. Furthermore, the inventors that would shift to trade-secret protection are likely to enjoy a shorter period of exclusivity than they would have had under patent protection. The very fact that they are close to indifferent when deciding between a patent and trade-secret protection indicates the invention is not easy to keep secret. Thus, the social loss from less disclosure is mitigated by the expectation of earlier access.

Table 10.1.
Percentage of Firms Who Read Patents for Given Reasons (Not Mutually Exclusive)

Reason Reads Patents (If Reads Patents)	Percent of Respondents
To check whether an invention may be patented	46%
To check that a product does not infringe an existing patent	44%
To keep track of competitors	27%
To keep abreast of technological developments generally	16%
To get information in response to a specific technological problem	13%
To license in new technology	9%
Other reason	1%

Note: Reasons given are not mutually exclusive.
Source: Oppenheim (1998).

Finally, survey evidence suggests that patents are not a major source for the diffusion of technical information. Only about half of the United States firms surveyed rated patents as an "important" or "very important" source of information (Cohen et al. 2002). Moreover, when firms do read patents, their reason is often not to obtain technical information but information about patents and about competitors' activities. Table 10.1 shows responses from a survey of small British firms (Oppenheim 1998). Only about half the firms read patents at all, and only about one-sixth of the firms read patents in order to obtain technical information. There are, in fact, sound theoretical reasons why patent disclosures might not be a very useful source of technical information (Bessen 2005): if firms *can* keep their valuable inventions secret, they will choose to do so rather than to patent them. They only choose to patent inventions that are likely to be revealed anyway—information that might well be public before the patent is even published.[19]

In any case, those who do learn from patents could benefit from enhanced notice. Today's software patents teach very little because the enablement standard, which is supposed to require patentees to disclose detailed information on how to make and use the invention, is so lax. A stricter enablement standard would especially improve software patent notice and the quality of the technical disclosure of software inventions. Also, the growth of technology licensing and accompanying knowledge transfer made possible by notice reform could more than offset any decline from a shift to trade secrets.

11 Reforms to Improve Notice

In chapter 3 we identified the factors that impair the notice function of patent law. Here we suggest reforms that address these factors. We do not present these ideas as a definite prescription for fixing the patent system in "a few easy steps." Rather, we just want to put forth policy suggestions that might improve notice, since reforms are rarely discussed from this perspective. We are sure reform is needed but it is hard to say how effective any one of these reforms will be or how successful they would be together at fixing the patent system. The kind of data that we find so helpful in diagnosing the problems in the current system are not available to assess the costs and benefits of most reforms. We will simply sketch the main features of possibly desirable reforms, and warn that reformers should be flexible and willing to modify or abandon reforms if it turns out they generate large, unforeseen costs.

The reforms to improve notice fall into three general categories:

- Making patent claims transparent so that innovators can obtain predictable information on boundaries as soon as possible.

- Making the patent claims and their interpretation clear and unambiguous.

- Improving the feasibility of clearance searches.

Some of these reform proposals require congressional action, while others could be implemented by either Congress or the courts—a few can be implemented by the Patent Office acting alone. There is a good chance that reform could come from any of these sources. As of this writing Congress has been more concerned about patent quality than patent notice, but both the Patent Office and the Federal Circuit have taken steps to improve notice. Concerned about its backlog of patent applications, the Patent Office has recently proposed increased disclosure requirements and limits on patent continuations. Many judges on the Federal Circuit have indicated they are eager to improve the notice function of patent law. Lobbyists from IT industries, too, are apt to make Congress more aware of the importance of patent notice. Many readers, however, will see some of these reforms as infeasible in the current political climate. We return to the issue of political feasibility in the next and final chapter, where we argue that the growing costs of the patent system might soon open the door to reforms that are impracticable today.

We think the main goal of reform should be to improve patent notice. This is *not* equivalent to simply improving the clarity, or certainty, of each aspect of patent law. Sometimes policies might increase uncertainty in one area but nevertheless improve notice overall. For example, the requirement that patents should not be obvious is sometimes difficult to interpret. This means that some patents have uncertain validity, leading to notice problems. Nevertheless, because a strong non-obviousness standard would eliminate a great number of trivial patents—ideally many more than the number for which obviousness is uncertain—it might serve to make it easier for innovators to conduct clearance searches. Thus a strong non-obviousness standard might improve notice overall despite being a standard that is less than perfectly clear.

Furthermore, there is more to clear notice than clear legal rules. Poor notice also occurs when innovators are not sure if anyone has a relevant patent and how broadly the observable patents will be construed. In other words, innovators need to know when they are at risk from a patent lawsuit and this involves more than "bright-line" legal rules.

Fuzzy Boundaries

Conscious of boundary problems, the Federal Circuit has struggled to find the best method of interpreting patent claims. The court seeks both predictability and an appropriate reward for inventors—no doubt legal scholars from outside patent law would be bemused by this quest. Interpretive problems are notoriously difficult, and the interpretive problems in patent law seem to be as hard as any in the law generally. We are not so presumptuous as to suggest that we know how to solve the problem of claim interpretation.

Instead, like many critics of the Federal Circuit, we take a step back and suggest that claim interpretation can be improved by reforming the process of generating claims and litigating infringement. Specifically, we recommend that the Federal Circuit defer more to the interpretive tasks performed by the Patent Office and trial courts. Further, we recommend reforms that improve the capacity of the Patent Office and trial courts to generate information relevant to interpretive tasks. Absent reforms at the Patent Office and trial courts it is not so clear that appellate deference is appropriate. Finally, we recommend procedural reforms that give innovators opportunities for early, cost-effective review of patent boundaries.

The case in favor of centralizing claim construction in the hands of the Federal Circuit is based on expertise and uniformity. In chapters 3 and 7 we presented evidence that the court's expertise has not created a predictable regime of claim construction. District courts have trouble implementing the interpretive methods devised by the Federal Circuit. As a result, claim construction is often reversed and for difficult subject matter like software, business methods, and biotechnology, it is often appealed. Even worse, both evidence (Wagner and Petherbridge 2004) and anecdote suggests that Federal Circuit judges cannot agree on interpretive methods, and thus the outcome of claim construction depends too much on the make-up of the panel that hears an appeal.

What would happen if the Federal Circuit routinely deferred to the claim construction selected by trial courts and the Patent Office? Assuming no other changes in patent law or institutions, there is no reason to assume that claim construction would be either more predictable or more appropriate. Indeed, it might deteriorate even further. Nevertheless, such a change would likely improve the performance of the patent system simply because the issue would be resolved more quickly and trial court judges would have an easier time managing patent lawsuits. Optimists believe claim construction would improve because trial court judges better understand the facts developed at trials that are relevant to claim construction, and, arguably, the Patent Office does a better job of claim construction because examiners have technical training in the field of the inventions they examine.

Quite possibly deference alone will not lead to a big improvement. Effective reform requires appellate deference to fact-finders, *and* improved tools to get important information in front of the fact-finders. We have several types of reform in mind that will improve the quality of fact-finding relevant to claim construction.

The first is easy to describe and understand—specialized patent courts. Currently, patent lawsuits can be tried in any federal district court in the United States, and, in fact, patent suits are widely dispersed across districts and judges. Consequently, few district court judges gain much experience handling patent cases. Rai (2003) and others have proposed reforms that channel patent lawsuits to a single, specialized federal trial court. Specialized patent trial courts have been established in the United Kingdom, Japan, Germany, and other countries. Judge Kimberly Moore, recently appointed to the Federal Circuit, testified in Congress (before her appointment hearings) in support of designating one (or more) judge in each district to hear patent cases and draft legislation has been introduced with such provisions. Both Rai and Moore argue that specialization will improve the quality of claim construction. HR 34, sponsored by Congressman Darrell Issa, proposes a pilot program to provide training and additional law clerks to district court judges specializing in patent cases.

Reforms are also needed in the Patent Office to improve the notice qualities of issued claims. Claim meaning, and thus the boundaries of patent based property rights, in the main depend upon the information contained in the documents prepared by the Patent Office: namely, the patent—with its claim language, drawings, and written description—and also the history of the negotiation between the applicant and the examiner (in patent law jargon, this is called the "prosecution history"). Examiners should ask for more information about the meaning of claims and reject vague and abstract claims more aggressively. Simply put, it is time to change the nature of examination. Reform should push the patent system toward the real property system by making patent claims more similar to the boundaries of land.

Under the current system, patent applicants have an incentive to draft vague claim language and examiners have little incentive to object.[1] Applicants value vague language that can be manipulated at trial or during licensing negotiations. Vague language can be read narrowly when necessary to avoid prior art, and broadly when possible to ensnare third-party technology. Applicants can avoid the risk of an unfavorable interpretation of a vague claim because they can write any number of other claims that create other versions of the property right to the same invention. Vague claims create headaches for examiners—they take longer to read, understand, and search, and they are hard to assess for compliance with the enablement requirement.

Instead of resisting vagueness, examiners take their cue from the Patent Office and the Federal Circuit, both of which have all but ignored the claim definiteness requirement in the Patent Act. Claims are considered sufficiently definite unless they are "insolubly ambiguous."[2] Recall from chapter 3 that indefiniteness is rarely sufficient ground for a patent's invalidation. Imagine how examination would change if instead the rule stated, *claims that can be given more than one plausible interpretation are invalid for indefiniteness.* Vigorous examination for ambiguity would force applicants to write clearer claims. When examiners identified ambiguity, the applicant would be forced to amend the claim to eliminate the ambiguity, or disclaim the broader interpretation, or successfully argue that the allegation of ambiguity was mistaken. Complete documentation of negotiations over claim ambiguity would greatly aid subsequent claim interpretation.

In addition, to facilitate genuine examination for vagueness the Patent Office could use default rules to force better claim drafting by inventors who are truly entitled to broad claims.[3] The Patent Office, or the various art units within the Patent Office, could establish glossaries of commonly used claim terms, or specify certain references as authoritative sources of definitions. Applicants would be free to explicitly deviate from default meanings and provide their own definition of a claim term. Deviations from default meanings flag nonstandard claim terms and help both examiners and third parties better judge the scope of a claim. Another interesting default rule requires examiners to parse the language of some representative claims in an application and record their understanding of what the claims mean. Once again, if applicants think this default rule sets too narrow a meaning, they can respond by clarifying their claim. Sidebar11.1, "Claim Charts," illustrates this second default rule in more detail.

Sidebar 11.1. Claim Charts

Petherbridge (2006) favors requiring examiners to create a *claim chart*. Claim charts are commonly used by patent practitioners to parse claim language into limitations (also called "elements"). In a process claim, the limitations typically correspond to the steps of the process. In a device claim, the limitations often correspond to the main components of the device. In some inventions, dividing a claim into limitations is easy, while in others it is difficult. A claim chart includes interpretations and prior art that correspond to each limitation.

Here is a claim chart for a mechanical invention that features components x, y, and z. Assume the examiner has associated these three components with the three limitations in the claim.

Limitation	Interpretation	Prior Art
x	A widget	U.S. Pat. No. 555,555,555
y	A gizmo	Gizmo and Widget Journal
z	A gadget	None

Courts and strangers interested in the scope of this claim can use the claim chart as a checklist. If a possibly infringing technology lacks one of the limitations in the claim chart, then it is not infringing; this is already standard practice in patent law. The innovation proposed by Petherbridge is to require the examiner to present a claim chart. If the courts show adequate deference to the examiner's interpretation of the

(Continued)

(Continued)

claim as revealed by the claim chart, then patent clearance becomes easier and more valuable.

An applicant might disagree with the claim chart. For example, she might argue that the gizmo and gadget are really a single integrated component, and thus that there are really only two limitations in the claim. (Normally, a claim with fewer limitations is broader.) The applicant might disagree with an interpretation, and, for example, argue that *y* should include gizmos and a broad class of equivalent components. Finally, she might disagree about what is relevant prior art or what the prior art discloses. She might persuade the examiner to change his claim chart, appeal decisions made by the examiner based on the claim chart, or change the claim language in question to alter the scope of the claim.

Once the applicant accepts the claim chart, then the public should be able to rely to some extent on the list of limitations, their interpretation, and the implicit admissions by the applicant about safe harbors created by prior art. Such a reform promises to add much clarity to patent boundaries at the date of patent grant, and help provide a valuable factual record for judges who later construe claim language.

Another reform that would address the "fuzzy-boundary" problem is an infringement opinion letter. We envision a new role for the Patent Office in which any party can approach the agency and request its opinion about whether a particular technology infringes upon a U.S. patent. The role of the Patent Office would be similar to the role played by attorneys who currently offer opinion letters addressing this question. The Patent Office opinion letter would provide an advantage over a private opinion letter if it were treated with some deference by the courts.

The British Patent Office has recently taken steps in this direction. They have established a program, aimed at low-cost dispute resolution, that provides nonbinding opinions on infringement or validity for £200. Also, they can perform a nonbinding freedom-to-operate search (a clearance search of all patents for possible infringement) beginning at £1,500.[4] The Japanese Patent Office offers a similar program that generated an average of 13 opinion letters per year from 1989–98 (Duffy 2000).

In the United States, opinion letters are already offered by other federal agencies like the SEC and the IRS, but in those settings there is no property owner with an interest in the substance of the opinion. A patent opinion-letter process should probably include the patent owner as well as the concerned third party;[5] the British procedure involves both parties.

This kind of opinion-letter procedure would, like the post-grant opposition proceeding, be a low-cost alternative to litigation, but it would also serve to reduce the risk of litigation even when none is imminent. As offered in the United Kingdom, these opinion letters cost far less than comparable private opinion letters in the United States. Ideally, users would not fully fund the process, because they probably provide a public good by clarifying the scope of economically important patents, and so they should enjoy some degree of public subsidy. Also, to the extent that the behavior of the Patent Office is shaped by the hand that feeds it, this process would help shift the mindset of the Patent Office away from the notion that their mission is to serve patent applicants to the more enlightened one of serving innovators and the public.

PUBLIC ACCESS TO BOUNDARY INFORMATION

It has become a virtual cliche among policymakers to ever and always emphasize the superiority of transparent government policies. This is certainly true for patents and other property rights. Property rights systems work badly if boundary information is hidden from the public. The U.S. patent system is relatively transparent—for example, patents are published when they issue, and interested parties can examine the published claims and assess the scope of the associated property right. Publication at issue might seem adequate, but earlier publication can improve notice significantly. Indeed, most other nations have mandatory early publication and they do not permit expansive U.S.-style continuations.

Chapter 3 described the socially harmful practice of hiding patent property rights, best illustrated by the Lemelson "submarine" patents. Inventors like Lemelson hide their patent applications hoping that others will independently invent and adopt the same technology. In cases in which the second inventor is locked into the new technology, the patent owner can negotiate a more profitable license than would have been possible if the potential licensee were aware of the patent. Certain patent reforms in the mid-1990s reduced the incentive to prosecute submarine patents, but the practice persists.[6]

The key to the submarine strategy is the ability to hide claim language from potential technology adopters. As was mentioned in chapter 3, Rambus disclosed a patent application to a semiconductor standard-setting organization, but it hid the claims that covered the standard for computer memory devices that was eventually adopted by the organization. It is bad enough that Rambus was allowed to hide these claims, but even worse that they drafted their claims *after* the standard was adopted.[7]

The Federal Circuit has recognized that submarine patents are still a problem and recently crafted the doctrine of prosecution history laches to address submarine patents.[8] This doctrine allows a judge to consider whether an applicant abused the patent prosecution process and refuse to enforce the patents when enforcement would not be appropriate. Lemley and Moore (2004) recognize that the Federal Circuit is working to reduce this problem, but they think bolder steps are required. They suggest several reforms, of which we will mention two. First, there should be some kind of restriction on the process of claim revision.[9] Second, they favor making patent publication mandatory instead of optional. We would take this second reform further by requiring publication of every new or revised claim in every patent. Recently, the Patent Office developed new rules that take steps to limit patent continuations.

POSSESSION AND THE SCOPE OF RIGHTS

Naturally, the act of inventing is at the heart of the patent system. It might also seem natural that the award and scope of a patent based property right should be tied closely to invention. That expectation is not always satisfied. Increasingly, patent law grants property rights that are not closely linked to possession of an invention. Reforms that tighten that link will improve patent notice. We have noted at least two areas where the link between invention and property rights needs to be strengthened. One, largely affecting biotechnology and discussed in chapter 3, concerns doctrines that determine when patents on early-stage inventions can claim later-developed technology; the other deals with abstract inventions, discussed in chapter 9. We will look here at reforms related to abstract inventions.

Chapter 9 explained that abstract inventions like so many related to the software industry are hard to propertize through the patent system. Abstractness often makes it hard for an examiner, a judge, or the public to understand what an inventor possesses. Abstract software inventions are harder to examine because the claim language unavoidably tends to be vague or difficult to distinguish from other technologies. With a Patent Office that errs on the side of granting patents regardless of vague claim language, we find that software patents are litigated more often and present over twice as many claim-construction appeals as the average patent. These problems are even worse for business methods.

Proscribing abstract patents has, however, proven to be a difficult task for the patent system for over two hundred years. Legal doctrines such as enablement (requiring that the patent disclose sufficient information so that a skilled practitioner can make and use all versions of the claimed technology), restrictions on patentable subject matter, and a doctrine that interprets some claim language narrowly ("means-plus-function" claims) have all worked to restrict abstract patents. But these restrictions are often ineffective. Inevitably, any policy to restrict abstract patents amounts to drawing a line between what is patentable and what is not, and, unfortunately, such lines are drawn in the shifting sands of words. This makes their interpretation uncertain and subject to the winds of judicial sentiment, as so often seems to have been the case with software patents.

We thus do not know what it will take to appropriately restrict abstract patents in general or software patents in particular. The empirical evidence makes us quite sure that *some* change is needed; however, we are uncertain what change is best. Singleton (2006) recommends a graduated approach, which we find appealing: more modest reforms can be enacted initially. If these fail to work sufficiently well, then more aggressive reforms can be implemented.

One modest change in the doctrine of enablement would improve the notice qualities of software patents. The Federal Circuit has been criticized for applying a lax enablement standard to software patents (Burk and Lemley 2002; Cohen and Lemley 2001). Several IT firms, including IBM

(Kappos and Strimaitis 2005), have proposed a change in the application of enablement to software patents. Currently, when deciding whether a patent has disclosed broad claims, judges consider whether the underlying technology is "predictable" or not. Life-science technology is considered "unpredictable," so biochemical patents must specifically identify a number of the compounds in a class of biochemicals in order to claim the whole class. On the other hand, software is considered a "predictable" technology. This means that a software patent can claim to cover technologies far beyond what is actually described in the patent. For example, the E-Data patent discussed earlier was interpreted to cover Internet-based transactions occurring in private homes, even though the patent described non-Internet transactions occurring in retail stores and public vending machines. The proposal by the IT industry simply mandates that software should instead be treated as an "unpredictable" technology, limiting claims more closely to the technology that the patent actually discloses.

A more aggressive policy would subject patents involving software to an additional test to see whether they are patentable subject matter or not. A policy of this sort was in effect in the United States during the 1970s and 1980s.[10] The Federal Circuit effectively replaced this test in 1994 with the requirement that a patent just needs to be "useful, concrete, and tangible." This new restriction has little practical significance. Another subject-matter test is employed in Europe; this test generally limits software patents to inventions that make a "technical contribution."[11]

As we noted in chapter 9, these policies, and the even more aggressive policy of eliminating all patents on software, have been controversial. Some, such as Jaffe and Lerner (2004), argue against *any* policy that treats technologies differently. They argue that any attempt to draw lines between technologies will be evaded, making policy unlikely to solve problems with patents in particular technologies, such as software or business-method patents. They also argue that policies that grant special rights to specific industries will encourage excessive lobbying.[12]

Although these concerns are plausible in the abstract, Jaffe and Lerner provide little supporting evidence. The limited available evidence cast doubt on their theory. First, almost *every* restrictive policy of any sort is subject to some degree of avoidance (think taxes); this does not mean that all such policies should be abandoned. Instead, what matters is whether a subject-matter test can be effectively implemented, in the sense that avoidance costs are tolerable compared to the savings in dispute and litigation costs. Jaffe and Lerner (2004) cite evidence of avoidance in one small-scale program to subject business-method patents to extra examination, but even here they do not demonstrate that the program failed to improve examination of business-method patents generally. On the other hand, there does seem to be evidence that the strictures against patenting software and business methods prior to the mid-1990s did, in fact, reduce firms' propensity to patent in these areas (see, for example, Bessen and Hunt [2007]). This occurred despite considerable avoidance in drafting patents; for example, it was common to word software patents as hardware inventions (one instance is U.S. Patent No. 4,931,783, for a "computer controlled display system" that is actually for a software interface). Moreover, the policy of the 1970s and 1980s apparently did not create litigation-causing uncertainty. Returning for the moment to figure 9.2, above, the gap between the litigation rates for software patents and that for other patents seems to have mainly emerged during the 1990s.

Second, this argument is a bit specious because patent law *already* differentiates with regard to technology, although many of these distinctions are in case law, not in the statutes.[13] Burk and Lemley (2003) identify a whole range of technology-specific policies. Above, we noted the technology-specific implementation of the enablement doctrine. Jaffe and Lerner (2004) neglect to explain whether they feel that avoidance causes all of *these* policies to fail, and if not, why.

Finally, public-choice theory does suggest that special privileges (or the opportunity to gain them) can encourage wasteful lobbying. It is hardly clear, however, that policies that *restrict* rights for specific groups generate special-interest lobbying in the same way. Indeed, there is little evidence that the strictures against software and business-method patents before the 1990s encouraged wasteful lobbying. In fact, as we discussed in chapter 9, industry groups were often opposed to software patents in the early going.

In sum, Jaffe and Lerner do not make a persuasive case against technology-specific policy. We recognize that the policies we mention above might be difficult to implement effectively, which is why we suggest beginning with more modest reforms. The evidence suggests, however, that the problems related to abstract inventions in general, and software

and business-method patents in particular, are large and stubborn enough
that patent reform will not likely be successful unless these areas are specifically addressed.

THE PATENT FLOOD

The patent flood disrupts the notice function of the patent system in
many ways. As the number of patents grows, so, too, does the cost of a
search. High search costs discourage patent clearance and lead to more unintended infringement.[14] As the number of patents grows, so, too, do delays at the Patent Office. Delays prolong the time that the final patent
claims are hidden from the public. Furthermore, a heavy workload reduces
the quality of examination; examiners can be worn down by persistent applicants who can avail themselves of unlimited opportunities to revise
their claims and argue their case. Low-quality examination means that invalid patents will be issued, and more troubling to us, vague and overly
broad claims will be allowed.

As noted above, the backlog of pending patents is becoming a crisis for
the Patent Office.[15] Reforms are needed to stem the patent flood. A simple
and effective first step is to increase patent fees. Sharply escalating renewal
fees and claim fees might be especially useful. Renewal fees have the advantage of weeding out deadwood and, as long as initial fees are low, easing liquidity problems faced by small firms. Inventors should be discouraged from
bombarding an examiner and the public with scores of claims that make it
hard to examine the patent or understand the scope of its property rights.
But the most important value of a steep renewal-fee schedule is not so much
that it would eliminate all bad patents—it will not—but that it will reduce
search costs by reducing the number of patents.

Given current institutional arrangements, fees are not likely to be used
as policy instruments to address the patent flood. If higher fees succeed in
reducing patent applications, then that will harm the business interests
of the patent bar. The Patent Office would find it hard to resist pressures
by lawyers to keep the fees low. But if fees were set elsewhere in the executive branch with input from economists, this type of reform could be

extremely effective. Better yet, a quasi-independent agency, similar to the Federal Reserve, should be able to set fees and evaluate overall perform- ance of the patent system, and do so largely free from political pressure.[16] Arguably, innovation policy might be as important to the long-run health of the economy as are interest rates, so a similar institutional arrangement for setting policy might well be warranted.

A complementary policy instrument to renewal fees is the non- obviousness standard. Renewal fees work by weeding out patents that are worth little to their owners. The non-obviousness standard works by bar- ring patent applications that are worth little to society. Intuitively, an ob- vious invention would be invented regardless of whether it was patentable. On this view, patents should be reserved for non-obvious inventions. Many critics of the Federal Circuit believe that today's anemic non-obvi- ousness standard is partly responsible for the patent flood, especially the surge in patents for software and business methods. But some patent lawyers sensibly object that it will be difficult to implement a rigorous non-obviousness standard, perhaps leading to greater uncertainty about patent validity. A heightened standard is also likely to make errors and deny patents to deserving inventions. Certainly, errors will be made. Nev- ertheless, the overall effect of a stronger non-obviousness standard, espe- cially when combined with steeper renewal fees, is likely to be positive. We are optimistic that policymakers can implement these reforms to cut back on the patent flood and improve notice while at the same time mitigating any harm to deserving inventors.

OTHER REFORMS THAT EASE NOTICE PROBLEMS

In addition to directly addressing the causes of notice problems, reform can and should indirectly mitigate the harm that notice failure causes to good-faith infringers. Mitigation might be achieved by sensible and selec- tive application of injunctions, improved calculation of patent damages, and an expanded prior-user defense.

Traditionally, good behavior of an infringer has had little significance in the patent system. Recall from chapter 3 that patent infringement is governed by strict liability rules. This means a defendant's behavior and intent is irrelevant to the determination of infringement. Regardless of how careful a firm is to avoid infringement, and regardless of whether a firm independently invented a technology, it still has to worry about losing a patent suit.

Good behavior by a defendant might play a role at the remedy phase of a trial, but it does not create a safe harbor. Good-faith infringers, like Kodak in the patent case with Polaroid discussed earlier, can still be forced out of a market by an injunction. Kodak did not have to pay enhanced damages or the patent owner's attorneys' fees, but in other cases good-faith infringers have been saddled with both.

It might be desirable to reform patent law by simply excusing good-faith infringers. This suggestion is not as radical as it sounds. Independent creation is a defense under trade-secret and copyright law. The value of this defense to software developers is limited, though, by the specter of patent liability. If firm X makes some software and protects it using copyright and trade-secret law, and later firm Y independently creates the same software, then firm X cannot successfully sue firm Y, because independent creation is a complete defense under trade-secret and copyright law. If firm X has a patent on some aspect of the software, then firm Y is liable for patent infringement, because independent creation is not a defense under patent law.

In 1999 Congress created a limited prior-user defense that applies to business-method patents—many other nations have prior-user defenses.[17] In August 2006, Senators Orrin Hatch and Patrick Leahy proposed legislation that would expand this defense. Hatch testified:

> These prior-user rights are, in reality, a defense to infringement liability for those making or preparing to make commercial use of an invention prior to a patent being issued. Prior to a patent's issuance, such a user often has no way of knowing that he is—or will be—infringing a patent. In some cases, the user has independently invented the subject matter in question, in which case it would be inequitable to subject him or her to infringement liability.

The breadth of any defense for good-faith infringers is an important question. The breadth can be adjusted to respond to concerns about its effect on patent value. A narrow defense would be limited to independent inventors like Lazaridis of RIM, whose dispute involving the BlackBerry personal digital assistant was discussed earlier.[18] A broader defense would also apply to anyone who started using the technology before the patent issued. Vermont (2006) recommends that an independent-invention defense should be available to a party who invented after the patent owner but who did not have notice of the prior invention. In the context of this defense, a patent owner can provide notice by directly communicating to potential infringers, or by publicly disseminating news of the invention.[19]

The downside of permitting an independent-invention defense is that it might undercut incentives in fields where inventors race to obtain patents in order to exclude others from the market. Possibly, the defense would be socially harmful to incentives in the pharmaceutical industry. Consider, for example, the race to patent various recombinant proteins (like recombinant human insulin) in the early days of biotechnology. If we assume that researchers knew they were in a race for a patent, knew with whom they were racing, and believed their research path was relatively sure to succeed but also likely to be quite costly, then changing a winner-take-all race into a race with many potential winners might greatly reduce incentives.

This negative incentive effect is easy to overstate, though, and it might not apply in many industries—indeed, it might not even apply in the pharmaceutical industry.[20] Near-simultaneous invention is evidence that achieving the invention was not so difficult, and weaker patent rights might not have slowed invention significantly (Scotchmer and Maurer 2002; Shapiro 2006; Vermont 2006). Anecdotal evidence suggests that simultaneous invention has occurred throughout modern history (Merton 1961) and occurs often in the computer and electronics industries today. For example, both Kilby and Noyce independently invented the integrated circuit at about the same time and many spreadsheet or desktop publishing features were introduced by different firms nearly simultaneously during the 1980s. These are industries where R&D managers do not consider patent exclusivity a major incentive (Cohen et al. 2002; Levin et al. 1987) and, although they might race to be first to market with a new technology ("first-mover advantage"), they might be less likely to race to obtain patents. We suspect that in many cases of near-simultaneous invention, the research target was not well defined in advance and that innovators were not necessarily racing for a patent, or at the least did not know with whom they were racing. In addition, the low standard of non-obviousness and the unpredictable scope of patent rights together create the false impression of simultaneous invention by researchers who actually pursued and achieved different inventions.

A sensible reform might expand the current prior-user defense to cover all computer and electronics inventions. Firms in these industries rarely battle over the rights to a patent on the same invention. Evidence on simultaneous invention comes from research on patent "interferences." When two inventors achieve near-simultaneous invention, and they both apply for a patent, the resulting dispute is resolved in an interference proceeding at the Patent Office. The interference establishes priority of invention and gives exclusionary rights to the first inventor. The high legal cost and delay associated with patent interferences discourages many inventors from provoking an interference hearing unless the exclusionary value of patents is high.[21] Research on interferences shows that a disproportionately large fraction of interferences involve chemicals, including pharmaceuticals. "The interference rate for chemicals is 1.46 times greater than the average and drugs are interfered at over three times the average. Computers and electrical patents are interfered at only half the average rate" (Cohen and Ishii 2005). This suggests that independent invention is not driven by patent incentives in the computer and electronics industries, but might well be in the chemical and pharmaceutical industries. For this reason, an independent-invention defense might be particularly helpful in the computer and electronics industries.

Reform to protect good-faith infringers can be calibrated in another way. Besides expanding the prior-user defense, reformers can adjust the remedies available for use against good-faith infringers. An easy reform would create a safe harbor that would shield independent inventors from enhanced damages for willfulness. As we discussed in chapter 3, the willfulness doctrine discourages innovators from reading patents, providing a perverse disincentive to patent clearance. Although enhanced damages make sense for outright copyists, we want to encourage independent inventors to read patents. The same safe harbor should also apply to attorney fee-shifting.

Other reform proposals specifically address the problems faced by infringers who make complex products. Recall certain technologies, like software and semiconductors, might incorporate many components, and many of the components, as well as aspects of the product design, might be subject to patents. Hundreds of patents cover 3G cellular technology, the WiFi wireless network standards, recordable DVD media, and radio frequency–identification devices (RFID) (Lemley and Shapiro 2007). As noted earlier, Senators Hatch and Leahy have proposed legislation requiring that damages should be apportioned to the contribution of the patented invention. The House of Representatives passed a bill with such a provision in 2007. The goal of this proposal is to counter case law that appears to measure damages based on the revenue generated by the entire product as opposed to the patented feature or component.

Makers of complex products cheered when the Supreme Court recently reversed the Federal Circuit's practice of routinely granting injunctive relief to successful patent owners. The contours of the new patent law approach to injunctions are not yet clear. Independent invention might provide a good reason to disallow an injunction. Alternatively, an injunction against an independent inventor could be delayed (stayed) to provide time to redesign its product to avoid the patent. Ongoing court supervision is helpful in making certain that the defendant's new technology is outside the scope of the claims the court has construed.

Strong remedies are a hallmark of property law. Thus, there is some reason to be concerned about whether weakening injunctive relief will undermine patent value too much. Potent injunctive relief might be especially valuable to small firms facing pirates. The courts should not have too much trouble attending to this concern by granting injunctive relief and enhancing damages against pirates. Calibrating remedies in recognition of the public interests advanced by more worthy defendants is entirely in keeping with U.S. property law. For example, trespassers are treated harshly under property law, but the remedies under nuisance law are calibrated more carefully. When a party that causes a nuisance also creates some social value, courts sometimes refuse to enjoin that party, and sometimes craft a narrow injunction that allows some of the offensive behavior to continue.

The earlier sections of this chapter suggested reforms that address each of the sources of notice failure. The goal of these reforms is to increase the probability that an innovator can see and understand the scope of relevant patent rights. Another goal is to reduce the clutter of rights and make patent clearance cost-effective for all technologies and all industries. In combination these reforms should reduce the risk of inadvertent patent infringement and its associated disincentives. The preceding section examined the behavior of the alleged infringer. Calibrating remedies and providing a defense to innovators who act in good faith can reduce the risk of inadvertent patent infringement and also reduce the expected cost of lawsuits.

Many of the reforms suggested in this chapter have been advanced by other people and we have highlighted them because we think they might improve patent notice. Some of these reforms might also bring other social benefits. We have insights, to be certain, but we must admit that we are not sure how to successfully implement these reforms or whether they are politically feasible. We turn to the politics of patent reform in the next and final chapter of our study.

12 A Glance Forward

In various guises, abstraction has been a recurring theme in this book. First, in keeping with our empirical focus, we stressed the need to distinguish the real operation of the patent system from the abstract ideal of a property rights system. Although patents are similar to rights in tangible property, there are important differences in implementation. Moreover, the realities of neither entirely fit the stylized version of property often found in abstract economic models. Economic models understandably make simplifying assumptions, but the actual operation of property systems might diverge significantly from those assumptions. We have shown, for patents in particular, that the laws and institutions supporting the notice function—laws and institutions that support the ability of third parties to efficiently determine patent boundaries and to clear rights—fall far short of the ideal.

Similarly, economists, lawyers, and policymakers too often view empirical evidence about general property rights as indicative of the performance of the patent system. Property rights have indeed been a powerful engine of economic growth. It does not necessarily follow, however, that just because patents share similarities with other property rights that they will have the same effect. Again, the performance of the patent system, as with all property systems, depends not on the potential benefits of an ideal system in the abstract, but on the details of the regulations, laws, norms, and institutions actually implementing the system. A large body of empirical research shows that patents have, in general, performed differently from other property rights. And we have shown that by the late 1990s, patents failed to provide net positive incentives for public firms generally, notwithstanding important exceptions for chemical patents and for small inventors. For the firms who perform the majority of R&D, patents have failed as a property rights system.

When setting patent policy, judges and other policymakers also sometimes seem to conflate abstract ideals of property with the practical requirements of a property system. The Federal Circuit did this with patent boundaries when it decided claim construction is an abstract question of law rather than a question requiring intensive fact-finding. The appeals court interprets the words in claims anew, discounting previous efforts by the Patent Office and the district courts and placing little weight on industry experts or industry terminology generally. This approach might appear reasonable from a distance, but up close we can see it harms clear, predictable, consistent notice of patent boundaries. We repeat Judge Mayer's lament that "[b]ecause claim construction is treated as a matter of law chimerically devoid of underlying factual determinations, there are no 'facts' on the record to prevent parties from presenting claim construction one way in the trial court and in an entirely different way in this court."[1]

Another abstract idea influencing policy is the notion that patents should cover "everything under the sun made by man"—as was feared by legislators during debate prior to the passage of the Patent Act—which judges have expansively interpreted to include software, modified biological organisms, methods of doing business, and even mental associations. Peter Menell (2006) has documented that judges have taken this quote out of context from the legislative history of the patent act. Lawmakers, in fact, never expressed the intent that patent coverage should be expanded without limits. Yet in the abstract, it might seem reasonable to expand patent coverage to every kind of invention, discovery, or new concept—if property rights provide strong economic incentives, then shouldn't these incentives be offered for all types of discoveries?

Real property rights, as opposed to abstract conceptions of property, have limits, however. The messy, practical details of defining boundaries, providing public notice, facilitating clearance, and so forth, place real constraints on where property can be effective. A reasonable property system recognizes such limits. A landowner gets no rights to untapped oil flowing beneath her land nor to migratory ducks who put down on it nor to the airplanes that fly over it. Property rights should be granted only when property owners can manage them efficiently, and only if third parties can effectively cope with them.

The same is true with property rights in inventions. Economics research confirms that the effectiveness of patents varies by type of invention. For example, patents have worked best where boundaries can be staked in verifiable physical characteristics, like small molecules. With many chemical patents, third parties can test alternative substances and unambiguously determine whether they fall within the patent claims or not. In this case, the boundaries are clear, disputes and litigation are relatively infrequent, and the economic benefits of patents are high.[2] On the other hand, patents work poorly when they are highly abstract, claiming technologies that are not known to the patentee or not even developed at the time of application. As was seen in chapter 9 with respect to software, it is sometimes difficult, or even impossible, to distinguish which technologies are covered by abstract patent claims; not surprisingly, software patents have high litigation rates and high costs, as do patents on financial and other business inventions.

And so we return to our theme of abstraction in another guise. As with limitations on other property, the law has long recognized that there are substantive limits on which inventions can be patented, including limitations on abstract patents. Yet implementing this limitation is one of the most intractable problems facing any property rights system for inventions. Since the eighteenth century, patent law has attempted to proscribe abstract patents, but the doctrines used and their application have not always been successful or uncontroversial. It bears repeating that we do not claim to know how to craft the best policy regarding abstract patents. Yet the empirical evidence convinces us that allowing patents on "everything under the sun" while simultaneously encouraging that patenting by relaxing non-obviousness and enablement standards for key technologies constitute a major departure from the policy of the past. And although this departure might sound good in the abstract, its record, like the record regarding claim construction, has been one of failure.

The problem with mistaking abstract conceptions of property for the real thing is that this substitutes rhetoric for reasoned policy, where performance can be measured, evaluated, and adjusted. The result is policy that loses touch with reality. In the worst case, abstract rhetoric about property rights or about the sanctity of the patent statute simply provides cover for special interests.[3] The antidote is empirical evidence, and the evidence we have assembled unequivocally shows an all-too-real patent system far removed from the ideal found in so much of the rhetoric. But the picture we paint is also far removed from what the patent system *could* be.

Some readers might find this gap discouraging. As we have noted, patent policy has long been the domain of those entrenched interests who have the most to gain from patents, including the patent lawyers and the pharmaceutical industry. In the short run, it is not clear that these groups have much, if anything, to gain from improving patent notice. Clearer notice might undermine patent lawyers' abilities to manipulate patents, narrowing scope to avoid invalidating prior art or broadening scope to catch an unsuspecting inadvertent infringer. Of course, the boom in litigation provides a boom in business for lawyers and the growth in the patent bar has outstripped the growth of R&D (Barton 2000). It ought to be remembered, too, that the pharmaceutical industry already has clear notice, so they might be loath to introduce changes that might unintentionally reduce the value of their patents. So in the near term these groups will most likely oppose improved notice.

The stance taken by these powerful lobbies has lead many people to conclude that only very modest reforms are politically feasible—in the near term, this view is undoubtedly correct. Yet things might be changing. In legislative negotiations regarding patent reform during the last three years, representatives beyond the "usual suspects" of the patent bar and pharmaceutical companies have participated, including representatives from computer, software, electronics, Internet, and finance industries. One factor that might have spurred some of this new participation is the role of patents on software and business methods. As we have noted, these patents now account for a disproportionate share of the cost of patent litigation (close to 40 percent) and these are some of the industries most directly and negatively affected by the poor performance of the patent system.

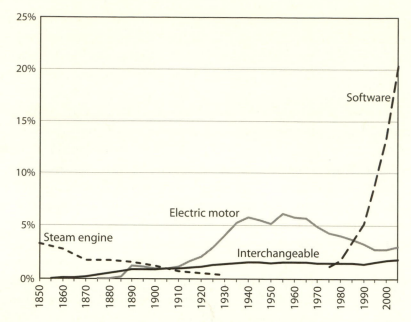

Figure 12.1. Shares of Patents that Use Given General-Purpose Technologies

There are strong indications that this problem is getting worse, not better. First, as we noted in chapter 9, the rate of litigation per patent has been increasing for software patents. Second, the number and breadth of use of software patents is also increasing rapidly.

In fact, a transformation in the use of software in patented technology appears to be occurring remarkably rapidly. The scale of this transformation can be seen by comparing software to other "general-purpose technologies." This term has been loosely applied to software, electric motors, the use of interchangeable parts, and, previously, steam engines. The defining attribute of these technologies is that they can be used in a wide variety of applications. The general-purpose nature of software is indicated by evidence that patents involving software are obtained mostly by firms outside of the software-publishing industry and they involve a large range of complementary technologies. Figure 12.1 shows the shares of patents granted that use various terms designating steam engines, interchangeable parts, electric motors, and software.[4] In comparison with the earlier general-purpose technologies, the use of software in patents appears to be growing much more rapidly and accounting for a much larger share of total patents.

This suggests that, so far as software technology is concerned, we have not yet seen the worst of patent performance. And we suspect that what is true of software patents is also true of business-method patents and other IT patents prone to abstract claiming. Litigation costs might continue to rise for a broad swath of the economy and modest reforms might do little to stem this tide. Our preliminary data from recent years suggest that the litigation crisis is, in fact, worsening. If trends do not change soon and the crisis deepens, then the political participation of people demanding patent reform will broaden beyond the "usual suspects." Reforms that seem politically impossible today will indeed become feasible.

The American public loves inventors, but the public image of the patent system waxes and wanes. In the early 1800s Eli Whitney was frustrated and bitter about the difficulty of enforcing his patent on the cotton gin. In the 1830s the patent system was revamped because of the low quality of patents that could be obtained without examination. In 1859 Abraham Lincoln, an inventor and patent owner, applauded patents for adding the "fuel of interest to the fire of genius." A generation later farmers complained loudly about "patent sharks" who bought up unused patents and used questionable licensing and litigation tactics to extract royalties on farm tools (Hayter 1947). At the end of the nineteenth century the patent system was praised for fostering electrical inventions. In the 1940s–1960s the Supreme Court worried about patent monopolies and was skeptical of a Patent Office that issued patents on obvious inventions.

We think the historical record is clear—the patent system can perform well, and it can perform badly. The legal and institutional details are critical. So is the economic and technological environment. Like other times in American history, we face a challenge today to improve the performance of the patent system. Yet the data in figure 12.1 give us pause. The challenge facing the patent system today might be more difficult and the stakes might be higher than they have been in the past. A unitary patent system simply cannot survive if it works well in some industries, but fails critically in others. If patent institutions prove inflexible, then perhaps we will be left with a patent system for chemicals and pharmaceuticals and little else. In any case, the future of the patent system will depend on getting beyond rhetoric and abstract thinking to build institutions that improve patent notice, even if this comes with realistic limits on what can be patented and how it can be claimed. Then, perhaps, the patent system can deliver on its promise as a property system for inventions.

Notes

Chapter 1
The Argument in Brief

1. BBC News, "Starvation strikes Zimbabwe," May 3, 2002, available online at http://news.bbc.co.uk/1/hi/world/africa/1966365.stm; The Heritage Foundation, Index of Economic Freedom, "Zimbabwe," available online at http://www.heritage.org/index/country.cfm?id=Zimbabwe.

2. E-Data sent out 75,000 letters to website developers offering "amnesty" from lawsuits for a fee.

3. Clifton Leaf and Doris Burke, "The Law of Unintended Consequences," *Fortune* 152, no. 6 (September 19, 2005).

4. Boldrin and Levine (2007)

5. Jaffe and Lerner (2004).

6. Frank Hayes, "Patents Pending," *Computerworld*, May 2, 2005, available online at http://www.computerworld.com/governmenttopics/government/legalissues/story/0,10801,101434,00.html.

7. MacLeod et al. (2003) found that a large portion of nineteenth-century steam engine patents were technically unviable. They go on to quote inventor Richard Roberts: "Our patent list now contains a great number of very silly things, which no man, who had been long in a workshop, would ever think of patenting; and the reason is that the patentee has money, though deficient in experience and mechanical talent; probably he thinks he cuts a figure by being in the patent list."

8. In fact, we suspect that the issues we raise in this book about patent notice are highly relevant to the comparison of patents to other forms of innovation incentives and to many other theoretical inquiries as well.

9. David Streitfeld, "Note: This Headline Is Patented," *Los Angeles Times*, February 8, 2003.

10. Some people argue that a major benefit of patents is that they disseminate information. The limited evidence available makes us skeptical of this claim, and it certainly seems unlikely this benefit could be large enough to justify a patent system that imposes a net tax on innovators.

11. The profit estimates are based on estimates of patent value (chapter 5) multiplied by a rate of return. The estimated profits are the value of the aggregate stock of patents held by public firms multiplied by the annual discount rate (the rate-of-return "hurdle" required to justify an investment compared to alternative investments). We use a discount rate of 15 percent, net of depreciation. We use estimates of the value of United States patents that economists have obtained using well-established techniques based on patent renewal behavior (decisions to pay maintenance fees reveal the actual value patentees place on patents). We also draw on several studies of the stock market value of firms to obtain estimates of their worldwide patent values (investors' valuations of firms reveal the value of firm assets including patents). And we check these estimates against several examples where information about the profits from patents is known. In chapter 6, we use stock market–event studies to estimate the total business cost of litigation. This, too, is an established technique that we have employed on a large scale— some 2,460 filings of lawsuits—to obtain an aggregate cost of litigation for public firms.

12. For this reason, patent infringement risk is not a general cost of doing business, but is specifically related to innovative activity. In fact, the risk of being sued increases with a firm's R&D spending. Of course, some lawsuits are filed against copyists, not inadvertent infringers. In chapter 6 we argue that most costly litigation is associated with inadvertent infringement rather than piracy.

13. Note that some, but not all, of the costs of litigation show up as profits for the firm holding the patent. To the extent that litigation costs represent a transfer to the patent holder—as we shall see, this is not largely the case—our calculation already includes these profits in the profit flow from patents.

14. There is some evidence of a modest increase in the cost per lawsuit during the 1990s. Because we have used conservative assumptions, however, our calculations in figure 1.1 do not factor in this increase.

15. Although the cost of patent litigation to alleged infringers might have increased modestly during the 1990s, we do not have evidence that there was a corresponding increase in the rewards to patentee litigants. In general, we find that what alleged infringers lose from patent litigation does not substantially accrue to patentee litigants.

16. The specific nature of the pharmaceutical industry might also play a role, but inorganic chemicals also have low litigation rates, while biotechnology patents that are not simple chemical entities have high litigation rates.

17. Trolls and their patent suppliers do profit from poor notice, but we doubt that they account for a large share of small inventors.

18. To be sure, the Supreme Court also contributed to this expansion during the early 1980s.

19. Of course, even if the patent system provides positive incentives, some people argue that it should be replaced by alternative incentives for other reasons. See, for instance, Hubbard and Love (2004a, 2004b) on pharmaceutical innovation. See also Wright (1983), Kremer (1998), and Shavell and van Ypersele (2001).

Chapter 2
Why Property Rights Work, How Property Rights Fail

1. Patents and property rights are sometimes described as "natural rights" or "moral rights." Contrary to this perspective, we take a strictly utilitarian view of property. Nevertheless, the practical problems we describe with the current patent system, such as unclear boundaries, pose significant philosophical problems for the natural rights view.

2. Although the popularity of the term "intellectual property" is recent, Adam Mossoff (2001, 2007) uncovers evidence that the rhetoric of property has long been used by judges in patent cases.

3. Many legal scholars argue that patent and copyright law are better thought of as regulatory regimes rather than property rights. We think that both of these metaphors are helpful. In this book, we embrace the property metaphor, but we do not mean to deny that important insights can be developed using the regulation metaphor.

4. Symmetrically, the first inventor also cannot use the second invention unless he gets permission from the owner of the patent on the second invention. Thus, there is a blocking relationship between the two patents—no one has the right to use the second invention. Typically, this impediment to use is overcome through assignment or licensing arrangements.

5. The pattern of exceptions is complicated, and on the whole quite limited. Two leading examples are: (1) the U.S. government can take tangible property or patents if it pays compensation; and (2) patent and property owners might lose the right to exclude if they "sleep on their rights."

6. *Raven Red Ash Coal Co. v. Ball*, 185 Va. 534 (1946); *Edwards v. Lee's Adm'r.*, 265 Ky. 418 (1936); *Laurin v. DeCarolis Constr. Co., Inc.*, 372 Mass. 688 (1977).

7. Copyright law follows tangible property law and allows disgorgement of profit, and patent scholars (Blair and Cotter, 2005) have recommended that patent law should, too. Tangible property is often supported with criminal penalties, as well. Proposed legislation in Europe would introduce criminal penalties for patent infringement. Even though U.S. copyright and trademark law both contain criminal penalties, there is no indication that U.S. patent law will follow suit.

8. The Federal Circuit favored routine use of injunctions in patent cases, but the Supreme Court recently ruled that a district court judge should weigh various policy concerns before granting an injunction, as in other property cases. See *eBay v. MercExchange*, 126 S. Ct. 1837 (2006).

9. In another contemporary example, Emmanuelle Fauchart and Eric von Hippel (2006) report how French chefs use norms to control access to and improvement on their recipes.

10. Similarly, protection against capital expropriation contributed to economic growth and the Industrial Revolution in England (North and Weingast, 1989).

11. This benefit might be offset by a negative effect on bargaining in the shadow of property law. There is a lively debate between those who argue that damages lead to more efficient contracting and use of property; see, for example, Ayres and Talley (1995) and Kaplow and Shavell (1995). The traditional view is that injunctive relief leads to greater efficiency.

12. A classic example comes from the law of leases, which recognizes four types of leases: "the term of years, the periodic tenancy, the tenancy at will, and the tenancy at sufferance." If a landlord attempted to create a lease "that lasted for the duration of [a] war," a court would refuse to respect that novel type of lease, and would either refuse to enforce it, or rewrite it to conform to one of the standard forms of lease (Merrill and Smith, 2000).

13. If fragmentation is less severe, the complementary nature of neighboring fragments causes social harm associated with a complementary product oligopoly. Economists have long recognized that complementary oligopoly leads to prices above the monopoly price, and the associated output restriction grows more severe as the number of fragments grows.

14. He also notes that the Homestead Act prevented consolidation of land grants that were too small to be farmed economically and thus the owners simply abandoned the property (Heller 1999).

15. Rent dissipation arises when an acquisition rule awards property to the first possessor and many parties have an equal chance of acquiring the property.

From a social perspective, the identity of the winner of the race is immaterial, but of course it makes all the difference to the contestants. Well-known social costs flow from socially excessive and duplicative acquisition investments. Government regulation and private ordering sometimes achieve coordination in search and acquisition efforts that avoid these costs. Also, the costs are small if contestants search in distinct parts of the commons, perhaps because of different skills. Finally, search might be underprovided if dry holes are publicly observed and provide socially valuable spillovers.

16. Libecap (1989) states that between 1861 and 1866 leading mines spent 11 percent of their total production costs on litigation.

17. "Tens of millions of dollars were spent in litigation on this issue in the effort to determine the apex and consequent ownership of ore bodies in the Comstock Lode. Millions were saved by a consolidation of Goldfield properties to avoid such battles in the courts" (Glasscock 1935). But in many areas, lode claims were limited by local constraints on subsurface claims to reduce these inefficiencies (Gerard 1998).

Chapter 3
If You Can't Tell the Boundaries, Then It Ain't Property

1. Barrie McKenna, Paul Waldie, and Simon Avery, *Patently Absurd*, [Toronto] *Globe and Mail*, January 28, 2006.

2. Many commentators credit this case with opening eyes in the business world to the growing danger from patents after the creation of the Federal Circuit. For a behind-the-scenes discussion of the case, see Fred Warshofsky, *Patent Wars: The Battle to Own the World's Technology* (New York: John Wiley, 1994), chap. 3.

3. The leading copyright treatise has a chapter on motion pictures that starts with a rights-clearance checklist and contains a variety of forms for standard contracts; see Nimmer and Nimmer (2006) § 25.

4. Campana developed pager inventions in the early 1980s and started working on pagers with text messages around 1985. The trial court judge noted: "It is apparent that RIM developed and conceived its BlackBerry products entirely independent of the Campana patents" (*NTP, Inc. v. Research in Motion, Ltd.*, 270 F. Supp. 2d 751, 755 [D. Va. 2003]). A decade before Campana, Geoff Goodfellow invented wireless e-mail and published the idea on an Arpanet mailing list. Like Campana, his start-up failed. He didn't patent the idea because he thought it was

obvious. RIM identified three other inventors who might have predated Campana. See John Markoff, "In Silicon Valley, a Man Without a Patent," *New York Times*, April 16, 2006.

5. Some of the NTP patent claims have been invalidated during reexamination by the Patent Office. These administrative decisions came too late to benefit RIM, however.

6. The failure of Kodak to negotiate a license from Polaroid might be explained by their divergent beliefs about the scope and validity of the relevant Polaroid patents.

7. *Polaroid Corp. v. Eastman Kodak Co.*, 1990 U.S. Dist. LEXIS 17968 (D. Mass. 1990), at 236.

8. Over the past three years there have been only four lawsuits in California concerning good-faith improvement of land. The disputes involved one party intruding onto another's property and making an investment that delivered value to the other's property. The investments involved tree cutting, a road, crops, and landscaping. California law defines a good-faith improver as "[a] person who makes an improvement to land in good faith and under the erroneous belief, because of a mistake of law or fact, that he is the owner of the land" (Code Civ. Proc., § 871.1.).

9. Richard S. Betterley, The Betterly Report (2006), available online at http://www.betterley.com/adobe/ipims_06_nt.pdf.

10. Melynda Dovel Wilcox, "Cut Your Title Insurance Costs," December 2005, available online at http://www.kiplinger.com/personalfinance/basics/managing/insurance/title.html. In other states the cost might be as high as $1,500. The $450 figure, at the low end of the range, is probably the best measure of the social costs of the land title system. There are complaints and recent government investigations of anticompetitive practices in the title insurance industry that drive up premium prices.

11. M. Martin Boyer and Charles M. Nyce, "Market Growth, Barriers to Entry, and Banks as Insurance Referral Agents: Evidence from the Title Insurance Industry," February 2005, available online at http://papers.ssrn.com/sol3/papers.cfm?abstract_id=886505.

12. For example, Chubb provides Reputation Injury and Communications Liability covers costs from copyright and trademark infringement lawsuits; more information is available online at http://www.chubb.com/businesses/cci/chubb1105.pdf.

13. See the IT Compliance Institute's website, available online at http://www .itcinstitute.com/display.aspx?id=160.

14. Obtaining an opinion letter reduces the likelihood that an alleged infringer will be found to have "willfully" infringed (*Knorr-Bremse Systeme Fuer Nutz-fahrzeuge Gmbh v. Dana Corp.*); opinion letters do not, however, accurately predict whether infringement will be found, as in the Kodak case.

15. Kimberly A. Moore, "Markman Eight Years Later: Is Claim Construction More Predictable?" 9 *Lewis & Clark L. Rev.* 231 (2005).

16. Giles Sutherland Rich, "Extent of Protection and Interpretation of Claims-American Perspectives," 21 *Int'l Rev. Indus. Prop. & Copyright L.* 497, 499 (1990).

17. Mark A. Lemley, "Rational Ignorance at the Patent Office," 95 *Nw. U. L. Rev.* 1495 (2001).

18. *White v. Dunbar*, 119 U.S. 47, 52 (U.S. 1886).

19. *United Carbon Co. v. Binney & Smith Co.*, 317 U.S. 228, 236 (1942).

20. *White v. Dunbar*, 119 U.S. 47, 51 (U.S. 1886).

21. 116 S. Ct. 1384 (1996).

22. Wagner and Pethebridge (2004). Both camps are relatively formal, and reject the use of policy considerations during claim construction. In a district court ruling, Circuit Judge Richard Posner, sitting by designation, worried that a broad claim construction of a drug patent that could cover only trace amounts of the claimed compound would be contrary to patent policy. The Federal Circuit reversed, stating that claim construction is not a policy-driven inquiry, but rather a contextual interpretation of language. *SmithKline Beecham Corp. v. Apotex Corp.*, 365 F.3d 1306 (Fed. Cir. 2004).

23. Judge Mayer, dissenting, *Lava Trading, Inc. v. Sonic Trading Management, LLC, et al.*, x F.3d x (Fed. Cir. 2006).

24. Burk and Lemley (2005) suggest that a great deal of scholarship about the textual interpretation of contracts points to the futility of relying too heavily on intrinsic evidence. Interpreting words can be difficult. They report that recent Federal Circuit cases have had to decide plausible disagreements over the meanings of the words "a," "or," "to," "on," "about," "including," and "through."

25. After a round of appeals, the case was sent back to the district court, where it was dropped or settled. The Supreme Court asked the lower courts to consider whether a doctrine called "prosecution history estoppel" should have prevented Hilton Davis from using the doctrine of equivalents. Prosecution history estoppel is one of several methods that courts use to screen cases and limit use of the doctrine

of equivalents. For more information about the doctrine of equivalents, see Meurer and Nard (2005a).

26. Courts resolve questions about the doctrine of equivalents about 55 percent as often as they resolve questions of literal direct infringement. More information is available online at www.patstats.org.

27. *Warner-Jenkinson v. Hilton-Davis*, 520 U.S. 17, 29 (1997).

28. The strategic benefits of hidden claim drafting probably explain why the average prosecution time of litigated patents is much longer than patents that are not litigated (Allison, Lemley, Moore, and Trunkey 2004).

29. The FTC recently ruled that Rambus violated antitrust law. That ruling is now on appeal.

30. That is, the time from initial application to patent issuance (Lemley and Moore 2004).

31. The rule of capture applies to oil and natural gas discoveries. A landowner owns the oil brought up from his wells, but the oil field itself is not owned, nor does the landowner have any definite claim on future oil withdrawals. Static physical boundaries do not work here because the underground structure of the oil field is not usually fully known until the field has been well developed. For example, if two wells that are twenty miles apart both strike oil, it might not be clear whether they are tapping the same underground reserve or not. Giving ownership of the entire field to one well-owner will cause costly disputes. Moreover, such a rule would inefficiently penalize the other well-owner if the fields are, indeed, separate. This would effectively discourage prospecting. Instead, the rule of capture works to reduce costly disputes and unearned ownership.

32. Some recent decisions have also read a "written description" requirement of possession into this paragraph, as well.

33. The Supreme Court noted other carbon filament, incandescent lamp inventions "by Greener and Staite in 1846, by Roberts in 1852, by Konn in 1872, by Kosloff in 1875, and by others."

34. In patent law jargon, the broad claim was not enabled. Of course, the current statute was not in effect at that time; however, a similar common law possession requirement existed. A modern counterpart can be found in *Amgen, Inc. v. Chugai Pharmaceutical Co.*, 927 F.2d 1200 (Fed. Cir. 1991). Amgen invented a recombinant version of EPO, a human protein that stimulates red blood cell production, used to treat anemia. Chugai was the licensee of a different patent on purified natural EPO. Amgen claimed any functional analog of the recombinant

EPO that it actually made. This claim was broad enough to cover Chugai's EPO. After five years of experimentation Amgen was unable to identify which analogs had the desired properties. The claim was invalidated because of excessive breadth.

35. *Amgen Inc. v. Hoechst Marion Roussel*, 314 F.3d 1313. For more information, see Feldman (2005).

36. In *Brenner v. Manson*, 383 U.S. 519 (1966), the Supreme Court held that "a patent is not a hunting license" and early-stage results that did not yet demonstrate a practical, useful application were not patentable. But in *In re Brana*, 51 F.3d 1560 (1995), the Federal Circuit held that the burden of proving a lack of useful application fell on the Patent Office; the court determined that a drug compound with promising test results against tumors in mice had sufficient evidence of practical utility. The Federal Circuit appears to be heading back into compliance with *Brenner*. In *In re Fisher*, (421 F.3d 1365 [Fed. Cir. 2005]), the court ruled that a gene fragment patent failed to meet the utility requirement.

37. Judges have recently developed new doctrines for interpreting the enablement and written description requirements found in Section 112; see, for example, Regents of *Univ. of Cal. v. Eli Lilly & Co.* , 119 F.3d 1559, and Plant *Genetic Sys. N.V. v. DeKalb Genetics Corp.*, 315 F.3d 1335, but these legal innovations have been controversial, even among the various judges of the Federal Circuit. See Judge William Bryson's concurrence in *Chiron Corp. v. Genentech, Inc.* , 363 F.3d 1261, and Judge Randall Rader's dissent in *LizardTech, Inc. v. Earth Res. Mapping, Inc.*, 433 F.3d 1376. Consequently, these doctrines have not been uniformly applied, possibly leading to increased uncertainty about patent boundaries.

38. Statement of Paul Misener before the Subcommittee on Courts, the Internet, and Intellectual Property, Committee on the Judiciary, United States House of Representatives, June 15, 2006.

39. The semiconductor and communication industries also face remarkable clearance problems. In 2002, Intel Vice President and Assistant General Counsel Peter Detkin claimed that there were about 90,000 CPU patents held by over 10,000 parties, and 420,000 semi/system patents held by over 40,000 parties. Also, the organization developing a standard for the third generation of wireless telephones, issued a call for disclosure of relevant patents and offers of licensing terms. In reply, they received notice of 7,600 patents and a combined royalty request equaling 125 percent of sales revenue (Lemley and Shapiro 2007).

40. Unless the firm intends to pirate the patented technology.

41. Henry and Turner (2005) studied reported patent opinions from 1953–2002. They selected opinions containing substantive holdings and placed them into three categories: invalid, valid and not infringed, and valid and infringed. The 27 percent figure is the fraction of substantive holdings that resulted in invalidity. The fraction in the pre–Federal Circuit era was 55 percent.

42. When different firms own patents that are complements, noncooperative pricing drives total license fees above the price that a monopolist would charge. Real estate developers are familiar with another bargaining problem created by the need to acquire a large number of property rights—the hold-up problem. If several specific parcels of land must be acquired before a development project is feasible, then a developer would worry that one of the landowners might hold out and refuse to sell her land unless she were to receive a substantial premium over the market price for the land. Additionally, when landowners first challenged plane flights over their land as trespass, the courts refused to enforce the traditional scope of property rights that extend out to space. The scope of property was sensibly limited to avoid the great social cost that would have arisen as airplane owners tried to obtain flyover rights.

43. Ziedonis (2004) studied a sample of 67 semiconductor firms from 1980-1994 and found "that capital-intensive firms patent more than five times as aggressively in response to average levels of fragmentation in markets for technology as firms of average capital-intensity, even controlling for differences in R&D spending and size. Moreover, and extending the earlier findings of Hall and Ziedonis (2001), I find that capital-intensive firms do not patent more intensively (again, controlling for other factors) unless they build on fragmented pools of outside technologies. There is little evidence to suggest that these findings are explained by underlying shifts in technological opportunity, divergent R&D efficiencies, or other unobservable sources of heterogeneity within the sample."

44. *Unique Concepts, Inc. v. Brown*, 939 F.2d 1558 (Fed. Cir. 1991).

Chapter 4
Survey of the Empirical Research: Do Patents Perform Like Property?

1. Mark Schultz, "The Ideological War over Intellectual Property," Tech Central Station, 2005, available online at http://www.techcentralstation.com/050205A.html.

2. "Patent Brochure," available online at http://www.ipo.org/template.cfm?Section=Patent_Brochure&Template=/TaggedPage/TaggedPageDisplay.cfm&TPLID=16&ContentID=7268&requestTimeout=500.

3. We assume that the IPO really means to say that strong patent laws make a *substantial* contribution to United States technological leadership.

4. James Boyle, "Geeks in software patent frenzy," *Financial Times*, June 25, 2005; idem, "More rights are wrong for webcasters," *Financial Times*, September 26, 2005; idem, "Deconstructing stupidity," April 21, 2005; idem, "A natural experiment," *Financial Times*, November 22, 2004.

5. Mark Lemley, "Property, Intellectual Property, and Free Riding," John M. Olin Program in Law and Economics, Working Paper no. 291, 2004.

6. World Intellectual Property Organization (WIPO), "Intellectual Property: A Power Tool for Economic Growth," 37, available online at WIPO's website, http://www.wipo.int/about-wipo/en/dgo/wipo_pub_888/index_wipo_pub_888 .html. This assessment is based, in part, on Keith E. Maskus, *Intellectual Property Rights in the Global Economy* (Washington, D.C.: Institute for International Economics, 2000).

7. This includes the "reward" theory, "prospect" theory, and theories that see major benefit arising from the licensing and sale of technology.

8. Mokyr (1999), 45.

9. Mokyr reviews the literature, concluding that "[t]he exact role of the patent system in Britain's Industrial Revolution is hard to determine."

10. Boldrin and Levine (2005) question whether Watt's patent might have even held up further improvements.

11. The percentage of patents contested grew from 1.5 percent during the late eighteenth century to 2.8 percent during the 1840s (Dutton 1984). The majority of court decisions went against patentees during the early nineteenth century but this trend reversed midcentury (Dutton 1984). Dutton quotes, among others, Charles Babbage, who wrote that patent law creates "factitious privilages of little value," where "the most exalted officers of the State in the position of a legalised banditto . . . stab the inventor through the folds of an Act of Parliament and rifle him in the presence of the Lord Chief Justice of England" (*Quarterly Review* 43, 1830, 333).

12. Dutton (1984) reports 69 inventors with 10 or more patents during the century from 1751 through 1852; there were 192 United States inventors with 10 or more patents during the shorter interval from 1790-1846 (Khan and Sokoloff 1990). Dutton (1984) reports about 19 percent of British patents were reassigned; Khan (2005) reports that the rate of reassignment for U.S. patents was about 80 percent during the 1870s.

13. Nard and Morriss (2005) argue that in 1790, the Americans fashioned a patent system superior to the British system because there were no forces organized to extract rents from the legislation—there was no independent inventors lobby, or any industrial lobby like that employed by today's pharmaceutical industry. Britain had to contend with royal prerogative and favored manufacturers at the start of its patent system.

14. They perform instrumental variable regressions, using instruments such as distance from the equator and the primary language of the country.

15. The index is based on five characteristics of the country's patent law: (1) the extent of patent coverage, including pharmaceuticals and chemicals; (2) whether the country participates in international patent treaties; (3) whether patent law includes compulsory licensing or working requirements that might result in a loss of patent rights; (4) whether patent law has features such as preliminary injunctions that make it easier for patent holders to enforce patents; and (5) patent term. Note that these measures reflect the law on the books, not the actual working of patent institutions.

16. Falvey, Foster, and Greenaway (2006) find a positive relationship between the strength of intellectual property rights and economic growth for wealthy countries and the poorest countries, but not for middle-income countries.

17. Italian firms did obtain more patents in the United States after the reform, but the authors attribute this to a change in the propensity to obtain a patent, not to a greater rate of invention.

18. Lerner (2000, 2002) classifies changes in patent policy as "strengthening" if they include: (1) increases in the subject matter covered by patents, including the initiation of patent coverage of any sort; (2) extensions in the length of the patent term; (3) reductions in patent fees; and (4) elimination of limitations on patent grants, including elimination of requirements that patents must be "worked" (put to commercial use) to avoid revocation or compulsory licensing.

19. See Lemley and Frischmann (2006) for an alternative view.

Chapter 5
What Are U.S. Patents Worth to Their Owners?

1. The entry is for March 3, 2006, and is available online at http://patentlaw .typepad.com/patent/2006/03/does_the_wall_s.html. Crouch goes on to cite another example of patent success, as well.

2. Certain theories of private patent value do not rely on exclusion. We are skeptical about the empirical significance of these theories, but our measures of value should capture these other sources of value, too.

3. There has been some confusion over this point. In personal correspondence with the authors from January 5, 2007, Alfonso Gambardella clarifies that their survey measured "the value of the invention plus the patent premium." This is important because the Patval study for the European Union has estimated that European patents are worth about 3 million euros on average, far higher than the value estimates we report below from other studies. Yet this makes sense because the survey values represent the value of the patented technology, not just the incremental profits earned from having a patent; it is the latter that we seek to measure.

4. There are several reasons survey responses might not provide the measure of patent value we seek. First, inventors might be rather optimistic about the value of their patents. That is, they might say that their patent is worth a lot more than what they would actually be willing to sell it for. This might be particularly true for patents assigned to large companies, where the inventor is not the person who makes the business decisions about the patent. (Gambardella, Harhoff, and Verspagen [2005] obtain some information from business managers tentatively suggesting that inventor-bias is not too severe.) Second, relatively few patents are actually sold in individual transactions (more typically, patents are sold along with other assets in corporate acquisitions) and data on these sales are not readily available. This means that these estimates are largely speculative. None of the survey studies have been able to validate their estimates against actual sales data. Third, and most important, survey respondents generally report the value of the technology, not the specific incremental value of the patent per se. That is, patents are often sold as part of technology-transfer agreements that also involve technical know-how and other complementary assets. These agreements typically have various terms of exclusivity and they might require the seller to exit the relevant market. It is sometimes unclear exactly what survey respondents have in mind when they answer simple survey questions. We suspect that they often think about a technology sale, since that is the most typical transaction involving patents. This is what Gambardella, Harhoff, and Verspagen assume, but this is a different concept than the one we seek to measure.

5. Pakes (1986) and Lanjouw, Pakes, and Putnam (1998) found an initial "learning" period where, for the first few years, patent value increases, after which, on average, it decreases at a constant rate. Nevertheless, care must be taken regarding this assumption because anything that distorts the time pattern of depreciation will affect value estimates. For example, Schankerman (1998) found that the oil shocks of the 1970s affected patent value. Much of this variation can be controlled by using patents from a variety of cohorts.

6. Note that because the value of a patent changes over time, our estimates are for the value at the time the patent was issued. Formally, this is the expected present value of the stream of rents the patent provides net of discounted renewal fees. A 10 percent discount rate is used in the estimates below.

7. Putnam (1996) reports that in 1974, 36 percent of United States patents were also filed in another country (table 3.3 in Putnam). Patents granted in the United States that were also filed abroad were worth $188,000 in 1992 dollars. Putnam also estimates that, in aggregate, domestic patents (estimated for Germany) add about 5 percent to the aggregate value of all international patents held in a country (p. 129). Worldwide rights associated with each United States international patent totalled $609,600 in 1974. Thus, the mean value of all patents should be ($188,355 + .05 × $609,600) × no. of int'l patents/total no. of patents = ($188,355 + .05 × $609,600) × .36 = $78,800. Alternatively, if the domestic-only patents are assumed to be worth $20,000 (the cost of applying for a second patent in an English-speaking country should be less than this), then the mean patent value is about $80,000.

8. The United States economy is about five to six times larger than the major European economies, so one would expect United States patent values to be larger. On the other hand, patentability standards appear to be substantially higher in Europe—the European Patent Office only awards patents to 72.5 percent of the inventions patented in the United States for a matched sample (Jensen, Palangkaraya, and Webster 2005), and some of the national patent offices (for example, Germany's) are believed to apply even stricter standards. A rough, back-of-the-envelope calculation suggests that United States patent values should be about four times larger than patent values in Germany, France, and the United Kingdom (6 × .725 = 4.3).

9. Half the patents have values less than the median patent and half have greater values. The most common patent value, the "mode," is less than the median in a lognormal distribution, about which see sidebar 5.2, "Estimating Patent Value Using Firm Market Value," at the end of this chapter.

10. The reason for this is that unobserved differences in the quality of a firm's R&D are correlated both with firm value and with the number of patents. This is because firms will obtain more patents per R&D dollar when the R&D has been "successful." This "endogeneity" is discussed further by Bessen (2006b).

11. One drawback of the renewal method is that it does not directly measure the values of the most valuable patents, those in the upper tail of the distribution. All

of the most valuable patents are renewed to term, so they are not directly reflected in the expiration data. This means that while estimates of median value using the renewal method are accurate, estimates of the mean could be misleading. This could occur if, for example, highly valuable patents occurred more frequently than would be the case with a strictly lognormal distribution. In Bessen's study (2006b) estimates of patent value based on market value regressions are not substantially larger than estimates based on renewal data, suggesting that the renewal method does not substantially understate patent value.

12. The United States Patent Office classifies patents according to a scheme of approximately four hundred technology classes. These do not correspond to conventional notions of technology nor do they correspond to notions of industry; rather, they are used to guide search for patented prior art. We identified sixty-eight classes that pertained to compositions of matter or molecules (this list is available from the authors). Note that the actual technology a chemical or pharmaceutical firm uses involves much more than just the molecules, including, for instance, processes, manufacturing apparatus, delivery devices, and so forth. But the chemical patents are the ones held to provide value by virtue of their clear, readily enforceable boundaries.

13. We counted the total number of patents listed per lawsuit in the Derwent LitAlert database from 1984 through 2000, obtaining an average for each technology class. We then identified the top quartile as "complex." A few complex classes were also chemical classes, so we excluded these from the estimation procedure.

14. These estimates were made using the market value method (see Bessen 2006b). More detailed breakdowns for the "Other Industry" group produce estimates of lower precision; however, the highest of these, for the instruments industry, is only $395,000, or not much larger than the estimate using pooled data shown in table 5.2.

15. The "large pharmaceutical" category consists of United States public firms whose primary industry is in SIC 2834, who have more than five hundred employees, and who are not identified primarily as manufacturers of generic drugs.

16. Bessen (2006b) found by one estimate that worldwide patent values declined from $373,000 in the 1980s to $353,000 in the 1990s. In another estimate, patent values declined from $482,000 to $300,000.

17. Jaffe and Lerner (2004) show a similar series in their figure 4.3, but only through 1978. Their figure also shows a series of win rates at trial beginning in

1983, but these two series are not comparable because most adjudications do not occur at trial (Kesan and Ball 2006). Our series is consistent over the time period shown. Note also that win rates must be interpreted with care because of a "selection effect": after a pro-patentee change in adjudication, the win rate should initially increase, but could then decline as defendants with weaker cases settle early rather than proceed to adjudication. Nevertheless, it is hard to reconcile a persistent continuing decline in the win rate with a further pro-patentee shift.

18. Bessen and Meurer (2007) looked at a large number of stock market event studies on lawsuit filings and found no significant increase in the wealth of plaintiffs in the 1990s compared to the 1980s.

19. Looking forward, the test of nonobviousness might be more rigorous after the Supreme Court decision in *KSR v. Teleflex*, 127 S. Ct. 1727 (2007).

20. For example, the *Festo* decision is widely held to narrow the patent holder's rights.

21. Lemley (2001), reviewing limited evidence, suggests that current prosecution costs are conservatively about $20,000 per application. This translates to roughly $15,000 in 1992 dollars.

22. They report that 70 percent of corporate assets are intangibles and that computer information and R&D constitute 47 percent of spending on intangibles (47 percent × 70 percent = 33 percent). They also report that the total market value of all United States equities is $15 trillion, so "intellectual property," by their definition, must be $15 trillion × 0.33.

23. The higher number is obtained when chemical and pharmaceutical firms are valued separately, using the worldwide estimates in table 5.3. For large pharmaceutical firms alone, this ratio is about 79 percent. The numbers reported here are based on firm-level data for both patents and R&D for United States data. Several authors (Lanjouw 1998; Pakes 1986; Pakes and Schankerman 1984; Schankerman 1998) estimate similar figures for European patents from the 1970s, but using aggregate-level data. They obtain ratios of (worldwide) patent value to R&D ranging from 4 percent to 35 percent, with a consensus around 10–15 percent. See Bessen (2006b) for a comparison of these different calculations and data sources.

24. This is a typical cost-of-funds rate for large public firms.

25. In 1992 dollars, total income over these eight years for this group of large pharmaceutical firms was $118 billion, total rents were $78 billion, and estimated patent rents were $73 billion.

26. Note that this figure is not in the actual income statement.

27. The category "Licensing/royalty based fees" was $340 million in 2003, and only about 40 percent of this amount was from pure patent licensing (as opposed to technology licensing). Note that this figure is not in the actual income statement. IBM has a large and highly successful licensing program; however, it is not nearly as great as has been hyped (IBM Annual Reports 2000–2003).

28. Because firms cannot adjust capital to its optimal level instantaneously, short-term cyclical fluctuations will cause firm market value to deviate from assets even in a competitive market.

Chapter 6
The Costs of Disputes

1. Note also that RIM had little opportunity to prove the patents invalid prior to litigation. Under current law, the validity of a patent can only be challenged in court by a party that has been sued or threatened with suit. The Patent Office does have a re-examination procedure; this procedure, however, places firms at a disadvantage if subsequent litigation occurs, so many are reluctant to use it.

2. Public firms are the targets of a larger share of lawsuits filed by other public firms (34 percent from 1984 through 2000) than they are targets of lawsuits filed by other types of plaintiffs (21 percent from 1984 through 2000). This is the reverse of what we would expect if litigation were mainly about small firms suing large firms.

3. Nor can this pattern be explained by greater "absorptive capacity" of firms that spend more on R&D. These firms might have greater incentive to adopt external technologies, but, for that reason, they can expect greater monitoring of their products by patent holders. A simple model of infringement monitoring shows that these firms will then be *less* likely to be pirates.

4. Cockburn and Henderson (2003) surveyed IPO members: 71 percent responded that it would be "straightforward to identify infringement of most of our product patents," but 79 percent disagreed with the same statement about their process patents.

5. Moore (2000) has investigated cases of "willful patent infringement" and found that enhanced damages are awarded in only 8 percent of the patent lawsuits that go to trial. We examined a sample of cases where a finding of willful misconduct had been made and we found that about half (30 of 68 = 44 percent) of these were cases where the infringer knowingly copied patented technology. Other reasons for a finding of willful misconduct include failure to adequately investigate infringement when informed by the patent holder, misconduct during the case, and attempts to

conceal misconduct. Of course, lawyers likely muck up the willfulness hearings to some extent, as well.

6. "Perspectives on Patents: Post-Grant Review Procedures and Other Litigation Reforms," testimony before the U.S. Senate Committee on the Judiciary, May 23, 2006.

7. We and other academics have alerted Myhrvold that his claims are inconsistent with the results of academic research and have asked him to clarify how he obtains his numbers. In personal correspondence with the authors of October 25, 2005, he promised to provide a paper detailing his methods; this paper, however, has not yet been made available.

8. The data in figure 6.3 have been adjusted for Derwent's under-reporting (see Bessen and Meurer [2005]). Part of this upward trend arises because each lawsuit involves more patents on average. Even after correcting for this factor, the data show an upward trend. There are other measures that academic researchers have also used to explore litigation rates relative to patents, such as the expected number of lawsuits per patent. In addition, some researchers (Lanjouw and Schankerman 2004; Bessen and Meurer 2005) estimate (projecting into the future) the expected number of lawsuits per patent over the entire patent term. All of these measures show an upward trend.

9. Including the filing of declaratory actions against a party who is asserting a patent.

10. Note that on average firms do *not* recoup their losses on settlement of patent lawsuits. In fact, Haslem (2005) finds that stock values decrease on announcement of a settlement.

11. When multiple defendants are named in a lawsuit, the estimation procedure is different and the results are also different. We find a much smaller mean loss in these cases. This might reflect indemnification agreements between the parties (in many of these cases, a number of retailers are named in addition to a manufacturer) or it might reflect a lower-quality lawsuit (for example, a troll names many alleged infringers in a tactic to arrive at a quicker settlement). For whatever reason, we focus our analysis on those lawsuits where only a single public firm is named as an alleged infringer, even though this might cause our aggregate-loss estimates to be somewhat understated.

12. The larger losses for lawsuits announced in the *Wall Street Journal* might reflect the possibility that suits reported in the *Wall Street Journal* are somehow larger or more important. Or instead, it might reflect that the news of lawsuits that are not

announced in the *Wall Street Journal* leaks out more slowly, so that the complete stock market reaction is not measured within the days of the event study. In that case, our large sample estimates will be too low. The Bessen-Meurer study used an event window of twenty-five days. We also looked for factors associated with announcement in the *Wall Street Journal*, but found that size did not make a difference.

13. These estimates are for the loss in wealth *divided* by Tobin's Q. Among other things, this normalization should correct for the stock market "bubble" of the late 1990s. Uncorrected estimates of loss of wealth are, of course, much larger.

14. These are simply calculated as follows: for each lawsuit, we multiply the common stock value prior to the lawsuit by the appropriate mean relative loss (.0056 or .0208), depending on whether the firm had fewer than five hundred employees or not. We deflate these loss estimates twice: first by the GDP deflator to correct for inflation, second by Tobin's Q (aggregate firm market value divided by the sum of accounting assets and R&D stock) to correct for any stock market disequilibria, such as a market "bubble." These individual losses are then summed for all lawsuits occurring each year.

15. We only show losses in the value of firms' common stocks, ignoring losses in other securities. Our event studies include some lawsuits where the firm studied is actually the patentee rather than the alleged infringer and we miss some lawsuits because we have incorrectly identified the alleged infringer as the patentee. We also did not include a number of lawsuits that failed to meet the technical criteria required for an event study.

16. See, for example, Strandburg (2004) and Bessen (2005).

17. To the extent that firms benefit from lawsuits in which they are neither plaintiff nor defendant, litigation costs might overstate the disincentive. There is no evidence, however, that this occurs in general and there is little theoretical reason to suggest that such benefits would be significant.

18. The former figure is from our sample of public firms; the latter figure is from the NSF survey. These measurements involve slightly different quantities, so they are not directly comparable, but by all reasonable interpretations, United States public firms perform a very large portion of privately financed United States industrial R&D.

19. Litigation costs in table 6.3 are assigned according to the patents at issue in each lawsuit, prorating the costs if patents fell in different classes. The United States profits from patents are based on table 5.3, as above, assuming a 15 percent net profit flow from the stock of patents.

20. Since most other countries have tighter restrictions on software patents, it seems likely that the average value of a worldwide patent might overstate the worldwide value of software patents.

21. For large pharmaceutical firms, profits from patents were even higher, at about 79 percent of R&D.

22. The litigation cost estimates here do not correct for under-reporting. Other researchers have estimated the ratio of patent value to R&D for all industries at around 10–15 percent (Arora, Ceccagnoli, and Cohen, 2003; Lanjouw, Pakes and Putnam 1998). For a variety of reasons, these various estimates are not directly comparable to the ones we have presented. See Bessen (2006b) and Bessen and Meurer (2007) for further discussion.

23. Jaffe has since coauthored a book arguing that the patent system is broken.

Chapter 7
How Important Is the Failure of Patent Notice?

1. This is the cost relative to a firm's stock market value. We also corrected stock market values for the "bubble" by deflating and dividing them by Tobin's Q.

2. We multiply the growth rate of the variable times its associated regression coefficient.

3. After 1996 disputes over claim meaning are relatively transparent. The district court judge interprets the claim, and that interpretation is subject to rigorous review by the Federal Circuit. Before 1996 claim interpretation was often hidden within jury deliberations. Therefore, it is harder to empirically assess the uncertainty of claim interpretation before *Markman*. After *Markman*, it is clear that claim interpretation is highly uncertain.

4. Software patents are selected by the method employed by Bessen and Hunt (2007). Business method patents (which are largely, although not exclusively, software patents) are selected as those in technology class 705 (Data Processing: Financial, Business Practice, Management, or Cost/Price Determination). Biotechnology patents are those in classes 435 (Chemistry: Molecular biology and Microbiology) and 800 (Multicellular Living Organisms and Unmodified Parts Thereof and Related Processes).

5. These probabilities are calculated for patents granted between 1983 and 1999 and use the Derwent LitAlert database of patent lawsuits through the year 2005. These figures have been adjusted both for undercounting (in the LitAlert

database) and for truncation (for the years past 2005) using the methods outlined in Lanjouw and Schankerman (2004). These data differ from Lanjouw and Schankerman's because these litigation rates count all the patents listed in a lawsuit, not just the first patent listed. If the litigation rates are restricted to just the first patents listed, the rates are 1.2 percent, 2.0 percent, and 2.6 percent for chemical, complex, and other patents, respectively.

6. These data come from Polk Wagner's database of all Federal Circuit claim-construction decisions from 1996–2005, available online at www.claimconstruction .com, and we thank him for making this information available.

7. About 60 percent of all trials are appealed and claim construction is often necessary to address other aspects of validity and infringement. There might be a selection effect where the most valuable patents are appealed. If, however, one assumes, for instance, that pharmaceutical patents are highly valuable, their relatively average rate of claim-construction review suggests that the selection effect is not driving these statistics.

8. These data are taken from Allison and Lemley (1998), with some slight violence to the categories. In our row labeled "Complex" we list Allison and Lemley's figure for "Electrical" patents; our row labeled "Other" contains their "General;" our row "Software" contains the combination of their "Computer-related" and "Software" (software alone was too small to be statistically significant).

9. A stronger argument can be made that the law regarding biotechnology patents is unsettled and thus contributes to litigation. In chapter 3 we identified controversies over the "written description" requirement and the claiming of future-developed technologies that add uncertainty to such patents. Biotechnology patents do not account for a substantial share of patent lawsuits, however (about 3 percent in 2002).

10. During the 1990s, the market value return to filing a lawsuit was only 0.09 percent higher than in the 1980s, well below any level of statistical significance.

11. The mean damage award during the 1990s was $11.1 million; it was $14.4 million (in 2000 dollars) from 2000–2006, but given the large variation in damage awards and the small number of cases, this difference is not statistically significant (data from PricewaterhouseCoopers 2006).

12. This view is supported by evidence, provided in Lerner (2006b), concerning the role of independent inventors in litigation over financial patents.

13. There is some evidence of an increase during 1999 and subsequent years; this increase, however, did not increase levels to those of the pre-CAFC era.

Chapter 8
Small Inventors

1. This includes patents not formally assigned at issue; by default, these are owned by the individual inventors.

2. Many of these are design patents. Not counting design patents, he has 928 utility patents, leaving Thomas Edison with a narrow lead. See Maney (2005) for details on other inventors.

3. Before 1995 U.S. patent law granted a patent term of seventeen years that started running at the date a patent was issued. Under current law, the twenty-year patent term is measured from the date of application rather than the date of issuance. This discourages submarine patents.

4. To his credit, Lemelson was honored as an inventor. At a minimum he was a clever futurist, with a talent for predicting the paths taken by many important technologies.

5. University technology transfer and patenting is a broad subject that lies outside the scope of this book. Two excellent studies are by Thursby and Thursby (2003) and Mowery et al. (2004).

6. Gross funds (gross of expenses of technology transfer offices) from patents account for less than 5 percent of university research funding (AUTM).

7. Domestic organizations that are small entities account for 22 percent of the patent citations made by domestic organizations. They also account for 22 percent of the patents in the top 1 percent of patents granted to domestic organizations as ranked by the number of patent citations received. (These statistics are for 1991).

8. Christensen 1997, 13; emphasis in original.

9. Ibid., xv–xvii.

10. Ibid., 147.

11. Arora, Ceccagnoli, and Cohen (2003) also found a large disparity between large and small United States firms. Gustafsson (2005) found a large disparity in patent value between individual and firm patents in Finland. On the other hand, Gambardella, Harhoff, and Verspagen (2005) found that individuals and small firms claim higher patent values than large firms in a survey. This, however, might reflect greater optimism on the part of smaller inventors rather than greater actual value. Hall (2005) found some indirect evidence for complex technology industries that patents might, in recent years, contribute more to firm value for entrant firms than for incumbent firms; however, this data does not necessarily imply that entrants' patents are more valuable (see Bessen [2006b]).

12. Of course, the mean patent value might not reflect the value of break-through inventions. Perhaps small inventors' inventions have a greater variance in value than other inventions, so that there are more high-value inventions relative to the mean. The last column of table 8.1 reports the estimated standard deviation of the log of realized patent value. Given the limitations of patent-renewal analysis, these estimates suggest that, if anything, the patents of corporate small entities actually have smaller variance in value than do the patents of large firms.

13. Mann and Sager (2005) reported that when they use a model that controls for firm duration, patenting has no significant relationship with the number of financing rounds or the total investment that the firm receives.

14. By "successful" patent application, we mean that it resulted in a patent grant by the end of 2002. This sample includes all newly listed firms; that is, it includes some firms that are not start-ups, such as spin-offs. If we restrict the analysis to newly public firms with fewer than five hundred employees, the percentages are very similar. The sample of firms is restricted to those that are matched to the United States PTO list of patent assignees and those for whom there is no match. The matching methodology is described in Bessen and Meurer (2005a).

15. Patents are probably most important to biotechnology start-ups. One indicator of their importance is the crash in biotechnology stocks that followed a joint statement by then-President Bill Clinton and then–British Prime Minister Tony Blair that was indirectly and mildly critical of gene patents. The share value recovered when it became clear that the statement did not signal any change in gene-patent policy.

16. In the business services/software industry, the share was 22 percent from 1995 through 1999 despite a major expansion in software patenting during the late 1990s.

17. Christensen (1997), 210.

18. Software, an industry with many small innovative firms, engages most frequently in trade-secret litigation.

19. Big firms might also have more opportunities to cross-license their patents and benefit from other forms of cooperative behavior because a broad scope of activities implies more chances to reciprocate with potential rivals. Evidence suggests, however, that these benefits are rather limited and pertain mostly to interactions between very close competitors (Bessen and Meurer 2005a).

20. With highly skewed distributions of patent value such as the lognormal distribution, an increase in a lower truncation threshold increases the mean value

of the truncated distribution by more than the increase in the threshold, as long as the threshold is sufficiently large.

21. Om Malik, "Technology's Clearinghouse: Yet2.com," *Forbes*, February 7, 2000.

22. These include: Ocean Tomo Bank, PL-X.com, a patent licensing exchange with former Patent Commissioner Bruce Lehman on its board; the aptly named Yet2.com, launched with backing from Dupont and other large companies; IPEX.net, launched by PricewaterhouseCoopers; VCX, a "virtual component exchange"; and others. These companies would seek, as Yet2.com claims, to make licensing "as easy as selling on eBay."

23. Robert Hunter, "Patent Marketplaces on the Web," *Web Patent News*, October 2000, available online at http://www.webpatent.com/news/news10_00 .htm.

24. The $33.7 billion in intellectual property licensing includes music, Hollywood movies, books, and, yes, a small portion of patent royalties. And IBM's oft-cited billion dollars in patent licensing is actually far less and has been declining since first reported in 1999; we dissected this claim in chapter 5.

25. VCX, which predicted two hundred transactions by the end of 2001, only managed to be involved in seven; see Robert McGarvey, "I Will Survive," *Electronic Business* 28, no. 2 (February 2002). Yet2.com, despite backing from Dupont, Toshiba, and NEC, only concluded four deals by the beginning of 2002. Many of the companies founded to take advantage of the coming patent-licensing boom folded or changed their focus. A few survived, including Yet2.com, which now claims to be the "global leader in intellectual property licensing, acquisition, and consulting"; see "Patent Auctions and Marketplaces: Leveraging Value from Under-employed Technologies," presentation by Tim Bernstein, Ben DuPont, and Jim Malackowski to IP Master Class, Fish and Neave IP Group of Ropes and Gray, January 10, 2006. Yet2.com claims to be growing at 100 percent per year for the last two years, but this appears to be on a base in the low single digits. Yet2.com press releases announced two deals in 2003, five in 2004, and eight in 2005.

26. Akerlof (1970). Lamoreaux and Sokoloff (1997) contend that evidence of a robust market for patents during the nineteenth century suggests that economists might have overemphasized the lemons problem. Lamoreaux and Sokoloff do not distinguish, however, between trade in patents and trade in technology. Trade in patents does not necessarily imply that technology transactions occur efficiently.

27. Arora (1996) also demonstrated that patents can facilitate contracting over tacit knowledge. This mechanism also only works when patent boundaries are well defined.

28. Anand and Khanna (2000) and Gans, Hsu, and Stern (2002) both interpret their results in terms of "stronger" and "weaker" patent rights. As we noted in chapter 5, however, this distinction is a bit ambiguous. The evidence seems most consistent with the interpretation that "stronger" patents are those where enforcement is more certain and vice versa.

Chapter 9
Abstract Patents and Software

1. A similar argument is made by David Kaefer, Microsoft's director of business development for the IP and Licensing group. In a recent interview (Kerner 2005), Kaefer argued that issues surrounding the patentability of intangibles are nothing new and that there was a debate over patents on electrically powered consumer appliances during the 1920s. According to Kaefer, it was argued that "electricity is a force of nature and no company should have control over nature." This seems to be a rather strange reading of history, since electrical devices were patented since the early nineteenth century and some of the most famous nineteenth-century patents were electrical (for example, the telegraph and telephone) and were held to be valid by the Supreme Court.

2. Many companies have changed their positions over time. IBM initially opposed software patents, then supported them enthusiastically during the 1990s; recently it has grown concerned about overly generous protection. In recent years, Microsoft has been a stronger defender of software patents than most IT firms, but even Microsoft supports certain substantive reforms that limit patent protection.

3. Merges's evidence is based on an analysis of the software-publishing industry as a whole. Usually studies of industry concentration and entry examine individual market segments separately. Indeed, Cockburn and MacGarvie (2006), using the same data set, looked at entry into individual market segments and found that patents do have a negative effect on entry rates.

4. And these might adversely affect firms in the software industry. The effect of these patents on software firms, however, is likely not as strong as the effect of a patent thicket within the software industry itself.

5. Bill Gates was among those who raised concerns during the early 1990s about the effects of patents on software innovation (Warshofsky 1994).

6. The source of these data are Derwent's LitAlert database, which is known to report only about two-thirds of the actual patent lawsuits (Bessen and Meurer 2005b; Lanjouw and Schankerman 2004). Following Bessen and Meurer, we correct for under-reporting by dividing the observed litigation rates by 0.64.

7. The first claim of the patent reads,

> 1. A method for reproducing information in material objects utilizing information manufacturing machines located at point of sale locations, comprising the steps of:
>
>> providing from a source remotely located with respect to the information manufacturing machine the information to be reproduced to the information manufacturing machine, each information being uniquely identified by a catalog code;
>>
>> providing a request reproduction code including a catalog code uniquely identifying the information to be reproduced to the information manufacturing machine requesting to reproduce certain information identified by the catalog code in a material object;
>>
>> providing an authorization code at the information manufacturing machine authorizing the reproduction of the information identified by the catalog code included in the request reproduction code; and
>>
>> receiving the request reproduction code and the authorization code at the information manufacturing machine and reproducing in a material object the information identified by the catalog code included in the request reproduction code in response to the authorization code authorizing such reproduction.

8. One relevant claim reads,

> 38. Apparatus for locally processing frames of information received from central videotex suppliers, different frames being encoded in accordance with different protocols, comprising:
>
>> means connected to locally store the information frames,
>> means connected to locally display the frames,
>> means connected to decode the locally stored frames as they are displayed, and

means connected to tag each stored frame with a header indicating one of said different protocols as having been used for encoding the frame,

means connected to decode being arranged to decode each frame in accordance with the protocol indicated by the header on the frame.

This claim is written in "means-plus-function" form but the court considered the term "frames" generally as well as the in the specialized context of a means-plus-function claim.

9. See, for example, Sandra Gittlen, "Netscape enlists help to fight Wang lawsuit," *Network World*, May 4, 1998.

10. One relevant claim reads:

43. A method of scheduling customer access to data from a plurality of data sources, comprising the steps of:

creating at least one customer profile for each eligible recipient of said data, said customer profile including a profile of data previously accessed by said customer;

creating content profiles for each data source of said data, said content profiles reflecting the customer profiles of those customers who have previously accessed said data from each data source;

relating at least one said customer profile with the content profiles for the said data available from each data source to the customer;

determining a subset of data having content profiles which are determined in said relating step to most closely match at least one said customer profile; and

presenting said subset of data to said customer for selection.

11. Another issue in the claim interpretation was whether the preamble to the claims that used the word "scheduling" limited that matching to temporal matching. Patent law has complicated rules for determining whether words in the preamble limit the claims.

12. To be sure, these are integer expressions as opposed to real number expressions, but integer expressions are a subset of real number expressions.

13. In patent law, these determinations start with the judge interpreting the relevant claim and fixing its scope. Then the jury assesses the allegedly infringing

technology to determine whether it falls within the scope of, or is equivalent, to the claimed technologies.

14. "Breakthrough in Problem Solving," *New York Times*, November 19, 1984.

15. *Northern Telecom, Inc. v. Datapoint Corp.*, 908 F.2d 931; *Fonar Corp. v. General Elec., Co.*, 107 F.3d 1543. Ironically, the E-Data patent makes claims that seem surprisingly similar to Morse's eighth claim: instead of printing at a distance, we have the production of digital media in material objects. E-Data adds some additional requirements about exchanging codes, but Morse limits the claim to techniques using electromagnetism.

16. One recent exception is *LizardTech, Inc. v. Earth Res. Mapping, Inc.*, 35 Fed. Appx. 918 (2005).

17. In *State Street Bank & Trust Co. v. Signature Financial Group, Inc.*, the Federal Circuit elaborated that "certain types of mathematical subject matter, standing alone, represent nothing more than abstract ideas until reduced to some type of practical application, i.e., 'a useful, concrete, and tangible result' (*Alappat*, 33 F.3d at 1544, 31 United States PQ 2d, at 1557). Unpatentable mathematical algorithms are identifiable by showing they are merely abstract ideas constituting disembodied concepts or truths that are not 'useful.' From a practical standpoint, this means that to be patentable an algorithm must be applied in a 'useful' way. In *Alappat*, we held that data, transformed by a machine through a series of mathematical calculations to produce a smooth waveform display on a rasterizer monitor, constituted a practical application of an abstract idea (a mathematical algorithm, formula, or calculation), because it produced 'a useful, concrete, and tangible result'—the smooth waveform."

18. In *Benson*, the Court notes that it is considering a subject-matter issue: "The question is whether the method described and claimed is a 'process' within the meaning of the Patent Act." Then the court uses language similar to ours: "Here the 'process' claim is so abstract and sweeping as to cover both known and unknown uses of the BCD to pure binary conversion. The end use might (1) vary from the operation of a train to verification of drivers' licenses to researching the law books for precedents, and (2) be performed through any existing machinery or future-devised machinery or without any apparatus" (*Gottschalk v. Benson*, 409 U.S. 63 [1972])

19. *WMS Gaming Inc. v. Int'l Game Tech.*, 184 F.3d 1339 (Fed. Cir. 1999); *Harris Corp. v. Ericsson, Inc.*, 417 F.3d 1241, 1253 (Fed. Cir. 2005)

20. Some recent exceptions are the LizardTech case, cited above, as well as *DE Technologies v. Dell Inc.*, 428 F. Supp. 2d 512, where the patent was held to be

indefinite, and *Ziarno v. Am. Nat'l Red Cross*, 55 Fed. Appx. 553, which was held to have an inadequate written description.

21. David Streitfeld, "Note: This Headline Is Patented," *Los Angeles Times*, February 8, 2003.

22. Mark Webbink, Red Hat Software, "Software Patents and Reality," presented November 17, 2006 at Boston University School of Law, available online at http://www.researchoninnovation.org/swconf/webbinkslides.pdf.

23. Oren Bar-Gill and Gideon Parchomovsky (2006) present a different argument.

Chapter 10
Making Patents Work as Property

1. The actual cost to the government's revenue was somewhat less because not all credits can be applied to reduce taxes.

2. Another policy instrument discussed by economists, but less frequently used, is prizes. See Wright (1983), Kremer (1998), and Shavell and van Ypersele (2001).

3. Lemley (2001) estimates patent prosecution costs at about $20,000 on average per application (closer to $15,000 in 1992 dollars). In 1991 there were about 1.7 applications for each grant and there were 56,000 patents granted to domestic firms and individuals: $15k \times 1.7 \times 56,000 = $1.4 billion. This includes the patent fees that fund the Patent Office. Patent fees alone were $0.4 billion in 1991 (United States PTO annual report).

4. To the extent that patents might provide incentives to a different group of innovators, however, these programs might be complements rather than substitutes. Consequently, high social cost relative to other programs does not necessarily rule out patents as welfare-enhancing.

5. Another complicating issue is that various policy instruments might "crowd out" other incentives; that is, firms might not increase R&D spending even though they receive positive incentives from an instrument. Instead, they might simply substitute one source of funding for another. Wallsten (2000) found some evidence that SBIR funding crowded out other investment and he attributed this to deficiencies in the SBIR selection mechanism. Goolsbee (1998) found evidence of crowding out from government programs generally, which he attributed to the inelasticity of the supply of scientists and engineers—subsidies served to raise salaries rather than to increase the quantity of R&D. Wilson (2005) found some

evidence of crowding out with the R&D tax credit. Depending on the nature of crowding out, patents might also crowd out R&D investment that would otherwise be made. The dominance of other means for protecting profits on innovation means that relatively smaller forms of incentives, such as subsidies or patents, need to be carefully studied to determine the extent to which they substitute for these other incentives.

6. Chapter 3 explains this doctrine in more detail.

7. Such uncertainty also provides a strong reason for *not* reading patents—their meaning will change depending on how courts interpret them.

8. Empirical evidence from Allison and Lemley (2007) shows that even though patent owners often raise the doctrine of "equivalents," courts have rarely relied on in it in recent years.

9. The low rate of invalidation might be from a selection effect—that is, disputes over invalid patents might settle early. In this case, however, it still means that patent validity is not the main source of *costly* litigation.

10. Challenges by generics often occur late in the life of a patent. Certain reform proposals limit the opportunity for opposition to a timeframe early in the life of the patent.

11. Evidence shows that pharmaceutical patents offer relatively clear notice.

12. The enormous scale and heterogeneity of examination activities creates a challenge for reformers who favor more predictable examination. Cockburn, Kortum, and Stern (2003) found significant variation across examiners in terms of their examination performance. Of particular interest, they found that certain examiners issue patents that are highly cited, but also frequently invalidated. After controlling for many relevant factors, they suggest the best explanation for their finding is that the highly cited patents are too broad. Another study suggests significant variation in the rigor of examination across examiners. Lichtman (2004) found significant variation across examiners in terms of the frequency of amendment of claims.

13. Duffy 2000, 156.

14. For example, Duffy (2000) argues that agency opinions improved judicial resolution of disputes over railroad tariffs. Like patent claims, railroad tariffs sometimes implicated difficult factual questions. Also like patent claims, the tariffs were proposed by private parties and approved by an agency.

15. This raises the question of whether effective patent notice is politically feasible. We address this important issue in chapter 12.

16. See the discussion of claim construction in chapter 3 and the different views on enablement and written description in chapter 3, n. 37.

17. Wagner and Petherbridge (2004) coded the claim-construction methodology used by Federal Circuit judges and found that there are two dominant approaches. One approach relies heavily on the plain language of the claim, while the other approach is more willing to interpret a claim in the context of the written description and the prosecution history. In a recent update to this study, Wagner (2007) found evidence that around the time of *Phillips*, the court temporarily coalesced around the more contextual approach, but, after a brief honeymoon period, disharmony had returned.

18. Menell (2006) points out that this phrase comes from the legislative history of the 1952 patent statute, but that it had no such expansive meaning then.

19. For evidence that inventors behave this way, see Moser (2006).

Chapter 11
Reforms to Improve Notice

1. Risch (2006) has criticized the Patent Office for using the broadest reasonable meaning in examinations because it harms the notice function of patent law.

2. *Xerox Corp. v. 3Com Corp.*, 458 F.3d 1310, 1323 (Fed. Cir. 2006).

3. Here is a quick list of other reforms that could be made by the Patent Office to improve claim construction. First, examiners could insist on greater precision in the written description of the invention. The written description is often used to interpret claims. Second, the Patent Office could require applicants to describe the most relevant prior art (see Miller [2005]); this is already required in Europe. Prior art disclosures help third parties identify safe harbors that the applicant has disclaimed. Third, the Patent Office could require applicants to explain the purpose of claim amendments. These reasons would be recorded in the prosecution history and available to the public.

4. For more information, see the British Patent Office's website at http://www.patent.gov.uk/patent/p-other/p-object/p-object-opinion.htm; see also http://www.patent.gov.uk/patent/p-manage/p-useenforce/p-useenforce-freedom.htm. These fees are far less than typical costs for lawyer's opinion letters.

5. The United Kingdom has initiated an experiment with a watered-down opinion-letter process that looks a lot like mediation.

6. These reforms required publication of certain patent applications after eighteen months, and changed the term of the patent. Under the old regime, the

patent term was seventeen years from the date of issuance; under the new regime, the patent term is twenty years from the date of application.

7. Apologists for Rambus argue that the written description of the invention in the Rambus application discloses the invention and provides adequate notice. Even though the set of claims contained in the disclosed application did not cover the standard, the apologists hold that any good patent attorney would have recognized that the standard falls within the set of technologies disclosed. Finally, they would surely contend that it is perfectly normal for claim language to change over time as the patent prosecutor perfects the claim language and negotiates with the examiner. The flaw in this argument is the assertion that it is a simple matter to predict the scope of property rights that will be awarded to the inventor of an information technology based on the disclosure he makes in his patent application. The low standard of obviousness, the low quality of disclosures, the abstractness of the technology, and the likelihood of related inventions make it very difficult to guess what an inventor thinks he has invented and what the Patent Office might grant him.

8. The Federal Circuit has also used equitable estoppel and the written description doctrine to improve patent notice and limit opportunities to profit from submarine patents and related tactics.

9. On July 10, 2006, the Patent Office proposed a rule change to limit the number of permitted claim revisions. More information is available online at http://www.uspto.gov/web/offices/pac/dapp/opla/presentation/focuspp.html#continuation.

10. The Walter-Freeman-Abele two-part test first asked whether a patent recited an algorithm. If so, it then asked whether the patent would preempt all uses of the algorithm, which would make the claimed invention unpatentable.

11. The European Patent Office generally takes a more liberal approach to software patents than the various national courts. The range of software that should be patentable has been hotly debated in Europe in recent years.

12. Jaffe and Lerner (2004) also argue that "there is no theoretical or empirical basis for saying specifically how patent treatment should differ across specific technologies." There is, in fact, a significant literature outlining both theoretical and empirical arguments for technology-specific policy, including Bessen and Maskin (2007), Burk and Lemley (2002), Cohen and Lemley (2001), and Hunt (2004). See chapter 9 for a discussion of the relevance of these issues for software technology.

13. There is differential statutory treatment for pharmaceuticals, semiconductor masks, surgical methods, business methods, and plant patents, among other things.

14. The perverse effects of the willfulness doctrine (discussed in chapter 3) also discourage patent clearance. Congress has considered reforming this doctrine to remove its disincentive to read patents.

15. In an April 2005 interview, Patent Office director John Dudas said that "without fundamental changes" at the Patent Office the average pendency for data-processing patents could double by 2008 (Molly M. Peterson, interview with John Dudas, April 26, 2005, available online at http://www.govexec.com/dailyfed/ 0405/042605cdam1.htm.

16. This was suggested by Bob Hunt of the Federal Reserve Bank of Philadelphia.

17. This statute is limited to first inventors (who did not patent). Broader prior-user rights are available as a defense against patent infringement in many countries.

18. Of course, the defense would have to extend to their customers, as well.

19. To be clear, this is notice of the invention, *not* the notice of patent-based property rights, the central concern of this book. If we wanted to implement this defense, we would have to think long and hard about how to determine whether notice of an invention was clearly communicated.

20. The "patent race" is prominent in the theoretical economics literature; however, the limited empirical evidence available suggests that it might not be an accurate description of actual behavior even in pharmaceuticals, about which see Cockburn and Henderson (1994).

21. Lemley and Chien (2003) report estimates of the average cost of an interference that range from $100,000 to $500,000. They also report the average pendency of an interference before the Patent Office is 30.5 months.

Chapter 12
A Glance Forward

1. Judge Mayer, dissenting, *Lava Trading, Inc. v. Sonic Trading Management, LLC, et al.*, 445 F.3d 1348 (Fed. Cir. 2006).

2. Even when patents work well as property rights, they might also create significant social costs that are outside the scope of this book.

3. It is perhaps telling that the FTC recommendation that received the most prominent rejection from the Intellectual Property Owners Association, a lobbying group dominated by patent lawyers for large firms, was the rather modest

suggestion to "Expand Consideration of Economic Learning and Competition Policy Concerns in Patent Law Decisionmaking."

4. The general-purpose technologies are cited in David (1990), Hounshell (1984), and Rosenberg and Trajtenberg (2001). The shares reported are the shares of patents using the terms "steam engine," "interchangeable" (for interchangeable parts), "electric motor," and "software" (or "computer program") (the last group also excludes some patents; see Bessen and Hunt [2007]).

References

Acs, Zoltan, and David Audretsch. 1990. *Innovation and Small Firms*. Cambridge, Mass.: The MIT Press.

Adams, John, Daniel Pare, and Puay Tang. 2001. "Patent Protection of Computer Programmes." European Commission, Directorate-General Enterprises.

Agrawal, Ajay, and Rebecca Henderson. 2002. "Putting Patents in Context: Exploring Knowledge Transfer from MIT." *Management Science*, 48(1): 44–60.

Aghion, Philippe, Nick Bloom, Richard Blundell, Rachel Griffith, and Peter Howitt. 2005. "Competition and Innovation: An Inverted-U Relationship." *Quarterly Journal of Economics* 120(2): 701–28.

Aharonian, Gregory. 2000. "E-data wins appeal, but exaggerates importance; EPC/EPO voting," PATNEWS, November 15, 2000.

Akerlof, George A. 1970. "The Market for 'Lemons': Quality Uncertainty and the Market Mechanism." *Quarterly Journal of Economics* 84(3): 488–500.

Allison, John R., and Mark Lemley. 1998. "Empirical Evidence on the Validity of Litigated Patents." *AIPLA Quarterly Journal* 6: 185–277.

———. 2002. "The Growing Complexity of the United States Patent System." *Boston University Law Review* 82(1): 77–144.

———. 2007. "The Unnoticed Demise of the Doctrine of Equivalents." *Stanford Law Review* 59: 955–84.

Allison, John R., Mark Lemley, Kimberly A. Moore, and Derek Trunkey. 2004. "Valuable Patents." *Georgetown Law Journal* 92(3): 435–79.

Allison, John R., and Emerson H. Tiller. 2003. "The Business Method Patent Myth." *Berkeley Technology Law Journal* 18(4): 987–1084.

American Intellectual Property Law Association (AIPLA). 2005. *Report of the Economic Survey*. Washington, D.C.: Fetzer-Kraus.

———. 2006. "Comments on Proposed Rules: "Changes to Practice for Continuing Applications, Requests for Continued Examination Practice, and Applications Containing Patentably Indistinct Claims.' " April 24, 2006, available online at http://www.aipla.org/Template.cfm?template=/ContentManagement/ContentDisplay.cfm&ContentID=11276.

Anand, Bharat N., and Tarun Khanna. 2000. "The Structure of Licensing Contracts." *Journal of Industrial Economics* 48(1): 103–35.

Anton, James J., and Dennis A. Yao. 1994. "Expropriation and Inventions: Appropriable Rents in the Absence of Property Rights." *American Economic Review* 84(1): 190–209.

————. 2002. "The Sale of Ideas: Strategic Disclosure, Property Rights, and Contracting." *Review of Economic Studies* 69(3): 513–31.

Armstrong, Jeff S., Michael R. Darby, and Lynne G. Zucker. 1998a. "Geographically Localized Knowledge: Spillovers or Markets?" *Economic Inquiry* 36(1): 65–86.

————. 2001. "Commercializing Knowledge: University Science, Knowledge Capture, and Firm Performance in Biotechnology." NBER Working Paper No. 8499.

Arora, Ashish. 1995. "Licensing Tacit Knowledge: Intellectual Property Rights and the Market for Know-How." *Economics of Innovation and New Technology* 4: 41–59.

————. 1996. "Contracting for Tacit Knowledge: The Provision of Technical Services in Technology Licensing Contracts." *Journal of Development Economics* 50(2): 233–56.

Arora, Ashish, Marco Ceccagnoli, and Wesley M. Cohen. 2003. "R&D and the Patent Premium." NBER Working Paper No. 9431.

Arora, Ashish, Wesley Cohen, and John Walsh. 2003. "Research Tool Patent and Licensing and Biomedical Innovation." In Wesley Cohen and Stephen A. Merrill, eds., *Patents in the Knowledge-Based Economy*. Washington, D.C.: National Academies Press.

Arora, Ashish, Andrea Fosfuri, and Alfonso Gambardella. 2001. *Markets for Technology: The Economics of Innovation and Corporate Strategy*. Cambridge, Mass.: The MIT Press.

Arora, Ashish, and Robert Merges. 2004. "Specialized Supply Firms, Property Rights, and Firm Boundaries." *Industrial and Corporate Change* 3(13): 451–75.

Arrow, Kenneth. 1962. "Economic Welfare and the Allocation of Resources for Invention." In Richard R. Nelson, ed., *The Rate and Direction of Inventive Activity: Economic and Social Factors*. Princeton: Princeton University Press, 609–25.

Arundel, Anthony, and Isabelle Kabla. 1998. "What Percentage of Innovations are Patented? Empirical Estimates for European Firms." *Research Policy* 27(2): 127–41.

Association of University Technology Managers (AUTM). "Licensing Survey Summary." *AUTM Publications*, various years, available online at http://www .autm.net/about/dsp.publications.cfm.

Atkinson, Scott, Alan Marco, and John L. Turner. 2006. "Uniformity and Forum Shopping in U.S. Patent Litigation." Working Paper.

Ayres, Ian, and Paul Klemperer. 1999. "Limiting Patentees' Market Power Without Reducing Innovation Incentives: The Perverse Benefits of Uncertainty and Non-Injunctive Remedies." *Michigan Law Review* 97(4): 985–1033.

Ayres, Ian, and Eric Talley. 1995. "Solomonic Bargaining: Dividing a Legal Entitlement to Facilitate Coasean Trade." *Yale Law Journal* 104(5): 1027–117.

Bar-Gill, Oren, and Gideon Parchomovsky. 2006. "A Marketplace for Ideas?" *Texas Law Review* 84(2): 395–431.

Barney, Jonathan A. 2002. "A Study of Patent Mortality Rates: Using Statistical Survival Analysis to Rate and Value Patent Assets." *AIPLA Quarterly Journal* 30(3): 317–52.

Barton, John H. 2000. "Reforming the Patent System." *Science* 287: 1933–34.

Baudry, Marc, and Beatrice Dumont. 2006. "Patent Renewals as Options: Improving the Mechanism for Weeding Out Lousy Patents." *Review of Industrial Organization* 28(1): 41–62.

Benjamin, Stuart, and Arti K. Rai. 2006. "Who's Afraid of the APA? What the Patent System Can Learn from Administrative Law." *Georgetown Law Journal* 95: 270–336.

Bessen, James. 2005. "Patents and the Diffusion of Technical Information." *Economics Letters* 86(1): 121–28.

———. 2006a. "The Value of U.S. Patents by Owner and Patent Characteristics." Boston University School of Law Working Paper No. 06–46.

———. 2006b. "Estimates of Firms' Patent Rents from Firm Market Value." Boston University School of Law Working Paper No. 06–14.

Bessen, James, and Robert M. Hunt. 2004a. "An Empirical Look at Software Patents." Working Paper 03–17/R, Federal Reserve Bank of Philadelphia.

———. 2004b. "The Software Patent Experiment." *Federal Reserve Bank of Philadelphia Business Review* 2004(Q3): 22–32.

———. 2007. "An Empirical Look at Software Patents." *Journal of Economics and Management Strategy* 16(1): 157–89.

Bessen, James, and Eric Maskin. 2007. "Sequential Innovation, Patents, and Imitation." *RAND Journal of Economics*, forthcoming.

Bessen, James, and Michael J. Meurer. 2005a. "Lessons for Patent Policy from Empirical Research on Patent Litigation." *Lewis and Clark Law Review* 9(1): 1–27.

———. 2005b. "The Patent Litigation Explosion." Boston University School of Law Working Paper No. 05–18.

———. 2006. "Patent Litigation with Endogenous Disputes." *American Economic Review* 96(2): 77–81.

———. 2007. "The Private Costs of Patent Litigation." Boston University School of Law Working Paper No. 07–08.

Bhagat, Sanjai, John M. Bizjak, and Jeffrey L. Coles. 1998. "The Shareholder Wealth Implications of Corporate Lawsuits." *Financial Management* 27(4): 5–27.

Bhagat, Sanjai, James A. Brickley, and Jeffrey L. Coles. 1994. "The Costs of Inefficient Bargaining and Financial Distress: Evidence from Corporate Lawsuits." *Journal of Financial Economics* 35(2): 221–47.

Blair, Roger D., and Thomas F. Cotter. 2005. *Intellectual Property: Economic and Legal Dimensions of Rights and Remedies.* Cambridge: Cambridge University Press.

Boldrin, Michele, and David K. Levine. 2005. "Against Intellectual Monopoly." *Economic and Game Theory,* November 11, 2005, available online at http://www.dklevine.com/general/intellectual/against.htm.

Branstetter, Lee, and Yoshiaki Ogura. 2005. "Is Academic Science Driving a Surge in Industrial Innovation? Evidence from Patent Citations." NBER Working Paper No. 11561.

Brewer, M. B., Michael R. Darby, and Lynne G. Zucker. 1998. "Intellectual Human Capital and the Birth of U.S. Biotechnology Enterprises." *American Economic Review* 88(1): 290–306.

Burk, Dan, and Mark Lemley. 2002. "Is Patent Law Technology-Specific?" *Berkeley Technology Law Journal* 17(4): 1155–1206.

———. 2003. "Policy Levers in Patent Law." *Virginia Law Review* 89(7): 1575–1696.

———. 2005. "Quantum Patent Mechanics." *Lewis and Clark Law Review* 9(1): 29–56.

Campbell-Kelly, Martin. 2005. "Not All Bad: An Historical Perspective on Software Patents." *Michigan Telecommunications and Technology Law Review* 11(2): 191–248.

Caves, Richard E., Harold Crookell, and Peter J. Killing. 1983. "The Imperfect Market for Technology Licenses." *Oxford Bulletin of Economics and Statistics* 45(3): 249–67.

Challu, Pablo. 1995. "Effects of the Monopolistic Patenting of Medicine in Italy since 1978." *International Journal of Technology Management* 10(2): 237–51.

CHI Research, Inc. 2003. "Small Serial Innovators: The Small Firm Contribution to Technical Change." Small Business Administration Office of Advocacy, February 2003.

———. 2004. "Small Firms and Technology: Acquisitions, Inventor Movement, and Technology Transfer." Small Business Administration Office of Advocacy, January 2004.

Chien, Colleen V., and Mark A. Lemley. 2003. "Are the U.S. Patent Priority Rules Really Necessary?" *Hastings Law Journal* 54(5): 1299–1333.

Christensen, Clayton. 1997. *The Innovator's Dilemma: When New Technologies Cause Great Firms to Fail.* Cambridge, Mass.: Harvard University Press/Harvard University Business School Press.

Clay, Karen. 2006. "Squatters, Production, and Violence." Working Paper.

Cockburn, Iain, and Zvi Griliches. 1988. "Industry Effects and Appropriability Measures in the Stock Market Valuation of R&D and Patents." *American Economic Review* 78(2): 419–23.

Cockburn, Iain, and Rebecca Henderson. 1994. "Racing to Invest? The Dynamics of Competition in Ethical Drug Discovery." *Journal of Economics and Management Strategy* 3(3): 481–519.

———. 2003. "The IPO Survey on Strategic Management of Intellectual Property." Intellectual Property Owners Association, Washington, D.C., November 2003.

Cockburn, Iain, Sam Kortum, and Scott Stern. 2003. "Are All Patent Examiners Equal? Examiners, Patent Characteristics, and Litigation Outcomes." In Wesley Cohen and Stephen A. Merrill, eds., *Patents in the Knowledge-Based Economy.* Washington, D.C.: National Academies Press.

Cockburn, Iain, and Megan MacGarvie. 2006. "Entry, Exit and Patenting in the Software Industry." Working Paper.

Cohen, Julie E., and Mark A. Lemley. 2001. "Patent Scope and Innovation in the Software Industry." *California Law Review* 89(1): 1–57.

Cohen, Linda R., and Jun Ishii. 2005. "Competition, Innovation and Racing for Priority at the U.S. Patent and Trademark Office." Working Paper.

Cohen, Wesley, Akira Goto, Akiya Nagata, Richard R. Nelson, and John P. Walsh. 2002. "R&D Spillovers, Patents and the Incentives to Innovate in Japan and the United States." *Research Policy* 31(8–9): 1349–67.

Cohen, Wesley, Richard R. Nelson, and John P. Walsh. 2000. "Protecting Their Intellectual Assets: Appropriability Conditions and Why U.S. Manufacturing Firms Patent (or Not)." NBER Working Paper No. 7552.

Cordes, Joseph J., Henry R. Hertzfeld, and Nicholas S. Vonortas. 1999. "Survey of High Technology Firms." Small Business Administration Office of Advocacy, April 1999.

Crafts, Nicholas. 2004. "Steam as a General Purpose Technology: A Growth Accounting Perspective." *Economic Journal* 114: 338–51.

Cukier, Kenn. 2005. "A Market for Ideas: A Survey of Patents and Technology." *Economist*, October 22, 2005.

Cutler, David, and Lawrence Summers. 1988. "The Costs of Conflict Resolution and Financial Distress: Evidence from the Texaco-Pennzoil Litigation." *RAND Journal of Economics* 19(2): 157–72.

Darby, Michael R., Andrew Wang, and Lynne G. Zucker. 2004. "Joint Ventures, Universities, and Success in the Advanced Technology Program." *Contemporary Economic Policy* 22(2): 145–61.

Darby, Michael R., I. I. Welch, and Lynne G. Zucker. 2001. "Going Public When You Can in Biotechnology." Working Paper.

Darby, Michael R., and Lynne G. Zucker. 2001. "Change or Die: the Adoption of Biotechnology in the Japanese and U.S. Pharmaceutical Industries." *Research on Technological Innovation, Management and Policy* 7: 85–125.

David, Paul A. 1990. "The Dynamo and the Computer: An Historical Perspective on the Modern Productivity Paradox." *American Economic Review* 80(2): 355–61.

de Laat, Paul B. 2000. "Patenting Mathematical Algorithms: What's the Harm?: A Thought Experiment in Algebra." *International Review of Law and Economics* 20(2): 187–204.

Demsetz, Harold. 1967. "Toward a Theory of Property Rights." *American Economic Review* 57(2): 347–59.

De Soto, Hernando. 2000. *The Mystery of Capital: Why Capitalism Triumphs in the West and Fails Everywhere Else*. New York: Basic.

DiMasi, Joseph A., Ronald W. Hansen, and Henry G. Grabowski. 2003. "The Price of Innovation: New Estimates of Drug Development Costs." *Journal of Health Economics* 22(2): 151–85.

Dreyfuss, Rochelle. 1989. "The Federal Circuit: A Case Study in Specialized Courts." *New York University Law Review* 64(1): 1–77.

———. 2004. "The Federal Circuit: A Continuing Experiment in Specialization." *Case Western Reserve Law Review* 54(3): 769–801.

Duffy, John F. 2000. "On Improving the Legal Process of Claim Interpretation: Administrative Alternatives." *Washington University Journal of Law and Policy* 2: 109–66.

Duffy, John F., and Craig A. Nard. 2006. "Rethinking Patent Law's Uniformity Principle." *Case Legal Studies Research Paper* No. 06–17.

Dutton, H. I. 1984. *The Patent System and Inventive Activity During the Industrial Revolution.* Manchester: Manchester University Press.

Eisenberg, Rebecca, and Michael A. Heller. 1998. "Can Patents Deter Innovation?: The Anti-Commons in Biomedical Research." *Science* 280: 698–701.

Ellickson, Robert C. 1991. *Order Without Law: How Neighbors Settle Disputes.* Cambridge, Mass.: Harvard University Press.

Evenson, Robert, and Sunil Kanwar. 2003. "Does Intellectual Property Protection Spur Technological Change?" *Oxford Economic Papers* 55(2): 235–64.

Falvey, Rod, Neil Foster, and David Greenaway. 2006. "Intellectual Property Rights and Economic Growth." *Review of Development Economics* 10(4): 700–719.

Fauchart, Emmanuelle, and Eric von Hippel. 2006. "Norms-Based Intellectual Property Systems: The Case of French Chefs." MIT Sloan School of Management Working Paper 4576–06.

Federal Trade Commission. 2003. "To Promote Innovation: The Proper Balance of Competition and Patent Law and Policy." Washington, D.C.: Government Printing Office.

Feldman, Maryann P., and Maryellen R. Kelley. 2003. "Leveraging Research and Development: Assessing the Impact of the U.S. Advanced Technology Program." *Small Business Economics* 20(2): 153–65.

Feldman, Robin. 2005. "Rethinking Rights in Biospace." *Southern California Law Review,* 79(1): 1–44.

Fisk, Catherine L. 1998. "Removing the 'Fuel of Interest' from the 'Fire of Genius': Law and the Employee-Inventor, 1830–1930." *University of Chicago Law Review* 65(4): 1127–98.

Frischmann, Brett M., and Mark Lemley. 2007. "Spillovers." *Columbia Law Review* 107: 257.

Gallini, Nancy, and Suzanne Scotchmer. 2004. "Intellectual Property: When Is It the Best Incentive System?" *Innovation Policy and the Economy* 2: 51–78.

Gallini, Nancy, and Brian Wright. 1990. "Technology Transfer under Asymmetric Information." *RAND Journal of Economics* 21(1): 147–60.

Gambardella, Alfonso, Dietmar Harhoff, and Bart Verspagen. 2006. "The Value of Patents." Working Paper.

Gambardella, Alfonso, Paola Giuri, and Alessandra Luzzi. 2006. "The Market for Patents in Europe." Working Paper.

Gans, Joshua, David Hsu, and Scott Stern. 2002. "When Does Start-Up Innovation Spur the Gale of Creative Destruction?" *RAND Journal of Economics* 33(4): 571–86.

Gerard, David. 1998. "The Development of First-Possession Rules in U.S. Mining, 1872–1920: Theory, Evidence, and Policy Implications." *Resources Policy* 24(4): 251–64.

Gill, P. E., W. Murray, M. A. Saunders, J. A. Tomlin, and M. A. Wright. 1986. "On Projected Newton Barrier Methods for Linear Programming and an Equivalence to Karmarkar's Projective Method." *Mathematical Programming* 36(2): 183–209.

Ginarte, Juan Carlos, and Walter G. Park. 1997a. "Determinants of Patent Rights: A Cross-National Study." *Research Policy* 26(3): 283–301.

————. 1997b. "Intellectual Property Rights and Economic Growth." *Contemporary Economic Policy*, 15(3): 51–61.

Glasscock, C. B. 1935. *The War of the Copper Kings: The Builders of Butte and Wolves of Wall Street*. Indianapolis: Bobbs-Merrill.

Goolsbee, Austin. 1998. "Does Government R&D Policy Mainly Benefit Scientists and Engineers?" *American Economic Review* 88: 298–302.

Gort, Michael, and Steven Klepper. 1982. "Time Paths in the Diffusion of Product Innovations." *Economic Journal* 92(367): 630–53.

Gould, David M., and William C. Gruben. 1996. "The Role of Intellectual Property Rights in Economic Growth." *Journal of Development Economics* 48(2): 323–50.

Grabowski, Henry, and John Vernon. 2000. "Effective Patent Life in Pharmaceuticals." *International Journal of Technology Management* 19(1–2): 98–120.

Graham, Stuart J. H., Bronwyn H. Hall, Dietmar Harhoff, and David C. Mowery. 2002. "Post-Issue Patent 'Quality Control': A Comparative Study of U.S. Patent Re-examinations and European Patent Oppositions." NBER Working Paper No. 8807.

———. 2004. "Prospects for Improving U.S. Patent Quality via Post-grant Opposition." In *Innovation Policy and the Economy 4*. Cambridge and London: The MIT Press/National Bureau of Economic Research, 115–32.

Graham, Stuart J. H. and Dietmar Harhoff. 2006. "Can Post-Grant Reviews Improve Patent System Design? A Twin Study of U.S. and European Patents." Working Paper.

Griliches, Zvi. 1981. "Market Value, R&D, and Patents." *Economic Letters* 7(2): 183–87.

Gustafsson, Charlotta. 2005. "Private Value of Patents in a Small Economy: Evidence From Finland." Working Paper.

Hall, Bronwyn H. 1990. "The Manufacturing Sector Master File: 1959–1987." NBER Working Paper No. 3366.

———. 1993. "Industrial Research During the 1980s: Did the Rate of Return Fall?" *Brookings Papers on Economic Activity Microeconomics* 2: 289–343.

———. 2000. "Innovation and Market Value." In R. Barrell, G. Mason and M. O'Mahoney, eds., *Productivity, Innovation and Economic Performance*. Cambridge: Cambridge University Press, 188–98.

———. 2005. "Exploring the Patent Explosion." *Journal of Technology Transfer* 30(2): 35–48.

Hall, Bronwyn H., and Dietmar Harhoff. 2004. "Post-Grant Patent Reviews in the United States: Design Choices and Expected Impact." *Berkeley Technology Law Journal* 19(3): 989–1015.

Hall, Bronwyn H., Adam B. Jaffe, and Manuel Trajtenberg. 2001. "The NBER Patent Citations Data File: Lessons, Insights and Methodological Tools." NBER Working Paper No. 8498.

———. 2005. "Market Value and Patent Citations." *RAND Journal of Economics* 36(1): 16–38.

Hall, Bronwyn H., and Rosemarie Ziedonis. 2001. "The Patent Paradox Revisited: An Empirical Study of Patenting in the U.S. Semiconductor Industry, 1979–1995." *RAND Journal of Economics* 32(1): 101–28.

———. 2007. "An Empirical Analysis of Patent Litigation in the Semiconductor Industry." Working Paper.

Hall, Robert E., and Charles I. Jones. 1999. "Why Do Some Countries Produce So Much More Output per Worker Than Others?" *Quarterly Journal of Economics* 114(1): 83–116.

Hansmann, Henry, and Rainier Kraakman. 2002. "Property, Contract, and Verification: The *Numerus Clausus* Problem and the Divisibility of Rights." *Journal of Legal Studies* 31(2): 373–420.

Harhoff, Dietmar, Frederic M. Scherer, and Katrin Vopel. 2003. "Exploring the Tail of Patented Invention Value Distributions." In Ove Grandstrand, ed., *Economics, Law and Intellectual Property*. The Hague: Kluwer, 279–309.

Haslem, Bruce. 2005. "Managerial Opportunism During Corporate Litigation," *Journal of Finance* 60: 2013–41.

Hayashi, Fumio. 1982. "Tobin's Marginal Q and Average Q: A Neoclassical Interpretation." *Econometrica* 50(1): 213–24.

Hayter, Earl W. 1947. "The Patent System and Agrarian Discontent, 1875–1888." *Mississippi Valley Historical Review* 34(1): 59–82.

Heller, Michael A. 1998. "The Tragedy of the Anti-Commons: Property in the Transition from Marx to Markets." *Harvard Law Review* 111(3): 621–88.

———. 1999. "The Boundaries of Private Property." *Yale Law Journal* 108(6): 1163–1223.

Henry, Matthew, and John L. Turner. 2006. "The Court of Appeals for the Federal Circuit's Impact on Patent Litigation." *Journal of Legal Studies* 35(1): 85–117.

Holbrook, Timothy R. 2006. "Possession in Patent Law." *Southern Methodist University Law Review* 59: 123–76.

Hounshell, David A. 1984. *From the American System to Mass Production—1800–1932*. Baltimore: The Johns Hopkins University Press.

Hubbard, Tim, and James Love. 2004a. "A New Trade Framework for Global Healthcare R&D." *PLoS Biology* 2(2): 52.

———. 2004b. "We're patently going mad: lifesaving drugs must be developed differently—for all our sakes." *Guardian*, March 4, 2004.

Hunt, Robert M. 2004. "Patentability, Industry Structure, and Innovation." *Journal of Industrial Economics* 52(3): 401–25.

———. 2006. "When Do More Patents Reduce R&D?" *American Economic Association Papers and Proceedings* 96(2): 87–91.

Hunter, Starling David. 2003. "Have Business Method Patents Gotten a Bum Rap? Some Empirical Evidence." MIT Sloan Working Paper No. 4326–03.

Jaffe, Adam B. 2000. "The U.S. Patent System in Transition: Policy Innovation and the Innovation Process." *Research Policy* 29(4–5): 531–57.

Jaffe, Adam B., and Josh Lerner. 2004. *Innovation and Its Discontents*. Princeton: Princeton University Press.

Jensen, Paul H., Alfons Palangkaraya, and Elizabeth Webster. 2005. "Patent Application Outcomes across the Trilateral Patent Offices." Working Paper.

Johnson, Simon, John McMillan, and Christopher Woodruff. 2002. "Property Rights and Finance." *American Economic Review* 92(5): 1335–56.

Kaplow, Louis, and Steven Shavell. 1995. "Do Liability Rules Facilitate Bargaining? A Reply to Ayres and Talley." *Yale Law Journal* 105(1): 221–33.

Kappos, David J., and Ray Strimaitis. 2005. "Collaborative Innovation and the Patent System—Replacing Friction with Facilitation." Unpublished Manuscript.

Keefer, Philip, and Stephen Knack. 1995. "Institutions and Economic Performance: Cross-Country Tests Using Alternative Institutional Measures." *Economics and Politics* 7(3): 207–27.

———. 1997. "Why Don't Poor Countries Catch Up? A Cross-National Test of an Institutional Explanation." *Economic Inquiry* 35(3): 590–602.

Kerner, Sean Michael. 2005. "A Primer on Software Patents." *Internetnews.com*, May 20, 2005, available online at http://www.internetnews.com/bus-news/article.php/3506836.

Kesan, Jay P., and Gwendolyn G. Ball. 2006. "How Are Patent Cases Resolved? An Empirical Examination of the Adjudication and Settlement of Patent Disputes." *Washington University Law Review* 84: 237–312.

Khan, B. Zorina. 2005. *The Democratization of Invention: Patents and Copyrights in American Economic Development, 1790–1920*. Cambridge: Cambridge University Press.

Khan, B. Zorina, and Kenneth Sokoloff. 1990. "The Democratization of Invention During Early Industrialization: Evidence from the United States, 1790–1846." *Journal of Economic History* 50(2): 363–78.

———. 1993. " 'Schemes of Practical Utility:' Entrepreneurship and Innovation among 'Great Inventors' in the United States, 1790–1865." *Journal of Economic History* 53(2): 289–307.

Kieff, F. Scott. 2001. "Property Rights and Property Rules for Commercializing Inventions." *Minnesota Law Review* 85(3): 697–754.

Kitch, Edmund W. 1977. "The Nature and Function of the Patent System." *Journal of Law and Economics* 20(2): 265–90.

Klemens, Ben. 2006. *Ma+h You Can't Use: Patents, Copyright, and Software.* Washington, D.C.: The Brookings Institution Press.

Klevorick, Alvin K., Richard C. Levin, Richard R. Nelson, and Sidney G. Winter. 1987. "Appropriating the Returns from Industrial Research and Development." *Brookings Papers on Economic Activity* 3: 783–820.

Klock, Mark, and Pamela Megna. 1993. "The Impact of Intangible Capital on Tobin's *Q* in the Semiconductor Industry." *American Economic Association Papers and Proceedings* 83(2): 265–69.

Kremer, Michael. 1998. "Patent Buyouts: A Mechanism for Encouraging Innovation." *Quarterly Journal of Economics* 113(4): 1137–67.

Lach, Saul, and Mark Schankerman. 2004. "Royalty Sharing and Technology Licensing in Universities." *Journal of the European Economic Association* 2(2–3): 252–64.

Lamoreaux, Naomi R., and Kenneth L. Sokoloff. 1996, "Long-Term Change in the Organization of Inventive Activity." *Proceedings of the National Academy of Sciences* 93: 12686–692.

———. 1997. "Inventors, Firms, and the Market for Technology in the Late Nineteenth and Early Twentieth Centuries." NBER Historical Working Paper No. 98.

———. 1999. "Inventors, Firms, and the Market for Technology in the Late Nineteenth and Early Twentieth Centuries." In Naomi R. Lamroeaux, Daniel M. G. Raff, and Peter Temin, eds., *Learning by Doing in Markets, Firms, and Countries.* Chicago: University of Chicago Press, 19–60.

Landes, William M., and Richard A. Posner. 2003. *The Economic Structure of Intellectual Property Law.* Cambridge, Mass.: Harvard University Press.

Lanjouw, Jean O. 1998. "Patent Protection in the Shadow of Infringement: Simulation Estimations of Patent Value," *Review of Economic Studies* 65: 671–710.

Lanjouw, Jean O., and Iain M. Cockburn. 2001. "New Pills for Poor People? Empirical Evidence after GATT." *World Development* 29(2): 265–89.

Lanjouw, Jean O., and Josh Lerner. 1997. "The Enforcement of Intellectual Property Rights: A Survey of the Empirical Literature." NBER Working Paper No. W6296.

———. 2001. "Tilting the Table? The Use of Preliminary Injunctions." *Journal of Law and Economics* 44(2): 573–603.

Lanjouw, Jean O., Ariel Pakes, and Jonathan Putnam. 1998. "How to Count Patents and Value Intellectual Property: The Uses of Patent Renewal and Application Data." *Journal of Industrial Economics* 46(4): 405–32.

Lanjouw, Jean O., and Mark Schankerman. 2004. "Protecting Intellectual Property Rights: Are Small Firms Handicapped?" *Journal of Law and Economics* 47(1): 45–74.

Lemley, Mark A. 2001. "Rational Ignorance at the Patent Office." *Northwestern Law Review* 95(4): 1495–1532.

———. 2005a. "Property, Intellectual Property, and Free Riding." *Texas Law Review* 83(4): 1031–75.

———. 2005b. "The Changing Meaning of Patent Claim Terms." *Michigan Law Review* 104(1): 101–129.

———. 2006. "Should Patent Infringement Require Proof of Copying?" *Michichigan Law Review* 105(7): 1525–536.

Lemley, Mark, and Kimberly Moore. 2004. "Abolishing Patent Continuations." *Boston University Law Review* 84(1): 63–123.

Lemley, Mark A., and Carl Shapiro. 2007. "Patent Holdup and Royalty Stacking." *Texas Law Review* 85: 1991.

Lerner, Josh. 1995. "Patenting in the Shadow of Competitors." *Journal of Law and Economics* 38(2): 463–95.

———. 1999. "Small Businesses, Innovation, and Public Policy." In Zoltan Acs, ed., *Are Small Firms Important?* New York: Kluwer, 159–68.

———. 2000. "150 Years of Patent Protection." NBER Working Paper No. 7478.

———. 2002. "150 Years of Patent Protection." *American Economic Association Papers and Proceedings* 92(2): 221–25.

———. 2006a. "Using Litigation to Understand Trade Secrets: A Preliminary Exploration." Working Paper.

———. 2006b. "Trolls on State Street?: The Litigation of Financial Patents, 1976–2005." Working Paper.

Levin, Richard C., Stephen A. Merrill, and Mark B. Myers. 2004. *A Patent System for the 21st Century*. Washington, D.C.: National Academies Press.

Libecap, Gary. 1989. *Contracting for Property Rights*. Cambridge: Cambridge University Press.

Lichtman, Douglas. 2004. "Rethinking Prosecution History Estoppel." *University of Chicago Law Review* 71(1): 151–82.

Long, Clarissa. 2004. "Information Costs in Patent and Copyright." *Virginia Law Review* 90(2): 465–549.

Lueck, Dean. 1995. "The Rule of First Possession and the Design of the Law." *Journal of Law and Economics* 38(2): 393–436.

Lunney, Glynn, Jr. 2001. "E-Obviousness." *Michigan Telecommunications and Technology Law Review* 7: 363–421.

———. 2004. "Patent Law, the Federal Circuit, and the Supreme Court: A Quiet Revolution." *Supreme Court Economic Review* 11: 1.

Lustig, Irvin, Roy Marsten, Matthew Saltzman, Avid Shanno, and Radhika Subramanian. 1990. "Interior Point Methods for Linear Programming: Just Call Newton, Lagrange, Fiacco and McCormick!" *Interfaces* 20(4): 105–16.

Macdonald, Stuart. 1998. "What the Patent System Offers the Small Firm." ESRC Summary Report.

Machlup, Fritz. 1958. "An Economic Review of the Patent System." Study No. 15, *U.S. Senate Committee on the Judiciary, Subcommittee on Patents, Trademarks and Copyrights.* Washington, D.C.: Government Printing Office.

Machlup, Fritz, and Edith Penrose. 1950. "The Patent Controversy in the Nineteenth Century." *Journal of Economic History* 10(1): 1–29.

MacLeod, Christine. 1988. *Inventing the Industrial Revolution: The English Patent System, 1660–1800.* Cambridge: Cambridge University Press.

———. 1998. "James Watt, Heroic Invention and the Idea of the Industrial Revolution." In Maxine Berg and Kristine Bruland, eds., *Technological Revolutions in Europe: Historical Perspectives.* Cheltenham: Elgar, 96–115.

MacLeod, Christine, Jennifer Tann, Andrew James, and Jeremy Stein. 2003. "Evaluating Inventive Activity: The Cost of Nineteenth-Century U.K. Patents and the Fallibility of Renewal Data." *Economic History Review* 56(3): 537–62.

Maney, Kevin. 2005. "You really can find identities of top patentholders." *USA Today*, December 23, 2005, available online at http://www.usatoday.com/money/industries/technology/maney/2005-12-13-patent_x.htm.

Mann, Ronald J. 2005. "Do Patents Facilitate Financing in the Software Industry?" *Texas Law Review* 83(4): 961–1030.

Mann, Ronald J., and Thomas Sager. 2005. "Patents, Venture Capital, and Software Startups." University of Texas Law and Economics Research Paper No. 57.

Mansfield, Edwin. 1986. "Patents and Innovation: An Empirical Study." *Management Science* 32(2): 173–81.

Mansfield, Edwin, Mark Schwartz, and Samuel Wagner. 1981. "Imitation Costs and Patents: An Empirical Study." *Economic Journal* 91(364): 907–18.

Maskus, Keith E. 2006. *Reforming U.S. Patent Policy: Getting the Incentives Right.* New York: Council on Foreign Relations.

Mass, William. 1989. "Mechanical and Organizational Innovation: The Drapers and the Automatic Loom." *Business History Review* 63: 876–929.

Menell, Peter S. 2006. "Are Software Patents 'Anything under the Sun Made by Man . . .'?" presentation at Boston University School of Law, November 17, 2006, available online at http://www.researchoninnovation.org/swconf/program.htm.

———. 2007. "A Method for Reforming the Patent System." Working Paper.

Merges, Robert P. 2005. "A Transactional View of Property Rights." Working Paper.

———. 2006. "Patents, Entry and Growth in the Software Industry." Working Paper.

Merges, Robert P. and Richard R. Nelson. 1990. "On the Complex Economics of Patent Scope." *Columbia Law Review* 90(4): 839–916.

Merrill, Thomas W., and Henry E. Smith. 2000. "Optimal Standardization in the Law of Property: The *Numerus Clausus* Principle." *Yale Law Journal* 110(1): 1–70.

Merton, Robert K. 1961. "Singletons and Multiples in Scientific Research." *American Philosophical Society Proceedings* 105: 470–86.

Meurer, Michael J. 1989. "The Settlement of Patent Litigation." *RAND Journal of Economics* 20(1): 77–91.

———. 2003. "Controlling Opportunistic and Anti-Competitive Intellectual Property Litigation." *Boston College Law Review* 44(2): 509–44.

Meurer, Michael J., and Craig A. Nard. 2005a. "Invention, Refinement and Patent Claim Scope: A New Perspective on the Doctrine of Equivalents." *Georgetown Law Journal* 93(6): 1947–2012.

———. 2005b. "Patent Policy Adrift in a Sea of Anecdote: A Reply to Lichtman." *Georgetown Law Journal* 93(6): 2033–36.

Miller, Joseph Scott. 2005. "Enhancing Patent Disclosure for Faithful Claim Construction." *Lewis and Clark Law Review* 9(1): 177–230.

Mokyr, Joel. 1999. *The British Industrial Revolution: An Economic Perspective.* Boulder: Westview.

Moore, Kimberly. 2001. "Forum Shopping in Patent Cases: Does Geographic Choice Affect Innovation?" *North Carolina Law Review* 79(4): 889–938.

———. 2002. "Judges, Juries and Patent Cases—An Empirical Peek Inside the Black Box." *Michigan Law Review* 99(2): 365–409.

———. 2005. "*Markman* Eight Years Later: Is Claim Construction More Predictable?" *Lewis and Clark Law Review* 9: 231–47.

Moser, Petra. 2002. "How Do Patent Laws Influence Innovation? Evidence from Nineteenth-Century World Fairs." NBER Working Paper No. 9909.

————. 2006. "What Do Inventors Patent?" Working Paper.

Mossoff, Adam. 2001. "Rethinking the Development of Patents: An Intellectual History, 1550–1800." *Hastings Law Journal* 52(6): 1255–322.

————. 2007. "Patents as Constitutional Private Property: The Historical Protection of Patents Under the Takings Clause." *Boston University Law Review* 87, forthcoming.

Mowery, David C., Richard R. Nelson, Bhaven N. Sampat, and Arvids A. Ziedonis. 2004. *Ivory Tower and Industrial Innovation: University-Industry Technology Transfer before and after the Bayh-Dole Act.* Stanford: Stanford University Press.

Nard, Craig A. 2001. "A Theory of Claim Interpretation." *Harvard Journal of Law and Technology* 14(1): 1–82.

Nard, Craig A., and Andrew P. Morriss. 2005. "Constitutionalizing Patents: From Venice to Philadelphia." *Berkeley Electronic Press Journal of Law and Economics* 2(2): 4.

National Science Foundation, Directorate for Social, Behavioral, and Economic Sciences. 2005. "The U.S. Research And Experimentation Tax Credit In The 1990s," Infobrief, NSF 05–316.

Newell, Allen. 1986. "Response: The Models are Broken, The Models are Broken." *University of Pittsburgh Law Review* 47(4): 1023–35.

Nimmer, Melville B. and David Nimmer. 2006. *Nimmer on Copyright.* San Francisco: Matthew Bender.

Noel, Michael C., and Mark Schankerman. 2006. "Strategic Patenting and Software Innovation." CEPR Discussion Paper No. 5701.

North, Douglass C. 1981. *Structure and Change in Economic History.* New York: W. W. Norton.

North, Douglass C., and Barry Weingast. 1989. "Constitutions and Commitment: Evolution of Institutions Governing Public Choice in Seventeenth-Century England." *Journal of Economic History* 49(4): 803–32.

Nuvolari, Alessandro. 2004. "Collective Invention during the British Industrial Revolution: The Case of the Cornish Pumping Engine." *Cambridge Journal of Economics* 28(3): 347–63.

Ocean Tomo, LLC. 2006. Results of Live Patent Auction, April 6, 2006, Ritz-Carlton Hotel, San Francisco, available online at http://www.oceantomo.com/auctions.html.

Oppenheim, Charles. 1998. "How SMEs Use the Patent Literature." Summary Report for the Economic and Social Research Council, United Kingdom.

O'Rourke, Maureen. 2000. "Toward a Doctrine of Fair Use in Patent Law." *Columbia Law Review* 100(5): 1177–1250.

Ostrom, Elinor. 1991. *Governing the Commons: The Evolution of Institutions for Collective Action.* Cambridge: Cambridge University Press.

Oz, Effy. 1998. "Acceptable Protection of Software Intellectual Property: A Survey of Software Developers and Lawyers." *Information and Management* 34(3): 161–73.

Pakes, Ariel. 1986. "Patents as Options: Some Estimates of the Value of Holding European Patent Stocks." *Econometrica* 54(4): 755–84.

Pakes, Ariel, and Mark Schankerman. 1984. "The Rate of Obsolescence of Patents, Research Gestation Lags, and the Private Rate of Return to Research Resources." In Zvi Griliches, ed., *R&D, Patents and Productivity.* Chicago: University of Chicago Press/NBER.

———. 1986. "Estimates of the Value of Patent Rights in European Countries during the Post-1950 Period." *Economic Journal* 96: 1052–76.

Petherbridge, Lee. 2006. "Positive Examination." *Idea* 46: 173–219.

Petherbridge, Lee, and R. Polk Wagner. 2004. "Is the Federal Circuit Succeeding? An Empirical Assessment of Judicial Performance." *University of Pennsylvania Law Review* 152(3): 1105–80.

Post, Robert C. 1976. " 'Liberalizers' versus 'Scientific Men' in the Antebellum Patent Office." *Technology and Culture* 17(1): 24–54.

PricewaterhouseCoopers. 2006. "2006 Patent and Trademark Damages Study," available online at http://www.pwc.com/extweb/pwcpublications.nsf/docid/b3a557aca66760b48525711c0074d8e7.

Putnam, J. 1996. *The Value of International Patent Protection.* Ph.D. Diss., Yale University.

Qian, Yi. 2006. "Do National Patent Laws Stimulate Innovation in a Global Patenting Environment? A Cross-Country Analysis of Pharmaceutical Patent Protection, 1978–2002." Working Paper.

Quillen, Cecil D., Jr. 1993. "Proposal for the Simplification and Reform of the United States Patent System." *AIPLA Quarterly Journal* 21(3): 189–212.

Quillen, Cecil D., Jr., and Ogden H. Webster. 2001. "Continuing Patent Applications and Performance of the U.S. Patent Office." *Federal Circuit Bar Journal* 11(1): 1–21.

————. 2006. "Continuing Patent Applications and Performance of the U.S. Patent and Trademark Office: Updated." *Federal Circuit Bar Journal* 15(4): 635–77.

Rai, Arti K. 2003. "Engaging Facts and Policy: A Multi-Institution Approach to Patent Law." *Columbia Law Review* 103(5): 1035–135.

Risch, Michael. 2006. "The Failure of Public Notice in Patent Law." Working Paper.

Rivette, Kevin G., and David Kline. 2000. *Rembrandt in the Attic: Unlocking the Hidden Value of Patents*. Cambridge, Mass.: Harvard University Press/Harvard University Business School Press.

Rosenberg, N., and Manuel Trajtenberg. 2001. "A General Purpose Technology at Work: The Corliss Steam Engine in the late Nineteenth-Century U.S." NBER Working Paper 8485.

Rosenberg, Nathan. 2003. "Property Rights and Economic Growth." Paper presented at the Gosta Bohman Foundation, available online at http://www.ratioinstitutet.nu/pdf/wp/nr_propertyrights.pdf.

Sakakibara, Mariko, and Lee Branstetter. 2001. "Do Stronger Patents Induce More Innovation? Evidence from the 1988 Japanese Patent Law Reforms." *RAND Journal of Economics* 32(1): 77–100.

Sales, Reno. 1964. *Underground Warfare at Butte*. Butte, Mont.: World Museum of Mining.

Saltzman, Matthew. 1994. "Internet Commentary. Re: The Karmarkar Algorithm (long)," available online at http://www.cs.uvic.ca/~wendym/courses/445/06/interiorpoint.txt.

Sampat, Bhaven N. 2004. "Examining Patent Examination: An Analysis of Examiner and Applicant Generated Prior Art." Manuscript, NBER Summer Institute 2004.

Samuelson, Pamela. 1990. "*Benson* Revisited: The Case Against Patent Protection for Algorithms and Other Computer Program-Related Inventions." *Emory Law Review* 39(4): 1025–1154.

Schankerman, Mark. 1998. "How Valuable is Patent Protection: Estimates by Technology Fields." *RAND Journal of Economics* 29(1): 77–107.

Scherer, F. M. 2006. "The Political Economy of Patent Policy Reform in the United States." Working Paper.

Scherer, F. M., and S. Weisburst. 1995. "Economic Effects of Strengthening Pharmaceutical Patent Protection in Italy." *International Review of Industrial Property and Copyright Law* 26: 1009–24.

Seabright, Paul. 2004. *In the Company of Strangers*. Princeton: Princeton University Press.

Scotchmer, Suzanne, and Stephen M. Maurer. 2002. "The Independent Invention Defence in Intellectual Property." *Economica* 69: 535–47.

Serrano, Carlos J. 2005. "The Market for Intellectual Property: Evidence from the Transfer of Patents." Working Paper.

Shapiro, Carl. 2006. "Prior User Rights." *American Economic Review* 96(2): 92–96.

Shapiro, Robert J., and Kevin A. Hassett. 2005. "The Economic Value of Intellectual Property." U.S.A. for Innovation Working Paper.

Shavell, Steven. 2002. "Economic Analysis of Property Law." Harvard University School of Law Discussion Paper No. 399.

Shavell, Steven, and Tanguy van Ypersele. 2001. "Rewards versus Intellectual Property Rights." *Journal of Law and Economics* 44(2): 525–47.

Singleton, Solveig. 2006. "Solutions for Software Patents: Notes From under My Desk." The Progress and Freedom Foundation, Progress on Point 13.33, available online at http://www.pff.org/issues-pubs/pops/pop13.33softwarepatents.pdf.

Smith, Henry E. 2003. "The Language of Property: Form, Context, and Audience." *Stanford Law Review* 55: 1105–91.

———. 2004. "Property and Property Rules." *New York University Law Review* 79(5): 1719–98.

Strandburg, Katherine J. 2004. "What Does the Public Get? Experimental Use and the Patent Bargain." *Wisconsin Law Review* 2004(1): 81–155.

Svejnar, Jan. 2002. "Transition Economies: Performance and Challenges." *Journal of Economic Perspectives* 16(1): 3–28.

Taylor, C., and Z. Silbertson. 1973. *The Economic Impact of the Patent System: A Study of the British Experience*. Cambridge: Cambridge University Press.

Thursby, Jerry G., and Marie C. Thursby. 2003. "University Licensing and the Bayh-Dole Act." *Science* 301: 1052.

Umbeck, John. 1981. *A Theory of Property Rights, with Application to the California Gold Rush*.

Ames: Iowa State University Press.

USPTO. 1994. "Public Hearings on Software Patents," available online at http://www.uspto.gov/web/offices/com/hearings/software/sanjose/index.html.

Vermont, Samson. 2006. "Independent Invention As a Defense to Patent Infringement." *Michigan Law Review* 105(3) pp. 475–504.

von Tunzelmann, G. N. 1978. *Steam Power and British Industrialization to 1860.* Oxford: Clarendon.

Wagner, R. Polk. 2007. "Did Phillips Change Any Thing? Empirical Analysis Of The Federal Circuit's Claim Construction Jurisprudence," available online at http://www.claimconstruction.com/.

Wagner, R. Polk, and Lee Petherbridge. 2004. "Is the Federal Circuit Succeeding? An Empirical Assessment of Judicial Performance." *University of Pennsylvania Law Review* 152: 1105–180.

Wallsten, Scott. J. 2000. "The Effects of Government-Industry R&D Programs on Private R&D: The Case of the Small Business Innovation Research Program." *RAND Journal of Economics* 31: 82–100.

Warshofsky, Fred. 1994. *The Patent Wars.* New York: John Wiley.

Wilson, Daniel J. 2005. "Beggar Thy Neighbor? The In-State vs. Out-of-State Impact of State R&D Tax Credits," Federal Reserve Bank of San Francisco Working Paper 2005–08.

Woodard, Colin. 2004. *The Lobster Coast: Rebels, Rusticators, and the Struggle for a Forgotten Frontier.* New York: Viking.

Wright, Brian D. 1983. "The Economics of Invention Incentives: Patents, Prizes, and Research Contracts." *American Economic Review* 73(4): 691–707.

Ziedonis, Rosemarie H. 2004. "Patent Litigation in the U.S. Semiconductor Industry." In Wesley Cohen and Stephen A. Merrill, eds., *Patents in the Knowledge-Based Economy.* Washington, D.C.: National Academies Press.

Index

Note: Page numbers followed by *f* or *t* indicate figures or tables, respectively.

technologies, 161; and notice reform, 236; opinions about, 227;
patent assignment by, 32; and
patent-citation practices, 153–54;
and patent quality, 223; reform of,
238–42; reforms instituted by,
220; role of, 25, 226–27, 237–38,
240–42; and software patents,
188–89, 192–93; technology classification by, 275n12. *See also* patent
examination
U.S. Supreme Court: and abstraction,
211; on claims, 56–58; on early-
stage technologies, 269n36; and
injunctions, 252, 264n8; and lower
courts, 229–30; and Morse's patent
claim, 204, 207–8; and patent coverage, 230; and patent policy, 24;
on patent system, 259
utility of inventions, 65–67, 150,
269n36

vague claims, 56–62, 200, 239. *See
also* claim construction
validity of patents: challenges to, 223,
277n1; court findings on, 158*f;*
Federal Circuit Court and, 157;
and Kodak-Polaroid case, 50–51;
as litigation factor, 154, 157, 224.
See also invalid patents
Vermont, Samson, 250
Vernon, John, 88
Videotex, 195–96
Vitronics v. Conceptronic, Inc., 150

Wagner, R. Polk, 291n17
Wagner, Samuel, 89

Walter-Freeman-Abele two-part test,
292n10
*Wang Lab., Inc. v. America Online,
Inc.*, 195–96, 286n8
Wang Labs, 195–96, 199–200, 286n8
*Warner-Jenkinson Co. v. Hilton Davis
Chemical Co.*, 61–62, 267n25
War of the Copper Kings. *See* Butte,
Montana copper mine disputes
water law, 64
Watt, James, 78
weaving shuttle, 78
Weber, Wilhelm Eduard, 206
Weder, Donald, 169
Weisburst, S., 85–86
Wheatstone, Charles, 206
Whitney, Eli, 79, 259
willfulness, 50, 70, 126, 251,
267n14, 277n5, 293n14
Woodruff, Christopher, 38
World Intellectual Property Organiza-
tion, 75
World's Fair (London, 1851), 79, 80
World's Fair (Philadelphia, 1876), 80
written description, 65, 268n32,
281n9, 291n3, 291n17, 292n8. *See
also* enablement
Wyeth v. Stone, 198

Xerox PARC, 195
Xerox Star, 195

Ziedonis, Rosemarie H., 71, 160
Zimbabwe, 1
zoning restrictions, 41–42
Zucker, Lynne G., 182
Zurko, In re, 163, 213, 227